RATIONALITY, ALLOCATION, AND REPRODUCTION

RATIONALITY, ALLOCATION, AND REPRODUCTION

Vivian Walsh

OXFORD · CLARENDON PRESS

1996

Oxford University Press, Walton Street, Oxford OX2 6DP

Oxford New York
Athens Auckland Bangkok Bombay
Calcutta Cape Town Dar es Salaam Delhi
Florence Hong Kong Istanbul Karachi
Kuala Lumpur Madras Madrid Melbourne
Mexico City Nairobi Paris Singapore
Taipei Tokyo Toronto
and associated companies in
Berlin Ibadan

Oxford is a trade mark of Oxford University Press

Published in the United States
by Oxford University Press Inc., New York

British Library Cataloguing in Publication Data
Data available

Library of Congress Cataloging-in-Publication Data
Walsh, Vivian Charles.
Rationality, allocation, and reproduction / Vivian Walsh.
Includes bibliographical references and index.
1. Economics. 2. Rationalism. I. Title.
HB175.W316 1996   95-46908
330—dc20
ISBN 0-19-828772-0

1 3 5 7 9 10 8 6 4 2

Typeset by Best-set Typesetter Ltd., Hong Kong

Printed in Great Britain
on acid-free paper by
Biddles Ltd., Guildford & King's Lynn

For my grandson,
William Molineaux Houldin, III

Acknowledgements

DURING the long development of this work, many people have read all or part of various versions, or have discussed some of the ideas involved with me at length. Early versions were commented on by Harvey Gram, Joseph Halevi, Heinz Kurz, Axel Leijonhufvud, David Levine, Gavin Reed, and Roy Weintraub. Later versions were commented on by Richard Cornwall, John Davies, David George, Harvey Gram, Michael McPherson, Robin Pope, Thomas Powell, Ted Schick, Gil Skillman, and Frank Thompson. Useful references were suggested by Paul Anand and David Laibman, and also by Regina Loughran and Ludwig Schlecht.

During the last five years I have benefited more than I can say from the continual advice and help of Amartya Sen and Hilary Putnam with the last two versions of the work. The help of Kenneth Arrow was indispensable. Needless to say, none of these people is responsible for its remaining faults. The last two complete versions were carried out with the assistance of Lisa Bendall-Walsh. Lisa and I are grateful to Grover H. Stainbrook Jr. for his kind permission to use the computer facilities at Lehigh Valley Industrial Park, Inc. after hours and at weekends. I am grateful to Arthur Raymond of the Muhlenberg College Economics Department for skilfully generating the Figures, and to Scherelene Schatz of Trexler Library at Muhlenberg College, for her assistance in locating needed material.

I wish to acknowledge the support of my research provided successively by the University of Tulsa, Guilford College, and Muhlenberg College. I also wish to thank the editors of the *American Economic Review* for permission to reproduce, as part of Chapter 5 below, work of which an earlier draft was previously published in that Journal (Walsh 1994).

V.W.

Muhlenberg College,
Allentown,
Pennsylvania,
January 1995

Contents

INTRODUCTION

WE would not ordinarily say that a choice or action was rational but unreasonable, nor that it was reasonable but irresponsible, nor that it was responsible but unwise, nor that it was wise but morally indefensible. Our ordinary concept of rationality is embedded in a delicate fabric of interconnected ideas which can be understood only in the context of the family of uses of words and expressions which are employed in making, explaining, and defending rationality claims. The concept of rationality in formal, axiomatized economic theory is not like this; it can be given a formal definition. A 'rational agent' in such a model is simply one who obeys certain axioms, and that is the end of it. When we ordinarily claim of someone that they acted rationally, on the other hand, we are not claiming that they satisfied a certain finite set of necessary and sufficient conditions. Our claim is a defeasible one—very crudely, it may be defeated by the production of various different sorts of evidence, some of which we may never have anticipated. If I claim that I have acted rationally, you may be able to point out that I have failed to take account of certain facts, that I have sacrificed a major goal for the sake of some trivial successes, that I have ignored the rights of people for whom I am responsible, etc., etc. On the other hand a charge of irrationality may be defeated by presenting various valid excuses, some of them peculiar to the special circumstances of an individual situation, or perhaps to a type of situation not hitherto distinguished.

As Hilary Putnam has observed, 'our values of equality, intellectual freedom, and rationality, are deeply interconnected. But the moral that I would draw from this is more Aristotelian than Kantian; we have a rich and multifaceted idea of the good, and the parts of this idea are interdependent' (Putnam 1987: 56). Our ordinary concept of rationality comes from the assimilation through the practices of daily life of ideas which, though long embedded in language, possess an ancestry which is partly philosophical and which goes back in the case of Europe and North Africa at least to Aristotle, and to Stoics like Cicero, in ancient Greece and Rome. Medieval theologians adopted some of these ideas, blending them with others of an even earlier origin from the Hebrew Bible: for instance Aquinas absorbed and adapted many of the ideas of Aristotle, seeing some of them through the eyes of Jewish and Islamic philosophers, and others through the partial translations of Aristotle from the Greek already available.[1] Hundreds of years later, in the New World, arguing about the nature of a community of reasonable people, 'the common man in Yankee towns consistently opposed the absolute powers of both kings and bishops, quoting the admonitions of Moses and Samuel against the corrupting powers of authority' (Rosenberg 1986: 102). Thus some of the practices through which, over the ages, people acquired their concept of rationality were those of religion. But this latter was only one element in a tradition which could at other times (as in the Enlightenment) be highly anti-clerical.[2]

Even those eighteenth-century figures in France or America, however, who claimed most for the rule of reason, did so precisely because of their belief in reason's ability to lead them to wisdom and the understanding of moral rights and obligations. Thus the concept of rationality which gradually became embedded in language never became a morally neutral one: to be rational was never merely to be consistent or efficient in the execution of *any* goal, irrespective of whether that goal was wise or foolish. It was always believed to be possible to argue rationally about the worthiness of goals, the legitimacy of claims to rights, the existence of obligations or duties. Argument concerning the rationality of a choice or action was never a purely technical value-free discourse.

[1] The most influential of the Jewish philosophers was Moses Maimonides (1133–1204), and the most influential of the Moslem philosophers were Avicenna (980–1037) and Averroës (1126–98). Parts of Aristotle had also been available to medieval philosophers in translations directly from the Greek into Latin. The reader who is not a specialist in medieval philosophy will find a classic introduction in Étienne Gilson ([1938] 1966). Gilson specifically stresses the views on rationality of key medieval thinkers, and their influence on Aquinas. The influence of Jewish and Islamic philosophy, and the role of the translations of Aristotle, is discussed in Frederick Copleston ([1950] 1962: 211–38).

[2] That a highly anti-clerical rationalism had been powerfully developed within the medieval period was stressed by Gilson, who observed that 'the Averroistic tradition forms an uninterrupted chain from the Masters of Arts of Paris and Padua, to the "Libertins" of the seventeenth and eighteenth centuries' (Gilson [1938] 1966: 65). The spirit of rationalism is often traced to the intellectual ferment of Galileo's Italy, and with some justice. The scientific renaissance in the sixteenth century certainly played an important role. But as Gilson remarked, there was an older rationalism: 'When Averroës died, in 1198, he bequeathed to his successors the ideal of a purely rational philosophy' (Gilson [1938] 1966: 38).

Then, early in the twentieth century if not before, versions of a fundamentally different and much narrower concept of rationality began to appear in the discussions of social scientists.[3] Beginning on the European continent, with Max Weber (1864–1920) as an important source, this concept later gained considerable momentum in the early 1930s from those influenced by the Vienna Circle, the early logical positivists. The newly debated concept of rationality perhaps first became widely known among English speaking economic theorists with Lord Robbins's famous *Essay* (1932). (Ironically, Robbins's little-quoted first edition was quite free from specifically logical positivist influence.) Rationality was now cut down to the exercise of efficiency in the allocation of scarce means towards the attainment of 'given' and unexamined ends. It was stipulated that the ends and means were strictly independent of one another, and that the ends were not the concern of the economic 'scientist': 'economic science', it was claimed, was a wholly value-free exercise.

Several versions of this constructed concept of rationality evolved, differing in their axiomatic foundations and therefore in the richness or austerity of their claims. The original version in orthodox (neo-classical) economics was the conceptually richest. It involved the claim that a rational agent maximized something called utility. This concept of utility had been borrowed from nineteenth-century utilitarian philosophy, and the account of rationality in terms of utility was never able to outgrow some of its ancestral traits, despite the austere axiomatic garb in which it was eventually clothed in the 1950s. We shall explore this in Chapters 2 and 3. The search for rigour led to a version of the constructed concept of rationality where a rational agent was simply one whose choices or actions were consistent. This line of thought can claim Robbins as an ancestor. It will be investigated in Chapter 4. Those dissatisfied with the bare notion of consistency sought to enrich this by means of the added claim that a rational agent was one whose choices or actions were directed towards maximization of the agent's self-interested aims. They claimed (rather misleadingly, as

---

[3] David Hume has often been put forward as an ancestor of the 'value-free' concept of rationality, and indeed he claimed in an often quoted passage '['t]is not contrary to reason to prefer the destruction of the whole world to the scratching of my finger' (Hume [1739–40] 1978: Book II, Part III, Section III). His position, of course, was radically revisionist—as his own examples make clear—and ordinary language did not adopt his sharp delimitation of the sphere of reason.

we shall see) that this was the view adopted in the eighteenth century by Adam Smith. This will be discussed in Chapter 5.

For any version of the economic concept of rationality to become a truly potent doctrine, capable of impressing and invading other fields of thought (including less mathematically developed social sciences) a vital ingredient was needed. The formal concept of rationality in economic theory had to be shown to be the core of an axiomatic structure from which could be derived proofs of the existence and 'optimality' of equilibrium in an extensive class of models of general economic equilibrium. This project, which began in the 1930s, was not completed until the developments of the 1950s. By then the axiomatic methods of formalist mathematics were being systematically applied to the fundamental concepts of economic theory. The choices of an agent were now said to be rational if and only if they satisfied the axioms of preference theory or (in models with risk) of expected utility theory. Widely applauded theorems were then proved to hold for model economies wholly populated by such agents. Other social scientists, outside economics, looked with some admiration (and perhaps a tinge of envy) at these newly erected mathematical edifices. Economics itself had earlier been invaded by wert-frei notions of rationality, by logical positivism, and by formalist mathematics; now it was in a position to return the compliment and invade other fields! It proceeded to do so.

Thus by the 1960s and 1970s views outside economics as to what it was for a choice or action to be rational were increasingly being derived from one or other version of the constructed concept found in economic theory. The age-old understanding of rationality built into our language was being replaced by the formal concept of a 'rational micro-economic agent'. Notions derived directly from economic theory came to underlie debate in a number of areas quite apart from fields which are part of economics proper. Social and political theorists, lawyers, philosophers, and many others all began to employ in their arguments what were originally theoretical constructions within economic analysis, and to do this both when engaged in modelling of their own and when taking part in the presentation and advocacy of particular policies.

This book is devoted to an examination of various formulations and interpretations of the concept of rationality which have been developed by economic theorists. It is also devoted to an examination of the philosophical implications of the replacement of the ordinary concept of rationality by such formal concepts from economic theory and decision theory, both for the character and significance of economic theory itself and for the nature of philosophical discourse upon matters of practical reason.

Both for the philosopher concerned with problems of practical reason, and for the lay person interested in appraising claims to the effect that various actions or policies are rational, the implications of this development and its widespread influence are, I believe, quite serious. An understanding of rationality which is the legacy of the ages has been to an alarming extent simply replaced by versions of a formal, constructed concept put together so as to fit the requirements of axiomatic general equilibrium theory, decision theory, or game theory.

That formalization should have burst into flower in economic theory, like a bulb for some time dormant in the earth, in the 1950s and 1960s is not in fact surprising. The flowering took place when the intellectual influence of formalism was nearing the end of its summer elsewhere; but philosophical ideas often reach economics somewhat late. Outside economic theory, the influence of the economic concept of rationality was again delayed, perhaps only reaching its peak in the 1970s and 1980s. It should be said that other social sciences are as slow in picking up new economic concepts as economics is in picking up new developments in philosophy. Meanwhile, however, the philosophical response to formalism has cooled. As Hilary Putnam has put it:

The hope for a formal method, capable of being isolated from our judgements about the nature of the world, seems to have been frustrated. And if we do widen the notion of a method so that a formalization of the complete psychology of an ideally rational human being counts as a 'method', there is no reason to think that a 'method' in this sense must be independent of the human being's judgements about metaphysics, aesthetics, or whatever. The whole reason for believing that the scientific method would not have ethical (or metaphysical) presuppositions was that it was supposed to be a *formal* method, after all. (Putnam 1987: 75, emphasis in original.)

As the spell of formalism dissipated, it could be seen that claims based on a formal system are not necessarily 'first class', nor are claims based on a judgement about the world and expressed in a natural language necessarily 'second class'. Furthermore it should be noted that when economists step away from their models, and offer advice as to the rational policy to adopt on some issue, they have to identify their rationality claims at key points with what is ordinarily understood as being rational. The austere limitations of what is entailed by calling a choice or action rational in the terms of the formal theory would not be very persuasive if they were fully understood. The impressive theoretical results of formal theory, however, depend upon the constructed concept of rationality with all its limitations, and that theory provides support for the gravity of the economist's advice. But the advice requires an appeal, at key points, to the hearer's quite different concept of rationality, one derived from experience and linguistic tradition. To borrow an expression used by Putnam (to describe certain philosophers), the economist is keeping a double set of books.

It is time to note that any study of rationality in the context of economic theory must involve a detailed examination of the role of the concept in neo-classical (or neo-Walrasian) theory. This is simply because, on a reading of the whole history of economic analysis, it is the neo-classical tradition which stands out sharply for its claim to make rationality the most fundamental concept of economic theory, and for its further claim to be able to discover what economic arrangements will most fully embody this rationality. The term 'neo-classical' is deeply confusing to non-economists. It suggests a revival of, and improvement upon, a classical tradition. 'Neo-classical' economic theory, however, differs profoundly from the classical tradition in economics, as we shall see in Chapters 8 and 9 of the present work. The classical tradition has been revived in the present day, but by theorists who would not on the whole want to call themselves neo-classics. The most important point at present, however, is that the fundamental role played by 'rationality' is a feature of the neo-classical tradition, which may be loosely described as the mainstream or orthodox tradition in present-day economics.

At its most sophisticated level, neo-classical theory offers a formal axiomatic characterization of a rational micro-economic agent. It is then shown that, if each agent in a model economy is in an equilibrium position (a rationally chosen position), then the model as a whole (given certain important restrictions) will also be in a *general* equilibrium. Such a demonstration is known as a proof of the (mathematical) existence of equilibrium. It is then shown that the general equilibrium in which all the agents find themselves possesses a certain kind of 'optimality' or 'efficiency'. This implies that no reallocation of goods could be made which any agent would prefer without some other agent being put in a less preferred position.

This work carried to its logical conclusion and formalized mathematically the historic contribution of Léon Walras (1834–1910) and so is often (reasonably) known as 'neo-Walrasian' general equilibrium analysis. The mathematical developments were begun in the 1930s, and their completion in the 1950s was chiefly the work of Kenneth J. Arrow (1951*a*) and Gérard Debreu (1951), Arrow and Debreu (1954), and Lionel W. McKenzie (1954, 1959). The formulation of neo-Walrasian general equilibrium which resulted from these works is standardly known as Arrow–Debreu general equilibrium. The essential properties of the concept of rationality most characteristic of the neo-classical tradition were formalized in this work, and have thus been around for quite a long time. By the 1970s, however, models were being constructed which branched out from the Arrow–Debreu structure in a number of different directions. Many involved rather exotic kinds of temporary equilibria, in which markets did not necessarily clear, and which differed enough from the canonical, complete Arrow–Debreu models for them to acquire the name 'non-Walrasian equilibria'.

Some of these new developments came about in the effort to capture features of the real world and its decision problems which the Arrow–Debreu equilibria could not depict. A typical example would be the extensive literature involving models where different agents possess different information. Key parts of the Arrow–Debreu construction require the (explicit or implicit) assumption that all agents in a model possess the same information. If they do not, the general equilibria may lack the prized 'optimality' or 'efficiency' properties which are a crucial element in some of the rationality claims made concerning such equilibria. (Asymmetric information will play a role in Chapter 4.)

It should be noted, however, that it was the original formalization of the concept of 'rationality' in the 1950s, embedded as it was in the elegance and architectural splendour of the original complete Arrow–Debreu models of those days, that was the source of the imperial influence of neo-classical economics. It was this synthesizing power and structural magnificence that so impressed the other less mathematically advanced social sciences that the concept of rationality on which it rested was willingly adopted by thinkers who would never in fact use it in the construction of existence theorems. But nowadays those of the more brilliant younger economic theorists who see themselves as in the neo-Walrasian tradition are engaged in generating, as has been noted, a plethora of special models. This fascinating but somewhat Balkanizing development, it may be suggested, would perhaps not have gained for economic theory the imperial dominion over thinkers and policy-makers in other fields which, many have felt, was attained by the complete Arrow–Debreu model in its gilded youth.

Meanwhile some of the axiomatic core of Arrow–Debreu has been increasingly questioned. Axioms which were thought to be necessary to the very idea of rationality have been shown to be questionable, and models constructed which no longer depended on them. Decision theorists have increasingly challenged the long reign of axiomatic expected utility theory in the form which it has had since the 1950s. Philosophers (including philosophically trained economic theorists) have increasingly subjected concepts of rationality from economic theory and decision theory to critical analysis on their terms. One cannot help the feeling that the tide is at last turning.

It is surely time, in the changed intellectual climate of today, to re-examine the concepts of rationality which scholars and policy-makers, many of whom were not economists, were ready to adopt directly or indirectly from economic theory in the recent past. This will be the task of Chapters 1–5, beginning with an examination of the individual micro-economic agent in neo-Walrasian theory and then considering several different interpretations of the concept of rationality which can be found in the neo-classical literature. Once the character of the individual agent has been established, neo-classical theory has always regarded the analysis of allocation among these agents as its supreme task, and indeed some treatment of this is vital if the reader is to see something of the use to which the rationality assumptions have in fact been put. Chapters 6 and 7 accordingly explore the neo-classical theory of allocation resulting from the choices of rational agents.

Finally, Chapters 8 and 9 are intended to contrast sharply with the rest of the book. Even a casual glance will reveal that there is much less that is directly *about* rationality in these final chapters; but this is exactly as it should be. Their whole purpose is to exhibit the strikingly different and much smaller role played by concepts of rational choice or action in the work of a present-day school which derives from the eighteenth- and nineteenth-century classical economists. In this tradition today, as in its historical forefathers, individual agents and their choices do not always occupy centre stage. Nor is it claimed by theorists in this tradition that economic outcomes, such as allocations among agents, will always exhibit rational properties from the point of view of all of the economic agents in a model.

The term neo-classical, as already noted, suggests (misleadingly) that the school it designates carries on the old classical tradition. The final chapters, however, will cast into sharp relief just precisely those respects in which neo-classical theory conflicts with the original classics and their present-day restatement in the technical language of our time. But it is of course just the possession of these contrasting properties that makes it possible for the revived classical analysis to construct general equilibrium models where axioms of rationality are not the cornerstone of the structure and where proofs of the 'optimality' of equilibrium are not the objective principally in view. Whatever may be the ultimate decision as to the strengths and weaknesses of these present-day classical models (and this is still a matter of controversy) they certainly perform the helpful task of offering another—and a strikingly different— perspective from that which is adopted throughout neo-classical analysis.

I conclude with a few points about how my own thinking has evolved. From 1954, when I began publishing on philosophy and economics, until 1967, I never published anything which was not in favour of the use of formal economic concepts of rationality in philosophy. Hilary Putnam has recently told me that I was questioning the axiom of completeness by 1958 in some of our long conversations on the relations between philosophy and economics. I do not recall this, but I do remember (as does he) our working on a joint paper on the necessity for a change in the axioms of choice theory (specifically, the need to drop the assumption of completeness) in the early 1960s. We never finished this, but I did publish a paper (1967) which discussed ways of extending the formal account

of choice to situations where not all alternatives could be compared. From then on I came to regard the rationality axioms with
increasing reservation.

My interest in formal choice theory, however, was never motivated by a desire to offer a value-free account of rationality. On the
contrary, I wanted to use some economic concepts in *moral* philosophy. Recall Aristotle's well-known claim that the lack of certain
external possessions could prevent the attainment of a person's
ethical objectives. I argued that the neo-classical economic concept
of maximization of an objective subject to constraints (resulting
from the scarcity of all sorts of means) could offer a more subtle
version of this idea of non-blameworthy failures of attainment
(Walsh 1958*a*, 1958*b*, 1961). That my use of the concept of scarcity
was for purposes of moral theory was understood at the time.
Kenneth Arrow, for example, noted that: 'The moral implications
of the position that many attributes of the individual are similar in
nature to external possessions have been discussed by V. C. Walsh
[1961]' (Arrow 1967: 21 n. 10).

Let me stress here that I still believe that philosophy has things to
learn from economic theory. That this is so has recently been
argued, for example, by Amartya Sen (1987) and by John Broome
(1991*a*), and Broome claims that this is now 'widely recognized'
(Broome 1991*a*: 1). I remember very well when it was not! I little
knew how much influence the formalists would later have outside
economics. But when all is said and done, the narrowness or arbi-
trariness of certain formalizations are not a reason for the philosopher to turn away from what is being contributed by economic
theory to the analysis of rationality, especially now when deeply
critical and exploratory work is being done within economics and
decision theory by a number of younger theorists who have seen
the dangers and are proposing escapes from the narrowness of
earlier formal conceptualizations of rationality. As for formalism in
economic theory: a healthy scepticism concerning the more hubris-
tic claims of formalism need not entail any desire to see less mathematics used in economic theory. Indeed I heartily agree with the
claim of Terence Gorman (1984) as interpreted by Amartya Sen
(1989: 318) that in some ways the need is for more mathematics,
not less. Again, whatever disagreements may remain between neo-
classics and those working on the present-day revival of classical
theory, these should not include any arguments concerning

the desirability of mathematics. One could almost say that the twentieth-century revival of classical theory arose when kinds of mathematics not available to the eighteenth- and nineteenth-century classics were applied to their concepts. Present-day classical theory has its existence theorems too!

On the other hand, I shall argue that more attention needs to be paid by economic theorists to the nature and force of claims made in natural languages. The relationship between things said in a natural language and theorems proved for a set of constructed concepts in a theory is often far from clear. Nor can the theorist aware of recent work in philosophy reasonably go on treating claims made in a natural language as 'second class'. It is ironic, but I believe true, that the claims that can be made for natural language have been strengthened by developments in the understanding of formal systems and their limits, and are stronger today than they were in the immediately post-Wittgensteinian days of the Oxford 'ordinary language' philosophy in the 1950s. But surely J. L. Austin was right even then to claim that, while ordinary language is certainly not the last word, 'only remember, it *is* the *first* word' (Austin 1961: 185, emphasis in original).

Nevertheless my concern for attention to the powers and subtleties of ordinary language (especially when engaged in moral argument) should not be mistaken for any endorsement of the nihilistic side of post-modernism—against which I have been inoculated over the years by Hilary Putnam with strong doses of 'internal realism'.[4] And I emphatically agree with his claim that 'what is wrong with relativist views (apart from their horrifying irresponsibility) is that they do not at all correspond to how we think and to how we shall continue to think' (Putnam 1987: 70).

---

[4] For the development of the concept of internal realism, see Putnam (1978, 1981, 1987, 1988, 1990).

1

INDIVIDUAL AGENTS VS. INDIVIDUAL PERSONS

THE constructed concept of rationality (in its various versions) embodied in neo-classical economic models primarily characterizes the choices or actions of an 'individual economic agent'. General equilibria with rational or 'optimal' properties are then the result of such choices by all of the individual agents in a given model. It seems reasonable therefore to begin our investigation by examining these individual agents. If problems arise in the interpretation of these agents, such problems would necessarily affect the neo-classical constructed concept of rationality at its roots and cause difficulties in turn for 'optimality' claims concerning the general equilibria which are wholly built up out of the choices or actions of the individual agents.

There is, I believe, a serious dilemma which confronts neo-classical theory concerning the proper interpretation of its concept of an individual agent. This dilemma is the subject of the present chapter. Let me say straight away that I do not offer an escape from the dilemma, indeed I am not at all sure that there is any escape which preserves what neo-classical theory actually needs. But in any case the task of finding an escape which will best serve neo-classical theory is most properly undertaken by philosophically self-conscious theorists who are fully committed to the neo-classical tradition. It is for them to decide what positions they are willing to give up and what positions must be defended at all costs. My purpose in this chapter is simply to draw attention to the character and complexity of the issues, and to the seriousness of their implications for the constructed concept of rationality derived from neo-classical theory.

A preliminary thumb-nail sketch of the dilemma might be put roughly thus. Weighty considerations impel the neo-classic towards interpreting the individual agent as a *person*. The individual person, hailed as independent, rational, and free to choose and act, has surely always been the protagonist of the neo-classical account of

life. It is not hard to show, however, that equally weighty considerations have in practice prevented neo-classics from adhering to this
interpretation of their agents. The theory usually requires, if its
models are to have any bearing on economic actuality, that organizations (made up of whole groups of persons) be interpreted as
'individual' agents. Households, partnerships, corporations, not-
for-profit organizations, colleges, rock bands, rugby clubs, and public utilities are just a few of the candidates for the role of 'individual
agent'. Indeed, an individual agent is often simply any entity which
acts on a market—one market actor among others. This, of course,
is simply what the exigencies of model building require.

Yet the motives for insisting that the individual agent should
be a person remain strong for the neo-classical tradition. Its most
fundamental concept, rationality, is a property which can most
correctly be said to apply to certain of the choices or actions of
individual persons. It was thus natural that neo-classics, as a result
of their prior vision of the economic aspect of life and of its nature
and significance, would be powerfully drawn to a doctrine which
enshrines an extreme claim concerning the role of individual
persons.

METHODOLOGICAL INDIVIDUALISM

This doctrine has been vividly expressed by James Buchanan:

> Only individuals choose and act. Collectivities, as such, neither choose nor
> act and analysis that proceeds as if they do is not within the accepted
> scientific canon. Social aggregates are considered only as the results of
> choices made and actions taken by individuals. The emphasis on explain-
> ing non-intended aggregative results of interaction has carried through
> since the early insights of the Scottish moral philosophers. An aggregative
> result that is observed but which cannot, somehow, be factored down and
> explained by the choices of individuals stands as a challenge to the scholar
> rather than as some demonstration of non-individualistic organic unity.
>   Methodological individualism, as summarized above, is almost univer-
> sally accepted by economists who work within mainstream, or non-
> Marxian, traditions. (Buchanan 1987: 586)

Buchanan is right to claim that this doctrine has links with the
early insights of the Scottish moral philosophers. These insights
were part of an old and morally non-trivial tradition which attached

great value to the choices and actions of individual persons, and to the ability of these persons to choose freely and act responsibly as members of and participants in a social covenant which respected the rights of each. This tradition was of course a part of the development of the concept of rationality which is embedded in our language. If neo-classical theory could truly embody this regard for the choices and actions of individual persons, and for the protection of their rights and the implementation of their responsibilities, it would thereby be able to claim to embody, in its formal models, some of what we ordinarily mean by rationality.

Buchanan notes that '[c]lassical political economy emerged from moral philosophy, and its propounders considered their efforts to fall naturally within the limits of philosophical discourse . . . How can persons live together in liberty, peace and prosperity?' (Ibid.) The concept of a society of freely choosing persons living together under a covenant which expresses their mutual obligations and respects their rights underlay much of the debate of the Scottish and French Enlightenments. Earlier it is to be found in the thinking of the seventeenth-century New England settlers. But its roots go all the way back to the Hebrew Bible; as W. E. H. Lecky wrote many years ago, 'in the great majority of instances the early Protestant defenders of civil liberty derived their principles chiefly from the old testament' (Lecky 1913: ii. 172). This tradition became deeply embedded in the conceptual scheme which underlies our ordinary concept of people living together in a community in a reasonable way, each with respected rights which in turn lay obligations upon all.

In appealing as he does to an aspect of this tradition, Buchanan demonstrates clearly that he is fully aware that economic theory must be able to forge links between its formal analysis of rational 'agents' and the traditional concept of rational persons embodied in natural language. The task, however, is a formidable one. Consider to begin with a faint echo of what Buchanan needs, which can be heard through the formalist constructions of Arrow–Debreu general equilibrium theory. When the existence of equilibrium has been proved for a class of such models, the theorist standardly proceeds to a proof that any such equilibrium will be 'optimal' in a certain sense. (The 'optimality' is of a highly restricted kind, as we shall see in Chapters 6 and 7, but let that go for the moment.) This optimality claim is expressed with great clarity by Debreu: 'Given two attainable states of an economy, the second is considered to be at least as *desirable* as the first if every consumer *desires his* consumption in the second state at least as much as *his* consumption in the first' (Debreu 1959: 90, emphasis added).

The personal pronoun used to express the ethical claim concerning 'desirable' states in this passage clearly implies that this ethical claim is about individual *persons*, as indeed it must be in order to make sense. If and only if each 'agent' can be interpreted as a person, the optimality theorem (as far as it goes) may resonate with echoes of those early insights as to the moral importance of individual citizens and of their free choices. This would forge links between the austere mathematics of the Arrow–Debreu proofs and a morally non-trivial concept of rationality.

Two problems immediately arise for the neo-classic, however. The first will occupy us in much of this book, but can be briefly dealt with here for present purposes. It is simply this: if neo-classical theory is to invest its concept of a rational agent with the penumbra of moral seriousness derivable from links to the Scottish moral philosophers and, beyond them, to the concept of rationality which forms part of the conceptual scheme underlying our ordinary language, then it must finally abandon its claim to be a 'value-free' science in the sense of logical empiricism. This will be a recurring theme of the present work, beginning with the next chapter; I leave it aside for now.

The second problem has already been briefly noted: it is what would confront neo-classical theory were it to decide to nail the flag of methodological individualism to its mast. It is thus what concerns us in the present chapter. If neo-classical theory were to pay more than lip service to methodological individualism, it would have to show that its individual agents can and must be individual persons. It is obvious that this would involve difficult tasks within economic theory: how do you open up the 'black box' of an 'agent' which is an organization and separate out the contributions (if any) made to 'its' choices or actions by the many different persons of which it is composed? It is perhaps less obvious that a serious defence of a methodological individualist position would also involve neo-classical theory in several highly controversial philosophical positions.

It would be folly to suggest that all this is not a tall order, and greater folly yet to encourage anyone not utterly committed to the task to attempt it. Yet we have seen the intimate links that for the neo-classic bind together the concepts of individual agent, of rationality, and of general equilibrium. This can be seen with special clarity in a passage from a philosophically thoughtful and life-long contributor to neo-classical analysis, Frank H. Hahn. He is explaining the sense in which he accepts the label 'neo-classical'. He tells us that there are three elements in his thinking which may justify it:

(1) I am a reductionist in that I attempt to locate explanations in the actions of individual agents.
(2) In theorizing about the agent I look for some axioms of rationality.
(3) I hold that some notion of equilibrium is required and that the study of equilibrium states is useful. (Hahn 1984: 1–2)

It is important to add that Hahn tells the reader that he is most comfortable with and feels most strongly about (1). He thus places methodological individualism at the top of his short list of those beliefs which he feels make him a neo-classic. What is more, he interprets his individualism strictly. Declaring that he has no difficulty with the concept of 'class', he stresses that nevertheless 'I have not been able to give meaning to "class interest" or the actions of a class until these interests and actions have been located in the individual member' (Hahn 1984: 2).

Since the individual member of a class is a person, it will be seen that Hahn's methodological individualism, like Buchanan's, is of pure undebased metal. It will also be seen that both Buchanan and Hahn are perfectly clear that the methodological individualist position involves philosophical claims. Buchanan acknowledges descent from the Scottish moral philosophers, while Hahn declares himself a 'reductionist', thereby associating himself with some well-known philosophical debates. The two authors whom I have chosen to quote are, I believe, fair representatives of the more sophisticated and philosophically aware thought on the subject by neo-classical theorists. But of course they are a far cry from run-of-the-mill neo-classical economics, where methodological individualism is naïve and philosophically unexamined. Standard treatments of the rationality of individual economic agents, however, depend for their force and consistency upon the successful resolution of philosophical issues which are left undiscussed and perhaps unnoticed by the average neo-classic.

We have seen why philosophically self-conscious and critical neo-classical theorists would want to embrace methodological individualism. We must now explore the philosophical problems which lie in the way of attempts to carry out the individualist programme. These problems, at their deepest level, constitute a specific case (within economic theory) of a set of philosophical problems which have arisen in numerous contexts throughout the present century. They are problems associated with 'reductionism'.

REDUCTIONISM

Very roughly, a 'reductionist' is someone who wishes to reduce claims about entities of one kind to claims about entities of another kind. Hahn, it will be recalled, wished to translate claims about classes into claims about their individual members. Reductionism often takes the form of the effort to translate talk about some puzzling or (supposedly) questionable aggregate into talk about its constituent parts.

Consider, then, some wholes and their constituent parts. A political assembly may be said to be made up of its members, while a house may be described as made of bricks, and a soufflé as made with eggs, flour, milk, etc. Clearly these sets of parts stand in different relations to their respective wholes. The assembly members can forsake the chamber, temporarily or for good. The bricks have to stay put, but can still be distinguished in the completed house ('the microfilm will be found in this hollow brick marked with a cross'). Whereas, the eggs, flour, milk, etc. become indistinguishably merged in the finished soufflé.

Now as we know an Arrow–Debreu general equilibrium is made up of the equilibrium choices of all of the agents in the model. If each agent has chosen a most highly ranked plan of action from those available to it and so has no incentive to change this, and the model economy possesses certain properties, then the model as a whole is said to be in a state of general equilibrium. This general equilibrium is in this sense the aggregative result of all the individual equilibria achieved by the individual agents. If some property of the equilibrium is then questioned, this property is typically justified by showing that it follows from a property of the individual agents, which has simply been aggregated.

In this way a philosophically naïve methodological individualism can enter the conduct and justification of general equilibrium modelling. To an important extent, the existence and optimality proofs in the Arrow–Debreu tradition can be said to be arguments from properties of the 'individual' agents to properties of the models as a whole. Of course these proofs typically also require that the agents (mathematically) exist in a formal milieu characterized axiomatically as possessing certain properties as a whole. More important for present purposes, however, is the fact that the 'individual' agents (whose interpretation is often left indeterminate) are usually not individuals in the sense required by a philosophically aware methodological individualism. The methodological individualism implicit in general equilibrium theory is thus philosophically naïve. Now, of course, claims about complicated wholes can be difficult to establish. One can easily see why neo-classical theorists, even if wholly free from philosophical aims or beliefs, might want to see if a puzzling aggregate could be reduced to hopefully less intractable parts. For this purely work-a-day purpose, the relevant 'part' might well seem to be the individual actor on a market. But this is not the 'factoring down' relevant to methodological individualism. A single person can act on a market, but so can a giant corporation. The individual market actor is a rather different kind of animal from the individual person. Having performed the technically important and demanding task of constructing general equilibrium models where each market actor plays a distinct role, it is possible for the theorist to confuse this with the quite different achievement of having produced a model where each *person* plays a distinct role. Unwarranted methodological individualist claims can then enter, as it were, through the back door.

Neo-classical economic theorists, it should be pointed out in fairness, were far from being the only thinkers to have embarked on the reductionist path in the present century. The twentieth-century history of philosophy (notably including logical positivism and later logical empiricism) is littered with the ruins of such attempts, some of them of truly heroic proportions. And scientists of a somewhat imperialistic temperament have from time to time tried to invade and colonize other sciences, bent on a reduction of the latter to their own more 'fundamental' science, with battle cries like 'everything is physical'!

Despite the enormous differences between their subject-matters, reductionist projects can exhibit remarkably similar problems. One of these is often signalled by the discovery that the entity being reduced has (or requires) properties as a whole which resist being decomposed. If every member of a political assembly voted for Bostwick, then saying that the assembly voted for Bostwick is literally equivalent to saying that Smith voted for Bostwick, and Jones voted for Bostwick, and so on for all the members of the assembly. But if the members of the assembly were not all of one mind, and there were more than two candidates, then what happened can depend on what sort of voting procedure was being used. And famous paradoxes can arise, as we shall see below. As for the house, even if each individual brick was sound, the house may not be so if the architect miscalculated some stresses. And, alas, even if every ingredient in the soufflé was correct, it still may not rise.

One feature which perhaps characterizes some reductionist projects more than others concerns the question as to where the reduction should stop. Sometimes this is evident. For the purposes of the theorist of voting procedures, the individual members of the assembly are presumably the relevant smallest components. For a psychologist studying phenomena suggesting 'multiple personalities' within a person, however, this might not be so. Some famous reductionist enterprises could find no satisfactory stopping-place, as we shall shortly see.

ONTOLOGICAL VS. LINGUISTIC/EPISTEMOLOGICAL CLAIMS

Aside from their very high failure rate, reductionist projects, at the best, involve the theorist in deep and controversial philosophical claims. Specifically, the doctrine of methodological individualism is seen today to have (at least) two components. First, an ontological claim, about what things exist. Secondly a claim about language, involving a translation of talk about 'aggregates' into talk confined to 'individuals'. This in turn can be presented in such a way that it involves an epistemological claim, about what things we can *know*, and therefore can talk about.

Sometimes the ontological claim is dominant, and the thrust of the argument lies in the effort to deny that certain sorts of things exist. People who saw the terrible results of the totalitarian states of the 1930s and who had read Hegel, tended to blame him for propagating the idea that the State (notice the capital letter) had some sort of superior existence, to which individual persons could be sacrificed. They were liable to react by insisting that only persons 'really exist'—the state was just a collection of individual people. I have always had a great deal of sympathy for those who sincerely saw this move as part of fighting the good fight against the forces of evil, but I wonder if in fact a cloudy ontology is most efficiently deflated by opposing to it an equally questionable 'individualist' ontology.

Whatever its appeal against certain dark doctrines of the 1930s, I think the ontological claim gets one into very deep water, and it is a claim of which economic theorists should be wary. This may be put simply by remarking that today, in different times, it will perhaps be readily accepted that, while the Inland Revenue does not exist in precisely the way in which Mary Smith exists, nevertheless there is a sense in which it certainly does exist. The ordinary common-sense view would be that if Mary Smith were to become persuaded that the Inland Revenue did not exist, then she would be dangerously misled, and the common-sense view would be right.

The doctrine of methodological individualism, as already noted, also needs to make a claim about *language*. If terms standing for 'improper' (i.e. aggregative) entities appear in the scientific discourse, then the doctrine calls for the translation of talk involving the 'improper' aggregative terms into talk consistent with the doctrine. This in turn can have epistemological overtones. The protagonist of a 'logical translation' is rather likely to think that what we truly know, or most directly experience, does not include the referents of the 'improper' terms which the translation is supposed to eliminate. The translation is seen as taking one nearer to the attainment of an 'ideal language'.

Early in the twentieth century, this epistemologically slanted version of reductionism gained great impetus from the logical positivists. If one referred to a material object, this was supposed to be capable of being analysed into a long statement about all the individual 'sense data' one might have of that object. The object was seen as a logical construction out of these sense data. This was part of their vast project of logical translation of every statement about something not 'given' into a set of statements about things which, it was thought, were 'given'. Later (after the movement changed its name from 'logical positivism' to 'logical empiricism') the project of reducing material object language to sense datum language was indeed dropped, but even then the project of reducing terms which refer to what is not immediately observable to 'observation terms' survived in one form or another until the deaths of Rudolf Carnap (1891–1970) and Hans Reichenbach (1891–1953), the movement's great figures.

The short answer to any effort to revive such projects is to point out that these heroic reductionist programmes failed. But it is useful to add that even had they succeeded they would have led to a result which the methodological individualist probably would not want. This is because the reduction would not stop with individual persons. Statements about persons (other than oneself) were first seen as constructions out of statements about one's 'sense data' of them, and later as constructions out of statements about their observable behaviour. Then even these statements were seen to contain elements of a sort that could not be part of perception uncontaminated by theory. The search for the pure 'observation term' and the pure 'observation statement' ended, as is well known, in defeat. The logical positivist/logical empiricist brand of reductionism was not a doctrine which a believer in a methodological individualism resting on the solid reality of individual persons ought to wish to revive.

Yet the linguistic/epistemological element in reductionism appears to be an essential component. It has been recognized by philosophers for some time that reductionism is not simply an ontological claim as to what sorts of entities there are; see, for instance, Geoffrey Hellman and Frank Wilson Thompson (1975). Nor, on the other hand, does the ontological element in reductionism appear to be dispensable. Writing about the specific case of methodological individualism, for example, Julius Sensat has argued persuasively and in detail that, while ontological and linguistic/epistemological elements in reductionism (here as elsewhere) are mutually independent, nevertheless some of the doctrines which the methodological individualist wishes to eliminate 'cannot be ruled out except on the basis of ontological individualism' (Sensat 1988: 193). Again he recognizes that ontological individualism on its own is an insufficient theoretical basis for the doctrine. For one thing, it does not 'rule out the possibility of *sui generis* social laws, long denied by individualists' (ibid.).

Sensat considers the question whether one can weaken the reductionist's 'reducibility' claim to a claim of 'determination' or 'supervenience', as has been attempted in some recent work on the philosophy of mind: 'The intuitive idea here is that fixing individual-level facts also fixed social-level facts; the latter are determined by (or "supervene upon") the former' (Sensat 1988: 192).

He doubts that this genuinely captures the underlying vision of methodological individualism, however, and I believe he is right to do so. 'Supervenience' is, I think, a tool that is likely to turn in the hand of the methodological individualist who takes it up. Whatever 'supervenience' may (or may not) accomplish for the philosopher of mind, its limitations for the methodological individualist can be suggested rather simply. 'Supervenience' cannot guarantee that irreducibly social-level explanation will not be indispensable. As Sensat pertinently notes, this has led to some critics of methodological individualism seizing upon this weakness of supervenience as support for their criticism of individualism (see, for instance, Kincaid 1986). If one distrusts the charms of supervenience, however, one is back with full-blown reductionism as necessary to individualism.

Even this brief sketch of some of the issues may be enough to show that the theorist committed to methodological individualism must be prepared to carry rather a heavy load of philosophical baggage. It is time to turn our attention to the other cost that must be borne if the doctrine is to be adopted seriously by neo-classics, and not simply paid lip service. This is the cost of the developments needed within neo-classical economic theory if its individual agents have to be individual persons.

AGENTS VS. PERSONS

Neo-classical theory, as we know, has not tried to construct its formal models of general equilibrium so that the micro-economic agents were persons. Now it is important for the reader whose background is philosophical (or at any rate outside economic theory) to see that this remarkable fact about the agents in neo-classical general equilibrium models, which so flagrantly violates the supposedly sacred principle of methodological individualism, is not due just to perversity on the part of the theorist.

Neo-Walrasian general equilibrium models are essentially about *markets*, and about the equilibria of markets. So it is perfectly natural for the participants in these models to be just exactly those who act on a market or markets. Hence if a corporation acts on a market as a single agency, then it is modelled as an individual agent. It will be useful to contrast the until recently dominant class of neo-classical general equilibrium models, namely the neo-Walrasian class of models, whose canonical form was as we know that of Arrow–Debreu, with another class of models which until recently constituted a less well-known expression of neo-classical theory: those deriving from the work of Francis Ysidro Edgeworth (1845–1926). Edgeworth will play a major role in Chapters 6 and 7. Meanwhile, it must suffice to note that Edgeworth modelled explicitly something which is off-stage in a neo-Walrasian model, namely the formation and disintegration of coalitions. This makes possible the exploration of the role of individual persons within (more or less unstable) groups, and potentially transcends what occurs on markets. Edgeworth's dazzling work, which was available by the 1880s, was not really appreciated until the 1960s, largely because the mathematical methods needed to give it full expression were only beginning to be applied to economic theory. Since the 1970s, however, a flood of non-Walrasian models for neo-classical theory have been appearing, and many of these are indebted to Edgeworth. If neo-classical theory were to undertake seriously the task of explicitly modelling individual persons, the Edgeworthian tradition in its present-day form might perhaps be the most promising place to start. And there are signs of activity. As has recently been noted by Hal R. Varian, it may be that 'the current "infant" subject of microeconomics is the research that is examining the "micro-microeconomics" of firms, consumers, and markets... the investigations that attempt to go behind the "black box" of the neo-classical firm, consumer and market, and try to understand the internal functioning of these economic institutions' (Varian 1987: 3, 463).

That canonical treatments of the 'individual agent' in the neo-Walrasian tradition *have* left that agent a 'black box' can be seen, for instance, from Debreu, who tells us that: 'When one abstracts from legal forms of organization (corporations, sole proprietorships, partnerships) and types of activity (Agriculture, Mining, Construction, Manufacturing, Transportation, Services) one obtains the concept of a *producer*, i.e., an economic agent whose role is to choose (and carry out) a production plan' (Debreu 1959: 37, emphasis in original). And likewise: 'A *consumer* is typically an individual, it may be a household, it might even be a larger group with a common purpose. His role is to choose (and carry out) a consumption plan made now for the whole future' (Debreu 1959: 50, emphasis in original).

How far Debreu was from taking care of Buchanan's concerns can be clearly seen by noting that Debreu was willing to let 'a larger group with a common purpose' pass muster as a consumer in models for his theory. An organized economic class, after all, could be described as such a group, and this would be anathema to Buchanan! Hahn, who is more tolerant of concepts like economic class than Buchanan, nevertheless insists, as is consistent with his methodological individualism, that class interests and actions be located in the individual member. Of course a corporation should be as much a black box to a methodological individualist as is an economic class. What is sauce for the goose is sauce for the gander.

In contrast with this, the Edgeworthian tradition seeks, as noted above, to explain how groups might coalesce through the forming, breakup, and reforming of coalitions. Two main problems, I believe, can be immediately seen to lie in the path of an attempt to use such an approach to the opening up of black boxes. The first problem is very simple to state. Most actual economic organizations are sharply hierarchical in structure. The overwhelming majority of the persons involved have little or no input into the 'organization's' choices or actions. These are made and acted on at the 'top', and simply imposed from above on those below. Edgeworth's coalitions, on the contrary, were composed of independent persons who felt it to be in their mutual interest to come together and co-operate. If a coalition was not bringing some if its members the hoped-for gains, these disaffected members would leave, break up the coalition, and form a new one (see Chapters 6 and 7 below). This is hardly a picture of a corporation, or even of a small business, unless it were a partnership. It is a *possible* picture of some co-operative organizations.

The second problem confronting an Edgeworthian attempt to break up black boxes would apply even where the black box was made up of a number of equally powerful persons—say partners. Let there be three or more such partners, and (since they are to be equal) give each of them one vote on any disputed choice or action. As long as they are unanimous, no black box develops. To paraphrase Buchanan, each aggregative result (each choice or action of the partnership) can be factored down and explained by the choices or actions of the individual partners. But the moment they need to act and cannot reach a unanimous decision, ancient problems arise on which a vast literature has been written in recent years. We are confronted with the problems of social choice theory.

Only the first few ideas in this field can be presented without the use of advanced tools, but these few elements may suffice for present purposes. The Marquis de Condorcet (1743–94), acknowledging the even earlier work of Jean-Charles de Borda (1733–99), published in the late eighteenth century his seminal treatment of elections (Condorcet 1785) which is now seen as the chief ancestor of the present-day theory of social choice. Amazingly, these works were forgotten until rediscovered by Duncan Black in our own time (Black 1958). Consider the problem where some voting body must choose one alternative from several. The alternative may be a candidate for some office (where only one can be elected) or it may be a policy decision (i.e. to reserve some land for a park rather than allow its commercial development). If there are only two alternatives, then simple majority voting has typically seemed a fair procedure. Once there are three or more alternatives, however, one is confronted with a variety of prima-facie reasonable voting procedures which unfortunately turn out to have serious defects. A central problem, known as the paradox of voting or the Condorcet Paradox, may be illustrated by a simple example where three agents (here called Tom, Dick, and Harry) vote on three alternatives. The alternatives (x, y, and z) are listed in Table 1.1 under each name in order of preference, starting from the top. Following majority rule, we have here x preferred to y, y preferred to z, and z preferred to x, resulting in a preference cycle where every alternative is beaten by another alternative. In such cases, one cannot speak of the group, or society, having a preference ordering—in other words (as it would be expressed nowadays) a social ordering does not exist. Another way of putting this is to say that a meaningful aggregation of the individuals' (Tom, Dick, and Harry's) preferences does not exist.

In a now famous work, Kenneth Arrow proved a general impossibility theorem on the possibility of aggregating individual preference orderings into a social ordering (Arrow [1951b] 1963), given a set of axioms which were believed to be very reasonable at the time. Following his work, an extensive literature developed, spreading beyond economic theory to embrace a wide field con-

TABLE 1.1

Tom	Dick	Harry
x	y	z
y	z	x
z	x	y

taining social sciences and political science, as well as philosophy and certain questions of symbolic logic and mathematics. Arrow's axiom set was later modified in a number of ways, in the search for an escape from the impossibility theorem. Different lines of enquiry were pursued, some of which yielded positive results depending on what exactly was being aggregated, and upon the different axiomatic restrictions imposed on these aggregations. Arrow had argued in his first edition that a great advantage of the axiomatic method was the considerable saving of time obtained by its use, since 'the same system may be given several different interpretations' (ibid. 87). And indeed this was a prophetic claim, destined to be echoed (with justice) many times in subsequent years with reference to various axiomatic developments in economic theory.

But the history of social choice theory has also shown that differing types of social choice problems can require strikingly different approaches. It then became clear that an abstract and general formalization could in fact conceal deeply significant differences between different classes of models for the theory of social choice. (It will be recalled from the Introduction that something similar was found to be the case in respect of general equilibrium theory. It was once argued that this theory had in effect only one significant class of models, the neo-Walrasian. Now everyone knows that strikingly different classes of non-Walrasian models for the theory of general equilibrium are proliferating.)

It is partly as a result of a similar proliferation of different classes of models for the theory of social choice that rather little can be said in general about the state of this field. The interested reader might, however, consult some recent works for a sampling of some strikingly different developments.[1] What can, I believe, be said in general is that, despite the first impression of a purely negative

---

[1] See, for instance, Sen 1982, Suzumura 1983, Nitzan and Paroush 1985, Arrow and Raynaud 1986, Schwartz 1986, and Elster and Hyland 1986.

result which is sometimes the reaction to Arrow's original impossibility theorem, a large number of positive discoveries have been made in respect of certain types of aggregation. But do these positive results with certain kinds of aggregation warrant confidence in the feasibility of opening up the black boxes of neo-Walrasian general equilibrium models, and of showing that the choices or actions made or carried out by each black box is a satisfactory aggregation of the choices or actions of each person in the black box? A reading of the literature suggests that this might still prove a daunting task.

THE PRIORITY OF 'PERSONS'

The philosophical defence of methodological individualism involves the theorist in a reductionist argument which would have to succeed where so many twentieth-century reductionist attempts have failed.[2] Ontological claims of a kind not natural to economic theory would be necessary, but would not be sufficient unless linguistic/epistemological claims could also be sustained. Within neo-classical economic theory, a class of general equilibrium models would have to be constructed wherein every choice or action embarked upon by a black box could be factored down and explained by the choices of all of the individual persons located within the relevant black box. Supposing that developments of the theory of social choice were to make this possible, the fact would still remain that the model economies so characterized were total utopias, without resemblance to or bearing upon a world of extreme inequalities of economic power, where the overwhelming majority of persons have no input into many of the choices most crucially affecting their lives.

All this has serious consequences for the evaluation of the constructed concept of rationality derived from neo-classical theory. In particular, it has serious implications for any non-economist user of the economic concept of rationality. This constructed concept is used to make claims about the rationality of economic agents. But we can now see that this 'agent' for which rationality is claimed is

---

[2] Readers interested in the philosophical background to methodological individualism might well consult Garfinkel 1981.

itself a constructed concept whose relation to a person and that person's choices or actions is at best problematical and at worst undiscoverable or non-existent.

As stated in the Introduction to the work, I wish to defend the concept of rationality which is part of the conceptual scheme embodied in natural language against any unwarranted inroads by the constructed concept of 'rationality' from economic theory. It should therefore cause no surprise that I also wish to defend the concept of a person, which is at least equally embedded in our language, against any unwarranted inroads by the constructed concept of an 'economic agent'. The concept of a person is a fundamental component of the conceptual scheme with which we live, and I can see why Sir Peter Strawson argued strongly for the primitiveness of this concept (Strawson 1959: 81–113). But this does not lead me to believe that those who care about, and wish to defend, the integrity and the rights, goals, agency, and responsibility of persons are at all well advised to follow Buchanan and become involved in methodological individualism. I believe with Strawson that some fundamental truths can only be expressed in terms of the concept of a person. But I believe that other truths of no less importance require, and are properly expressed in terms of, aggregative concepts such as the concept of a community and the concept of a class. Indeed it is for this reason that I shall devote Chapters 8 and 9 of the present work to classical economic theory, where the concept of class is centre stage.

Unquestionably there are legitimate uses in neo-classical theory for the concept of an 'economic agent', left as an unopened black box. This is true provided that there is no pretence that such constructed 'agents' can be treated as the bearers of the rational and moral properties of persons. And (as I shall argue in Chapters 8 and 9) there are by the same token legitimate uses in classical models for the concept of an 'economic class', provided that such constructs are not endowed with the unique properties which belong only to persons.[3]

But now it is time to turn our attention to the first of the different versions of the constructed concept of rationality, which it is our next task to consider.

---

[3] The argument that conflicting classes can result from the rational choices of individual persons, which has been developed by John Roemer (1981, 1982*a*, 1982*b*, 1988, 1992) will be discussed in Chapter 9.

2
RATIONALITY AS
MAXIMIZING UTILITY

IT will be argued in this chapter and the next that the axiomatic utility theory developed by neo-Walrasian economists and by decision theorists, for all its formal austerity, presents a view of rational choice or action which favours teleological (or consequentialist) moral philosophy in general and utilitarianism in particular. Now, of course, most people would agree with John Broome (1991a) that part of ethics is concerned with good. A teleological ethical theory, however, claims (roughly) that the whole of moral philosophy is about maximizing good. Utilitarianism, in its various versions, belongs among teleological theories. Such theories have been shown to lend themselves to formalization in terms of the structure of utility theory, specifically of axiomatic expected utility theory. The structure of concepts like 'good' and 'well-being' (more precisely the structure of the 'betterness' relation) and the formal structure of axiomatic utility theory, have been shown to have important features in common. As we shall see, the economic theorists and decision theorists who developed expected utility theory in the 1950s and 1960s embraced axiomatizations which happen to favour a particular moral philosophy (utilitarianism), all the while believing that they were producing 'value-free' science.

This must not, let me repeat, be taken as a denial of the importance of teleological or consequentialist moral claims. The moral importance of the consequences of our choices or actions has always been recognized in our ordinary moral discourse. But so has the importance of non-teleological moral claims, with which our ordinary language abounds. It has always been thought that some actions were wrong despite their consequences. These claims must have a place in any serious moral theory, and economic theory and decision theory should not be allowed to foreclose what is properly an issue for moral philosophy, simply by adopting particular formal structures as constitutive of rational choice without explicit dialogue on the philosophical issues raised by doing so. That utilitarian properties should lie beneath the surface of an analysis of rationality, rather than being prominently visibly parts of its structure, is a feature of the neo-classical economic theory of the 1930s and after, and of the decision theory which economic theorists adopted in the 1950s. It was not at all characteristic of the original neo-classical economists, who adopted on the whole a full-blooded utilitarianism from classical nineteenth-century utilitarians like Bentham.

BENTHAMITE UTILITARIANISM AND EARLY NEO-CLASSICAL ECONOMICS

Broome has recently observed that, as economists use it, 'the term "utility" has become so ambiguous as to cause immense confusion' (Broome 1991*b*: 3). Not all of this ambiguity, however, was the doing of economists: some of it entered economics from philosophical utilitarianism when William Stanley Jevons (1835–82)[1] happily adopted Bentham's definition of utility (Jevons 1871: 46).[1] Utilitarian philosophy, as we shall shortly see, has had an unhappy relationship with ordinary language since Bentham's time at least, and naturally when the early neo-classical economists brought the concept of utility from philosophy into economic theory, economics inherited these philosophical problems. Nowadays, as the philosophical implications of the uses of utility in economic theory are increasingly probed by philosophically sophisticated economists and economically sophisticated philosophers, questions concerning exactly what economics took over from philosophy with the concept of utility are being re-examined.[2] Some of the current debate reminds me of some earlier thoughts of mine:

---

[1] In our treatment of Jevons, Harvey Gram and I argued that '[t]he core of Jevons' theory is the theory of exchange' (Walsh and Gram 1980: 129). We treated his utilitarianism as unimportant for our purpose. But then we were interested in the contrast between classical theory, where what is allocated is surplus output, and neo-classical theory, where given resources are allocated. So for us the key feature of Jevons's work lay in his development of the theory of the exchange of given stocks. If Philip Mirowski is right, however, the mathematics of maximization and utilitarianism are more deeply interwoven in the neo-classical beginnings than we saw. In any case, Jevons certainly followed Bentham on utility—see for instance Jevons 1879.

[2] See for example, the exchange between John Broome (1991*b*, 1991*c*) and Amartya Sen (1991).

Now *utility* is an ordinary word but it was not used in economic theory simply in the ways in which it is used in English. In economic theory whatever satisfied a desire was said to have 'utility', whereas we ordinarily speak only of things like a Jeep or a plain kitchen table as having utility—we would not say this of a Jaguar or a Chippendale desk. Economic theory took over the constructed concept of 'Utility' from philosophers who had given it a set of uses specifically constructed to make it adapted to expressing their point of view. It was an ethical point of view: The English Utilitarians had an axe to grind. The economists thus inherited a concept burdened with old philosophical debts. (Walsh 1964: 154)

In the early nineteenth-century, Jeremy Bentham (1748–1832) was already worried by the resistance he detected in people to accepting his concept of utility and to admitting it into their moral discourse. Such problems were hardly surprising. Bentham was proposing a thoroughgoing reductionism: he wanted his term 'utility' to stand for 'that property in any object, whereby it tends to produce benefit, advantage, pleasure, good, or happiness (all this in the present case *comes to the same thing*) or (what *comes again to the same thing*) to prevent the happening of mischief, pain, evil, or unhappiness)' (Bentham [1789] 1970: 12, emphasis added).

Bentham did care about language, however, as shows in a touchingly rueful note which, as Sen has pointed out (Sen 1991: 280), Bentham added to the first page of the work already cited in 1822:

The word *utility* does not so clearly point to the ideas of *pleasure* and *pain* as the words *happiness* and *felicity* do... This want of a sufficiently manifest connection between the ideas of *happiness* and *pleasure* on the one hand, and the idea of utility on the other, I have every now and then found operating, and with but too much efficiency as a bar to the acceptance that might otherwise have been given, to this principle. (Bentham 1822: 1 n., emphasis in original).

Bentham, worried about whether language could be made to fit his Procrustean bed, saw only a small part of his problem. For example he treats pleasure as if it belonged to the same logical family as happiness. But words like pleasure and satisfaction are typically used to characterize some occurrence or occurrences, while happiness is typically a dispositional word. The special significance of dispositions in the formation of moral character is an ancient insight, having been well known to Aristotle. Similarly one *makes* choices or *performs* actions on particular occasions—they are occurrences. Preferences on the other hand are dispositions

(Walsh 1954*b*), as are tastes, and for that matter, virtues and vices. An actress may deliver a sentence in French which the director has taught her, but she may not be a French speaker. The analysis of dispositions was revived and much developed by Gilbert Ryle (1949).

One is observing this distinction of logical category when one makes the age-old observation that an excessive pursuit of pleasures may well destroy someone's chances of happiness. Happiness, in this very Aristotelian yet very ordinary sense, is a disposition of character resultant upon having acquired the habit of choosing well. It is certainly not a sum of pleasures—indeed many of the choices through which it was acquired may have been, in themselves, far from pleasant. It will be evident that such uses of language are not 'value free'. The same holds for comparisons of happiness: 'an ancient and quite respectable ethical tradition, begun, I suppose by Aristotle, would claim that "A is happier than B" is a most important kind of ethical utterance' (Walsh 1964: 151).

Of course there are non-ethical uses of words like happy and happiness. Consider this sort of claim: 'I can't think how she can live with herself after what she did, but she takes it in her stride and I swear she seems as happy as a clam.' The important point to see, however, is that this use of happy would not have served Bentham's turn. He was by choice doing explicit moral philosophy. He could not afford to have his readers say: 'I quite understand what you mean by your use of words like happiness and utility, but I see no reason to approve of or follow your utilitarian program.' For Bentham, happiness must be something which it can be seen to be our sole and whole duty to promote. But for this its simple identification with pleasure is fatal.

The sadly ironic thing to note here is that his concept of utility was putting at risk precisely what was most humane and enlightened in Bentham's own thought and in his dedicated efforts at reform. He wanted to subject institutions, such as the savage British penal law of his period, to the devastatingly simple test: did it promote human happiness and reduce human misery as much as possible? Bentham was both a psychological and ethical hedonist. He wanted to say that we necessarily always pursue pleasure and avoid pain because they are our two sovereign masters *and* that it our moral duty to do so. The moral claim, however, was clearly what was vital to the advocacy of his reforms, so let's let him off the logical impropriety of having added psychological hedonism, as it were for good measure. He was still burdened by the drastic reductionism of his boiling down of the concepts of benefit, advantage, pleasure, good, or happiness, into utility. But he was acute enough to see that there was a bar which could prevent acceptance of his principle into ordinary moral discourse as other ideas of philosophical origin or development had been accepted in the past.

He was trying to eliminate hard-won distinctions which were not going to be given up by ordinary language. Pleasure covered a multitude of diverse enjoyments as richly various as an oriental bazaar, with everything from innocent joys to soul destroying drugs. The common moral consciousness was never willing to endorse or condemn these as a job lot. Happiness cannot come to Bentham's aid as he fails to distinguish it logically from pleasure. Even if he had, it would not have been accepted as the whole subject of moral obligation, since it has always been recognized that it can sometimes be our duty to sacrifice our happiness. It is neither accidental nor trivial that our moral discourse developed in such a way as to embody such distinctions, and even reforming zeal (which Bentham possessed in a high degree) was powerless to sweep them away.

Axiomatic decision theorists in the present century, as we shall see, went to great pains to exorcize the ghost of classical Benthamite utility theory, which had been a central concept of the neo-classical economics of Jevons and other early neo-classics (especially Edgeworth, as we shall see in Chapters 6 and 7). But when you expel Bentham from the front door of a building whose formal structure is a natural home for a pure maximizing morality, you are liable to find that he has quietly climbed back in through a rear window. Both the first exorcism, which took place in the 1930s with the blessing of logical positivism, and the second exorcism, which took place in the 1950s with the blessing of logical empiricism, failed, as we shall see, to expel all elements of classical utilitarianism from economics and decision theory.

The roots of these matters go very deep. It has recently been suggested that another piece of borrowing may have had profound significance for the way in which neo-classical involvement with utility developed. Philip Mirowski, in a series of publications, has argued that the nineteenth-century neo-classics borrowed the mathematics of utility theory wholesale from physics: 'There is nothing obvious about the definition of human rationality as the maximization of an objective function over a conserved entity' (Mirowski 1987: 84). He argues that the adoption of this metaphor was far from harmless: 'It surreptitiously presumes an inordinately large amount of structure about the nature of desires and objectives, the role of time, the understanding of causality, the unimportance of process, the conservation of the domain of the objectives...the strict separation of the thing desired and the act of choice, and much, much more' (ibid.)

For the detailed development of the thesis that nineteenth-century economic theory had its hands in the pockets of the mathematical physics of the same period, the reader may be encouraged to sample Mirowski's works.[3]

THE HICKS–ALLEN REVOLUTION

It should be noted that for a long time—from the work of Jevons in the 1870s until the end of the 1920s—neo-classical economics and utilitarianism were quite happy bed-fellows. One can see this from the fact that the theoretical apparatus needed to 'free' economic theory from some of its Benthamite implications had been published, beginning with Edgeworth (1881) and continuing in the early twentieth century at the hands of others. Francis Ysidro Edgeworth (1845–1926) was of course himself a utilitarian, as we shall see in Chapters 6 and 7. But the possibility of using his indifference curves in order to give an account of choice simply in terms of ordered preferences was seen in the very early twentieth century. This possibility did not excite much interest, however, until the avoidance of classical utility theory became a burning issue for economic theorists in the 1930s. Arthur Cecil Pigou (1877–1959), who was a neo-classic of the old school if anyone was, made a striking use of utilitarianism in his welfare economics as we shall see in Chapter 6, and seemed quite at ease with this. But indeed it was partly as a result of this controversial and morally non-trivial welfare economics of Pigou and his followers that utilitarianism had become an embarrassment to neo-classical economists by the 1930s.

[3] See for example Mirowski (1984*a*, 1984*b*, 1987, 1988, 1989).

There were perhaps two outstanding reasons why the tide of opinion turned and began to run strongly against utilitarianism at this time. The first of these lay within economic theory itself, and can be seen most clearly in the work of Lord Robbins (1932, 1935, 1938), during that decade. Pigou's work had supported the 'daring' idea that the well-being or utility of the population of Britain might be greater if income and wealth were less unequally distributed than was the case in that country in the 1930s. This idea was deeply disturbing to orthodoxy, but of course was not new. Pigou was availing himself of the assumptions required to draw out one of utilitarianism's few egalitarian features. (We shall have to discuss utilitarianism and equality in Chapter 7.) Robbins, however, launched a series of attacks on the possibility of making inter-personal comparisons of utility of the sort needed by Pigou's argument. As I wrote many years ago 'part of the motive for the development of theories of [choice] that ran solely in terms of ordered preferences was to offer no basis in the structure of pure value theory for what were regarded as illegitimate developments of welfare economics,—i.e., those dependent on interpersonal comparisons' (Walsh 1964: 149). Economic theorists had been alerted by the work of Pigou and his followers to the fact that utilitarianism could have embarrassing implications: they might have to discuss the distribution of income and wealth, in the depths of the great depression.

Meanwhile the philosophical tide had turned against utilitarianism on a much wider front than economic theory. Early logical positivism had arrived in Britain. Utilitarianism, narrow and constraining though (as we shall see) it can be, was and is a non-trivial *moral* philosophy. And economists were among those who picked up the logical positivist idea that 'real' science was supposed to be value-free and to have no truck, therefore, with a doctrine like utilitarianism. Interestingly enough, Robbins's (1932) original argument against interpersonal comparisons made no use of logical positivism, and was in fact inconsistent with that philosophy (as we shall see in Chapter 7). In his later edition of the same work, however (1935), some positivist tints appeared.

Meanwhile a systematic effort was being made to banish what was regarded as the substance of utilitarianism from neo-classical economics. This task was undertaken by two theorists then at the London School of Economics, Sir John Hicks (1904–89) and Sir

Roy Allen (1906–83), in some widely known joint work (Hicks and Allen 1934).

Essentially what they did was to show informally that the concepts of preference and indifference were enough to account for the choices of an agent, under assumptions of certainty. If I am certain that I can have any of a given set of alternatives, then I can simply pick the one which I prefer. If there are several most highly ranked options available, I can just pick one of these. (In choices under risk, as we shall see, this is not enough: if I am very unlikely to be able to have one alternative, then I must want it very much to try for it instead of some other alternative where the chances of success are far better.)

It will be recalled that the theoretical apparatus that Hicks and Allen used to give a purely 'ordinal' account of choice has been available since Edgeworth's (1881) early work. But neither Edgeworth nor any subsequent theorists until well into the twentieth century saw any great point in the specific use of indifference curves to avoid utilitarianism.[4] Now, however, an account of choice solely in terms of preference and indifference was an idea whose time had come. It should cause no surprise that the joint work of Hicks and Allen won rapid and widespread recognition, and became known as the Hicks–Allen revolution.

This transformation from analysis of rational choice as the maximization of utility to analysis in terms of choice of the most preferred attainable option led, however, to the unwarranted belief that neo-classical theory had been purged of all elements of utilitarianism. Hicks, looking back at his joint work with Allen, wrote, 'If one is a utilitarian in philosophy, one has a perfect right to be a utilitarian in one's economics. But if one is not (and few people are utilitarians nowadays), one also has the right to an economics free from utilitarian assumptions' (Hicks 1939: 18).

---

[4] Around the end of the nineteenth century, it had been seen by the Marquis Vilfredo Pareto (1848–1923) that the choices of an agent in a timeless equilibrium model with certainty could be analysed by means of indifference and preference without using the utility theory then standard in neo-classical economics. (He had, by the way, been in touch with Edgeworth, and discussed aspects of the latter's work in print.) Beginning with a piece addressed to the 'Stella' society, posthumously published (Pareto [1898]) 1966), and from the turn of the century on, he treated this question. But, as Allais (1968, 1979a: 510) has pointed out, Pareto continued to use classical utility in his mature work wherever it was needed. Even the later contribution of Eugenio Slutsky (1915) caused little comment until Hicks and Allen, and others, had drawn attention to the issue.

Now as we shall shortly see, the axiomatic formalizations of neo-Walrasian theory in the 1950s were true to the spirit of the Hicks–Allen revolution. The same component of utilitarianism which had been eliminated informally by Hicks and Allen was later eliminated formally by Arrow and Debreu. Once again a certain specific aspect of utilitarianism, having to do with quantities of utility was left behind. As we shall see, a utility function, in Arrow–Debreu theory, was a representation in real numbers of an ordering.

The 'ordinal' utilitarianism which this left in place would hardly have satisfied the original utilitarian philosophers, who wanted to be able to speak of each person in a society as experiencing a quantity of utility, and also to be able to add these quantities and speak of the sum total of a society's utility. But a number of recent developments have led to a 'thickening' in the utilitarian brew once more. Some of these have to do with the development of various concepts of 'cardinality' and some have to do with the development of different degrees and kinds of interpersonal comparability, including partial comparability. And some result from implications which have been seen to lie in axiomatic expected utility theory.

Hicks and Allen's project, of freeing economic theory from utilitarianism, does not appear to have succeeded after all. Present-day utilitarians have been able to formalize their theories in terms of the axiomatic structure of expected utility theory. In so doing they have produced a philosophical position which has intricate new conceptual implications, but which is none the less unmistakably utilitarian in the character of its moral claims. It is also a position securely based on the constructed concept of rationality in neo-Walrasian theory.

The period during which economic theory contained only those elements of utilitarianism undetected by the surgical probing of Hicks and Allen was remarkably short. Nevertheless, it is worthwhile setting out briefly what these utilitarian elements remaining in even a purely 'ordinal' utilitarianism were. For one thing, it shows how difficult this philosophical position proved to be to eradicate from the structure of neo-classical theory. For another, it sets the stage for the arrival of expected utility theory in economics, for the initial resistance of the economics profession to expected utility, and for the efforts to give the latter as far as possible an 'ordinal' interpretation.

The breakdown of the components of utilitarianism which shows what survived Hicks and Allen's knife, is one which has been widely adopted in the literature of the last fifteen years or so, but it is a broad classification, and should not be assumed to be exhaustive.

SOME ELEMENTS OF UTILITARIANISM

Hicks's claim that an economics based on preference orderings was free from utilitarian assumptions must surely have been one of the most widely accepted philosophical claims ever made by an economic theorist, and the ramifications of this claim throughout neoclassical economics are still important today. After many years of acceptance, however, it has in recent years been increasingly questioned. Indeed, the whole significance of the Hicks–Allen revolution has been the subject of recent controversy; see for example Davis 1990 and the sources cited there.

As already noted, certain key components of utilitarianism survive the informal adoption of the concepts of preference and indifference as sufficient for the explanation of rational choice or action under certainty by Hicks and Allen, and the later axiomatic characterization of rationality in terms of the concept of an ordering by Arrow and Debreu. Most generally, utilitarian theories are members of the class of teleological or consequentialist theories. Consider a well-known definition owing to John Rawls: a moral philosophy, he claims, is teleological if 'the good is defined independently from the right, and then the right is defined as that which maximizes the good' (Rawls 1971: 24). A teleologist should never face insoluble moral conflict: choices or actions are to be judged by their contribution to good—there is a *single maximand*. As John Broome has put it: 'A teleological theory...will have to supply a mapping from goodness to rightness. The standard sort of teleology is *maximizing*' (Broome 1991*a*: 6, emphasis in original). The links between teleology and the Hicks–Allen concept of a preference ordering show very clearly in Broome's position: 'That rightness is determined by goodness is genuinely a constraint on teleology. It means that teleology is constrained by the *structure of good*...A teleological theory implies that between acts there is a *betterness* *relation*: —— is at least as good as —— (where the blanks are to be filled in with acts), and that this relation determines the rightness of acts' (Broome 1991*a*: 11, emphasis in original). Broome argues that a betterness relation is necessarily an ordering. This will call for comment in Chapters 3 and 4, where choice under unresolved conflict will concern us. Leaving this deep question aside for now, one can see what Broome is claiming when he writes: 'Any ethical theory with a maximizing structure is teleological, and what it aims to maximize is what it takes to be good' (Broome 1991*a*: 13).

Secondly, utilitarian theories have traditionally been a special class of teleological theories, where what the theory aims to maximize (and therefore sees as the content of 'good') is identified with welfare, happiness, satisfaction, or desiredness. One (or some combination of) these is then what the theory refers to as 'utility'. This property, usually known as 'welfarism' characterized classical nineteenth-century utilitarianism, and as we shall shortly see it still characterizes utility theory in its axiomatic dress and particularly in its formulation as axiomatic expected utility theory. Teleology (or consequentialism) alone, it will appear in due course, is necessary but not sufficient for a theory to be utilitarian. Neo-classical utility theory thus remained utilitarian because it remained a welfarist consequentialism, or welfarist teleology, despite the labours of Hicks and Allen (and the later labours of Arrow and Debreu and of the decision theorists who shaped axiomatic expected utility theory).

Finally we have a third property, or more precisely a group of properties, which characterized classical utilitarianism and which were indeed eliminated by Hicks and Allen from their treatment of rational choice under certainty. Classical utilitarianism had been interested in the maximization of the sum of all the utilities enjoyed by the individual persons in a society. States of that society would then be ranked according to the size of that sum. This has been referred to in the recent literature as 'sum-ranking'.[5] So a strictly ordinal theory, which therefore lacks sum-ranking, is nevertheless recognizably utilitarian by virtue of being teleological (or consequentialist) and welfarist, and is thus seen as a version of

[5] On sum-ranking, see Sen and Williams 1982: 3–4 and Sen 1982: 28, 1987: 39, 1992: 13–14, and the sources cited in these works.

utilitarianism—albeit a 'thinner' one than the classical—by friend and foe alike. Utilitarianism is a deeper and more complicated doctrine than has sometimes been realized, and a number of its most significant features, as well as its most serious defects, still show up even in its 'thinnest' form.

AXIOMATIC UTILITY THEORY

If the utility theory with the 'richest' mixture of philosophical utilitarianism was that of the classical utilitarians, then that with the thinnest mixture (or with the lowest 'octane level') was surely that of the canonical Arrow–Debreu formalization of the case of choice under certainty. If every agent can make a plan for the complete future of a model, knowing all relevant facts about that model with certainty, then we have the beginnings of a formalization of the situation which Hicks and Allen considered informally. All an agent needs for choice is to be able to rank all the relevant alternatives, and choose a plan which yields a most preferred alternative in every case.

In the axiomatizations within this class of canonical Arrow–Debreu models utility, or rather the concept of a utility function, was not even the starting-point of the theory: it was defined in terms of other prior concepts of the axiomatizations. The concept of a ranking (generally an ordering) was first formalized, and then the concept of a utility function was defined in terms of this (with the addition of a concept of continuity).

This feature of Arrow–Debreu theory is sometimes used to make the claim that, since a 'utility function' has just exactly the sense given to it by the axioms from which it is derived, no elements of utilitarianism cling to it. The claim that the canonical Arrow–Debreu utility function has utilitarian properties, however, is a claim about its structure. This structure comes to it from the ordering from which it is derived. Anyone who accepts this structure as characterizing the formal nature of rational choice or action will never have to make judgements whose form is not teleological and welfarist. Present-day formalizations of philosophical utilitarianism can take up residence and live happily within the axiomatic structure of Arrow–Debreu utility theory (and within the structure of axiomatic expected utility theory, as we shall see in due course). A utilitarian resident within this kind of moral economy lives in a world whose constructed language especially favours utilitarian claims as to what is rational and what is good.

But none of this, let me repeat, requires challenging the claim that the concept of a utility function is a derived concept, wholly defined in terms of the prior concepts of ordering and continuity. To see this, however, it will be necessary to glance at that part of the Arrow–Debreu axiomatization which directly concerns rational choice or action. I shall be as informal as possible (with the interests of non-economist readers in mind) and avoid any discussion of the merits of alternative formalizations. In common with other axiomatic work, the Arrow–Debreu tradition had some freedom as to what exactly to adopt as primitive (or undefined) notions of the axiomatization. It has been fairly usual, however, to treat as primitive the binary relation 'is preferred or indifferent to', often written R. Where x_1 and x_2 are two choices from the set of X, of all those possible for an agent, we can then write 'x_1 is preferred or indifferent to x_2' as 'x_1Rx_2'. (Recall that in Arrow–Debreu models, a choice was of an entire plan for the whole future of an agent.) It was then assumed that the relation R was an ordering.[6] A binary relation is an ordering if and only if:

(1) For all x in X, xRx.
(2) For all x_1, x_2, x_3, in X, if x_1Rx_2 and x_2Rx_3, then x_1Rx_3.
(3) For all x_1, x_2 in X, either x_1Rx_2 or x_2Rx_1. (Note that 'or' is used in its non-exclusive sense.)

I shall not pause long over the first requirement, known as 'reflexivity': clearly every alternative must be at least as good as itself. The requirement listed as (2) above, transitivity, used to be regarded as virtually a matter of logical necessity, but as we shall see in the next couple of chapters, it has recently come under heavy fire. Finally, requirement (3) above is usually known as 'completeness', and is far from trivial. The assumption that an agent can rank every single element in X is a deep and highly restrictive one to impose on a ranking, as we shall see in Chapters 3 and 4. When made for a class of formal models of general equilibrium endowed

---

[6] A binary relation which is reflexive, transitive, and complete, is also known in the literature as a 'weak ordering', a 'complete pre-ordering', and a 'complete quasi-ordering'.

as well with other unreal features, such as complete futures markets, a fantasy world is created in which the assumption of completeness may not possess a degree of unreality greater than that of other properties of such models, such as the assumption of perfect competition. One of the principle tasks of Chapters 6 and 7 will be to provide the non-economist reader with a sufficiently detailed sketch of a simple class of neo-classical general equilibrium models for it to be clear in what kind of theoretical context economic theorists have in fact used the axiom of completeness. It should be said immediately that for a moral philosopher, who is presumably writing about real persons, and not formal 'agents', and about choices made in the totally uncertain world in which we live, the axiom surely stands in need of more defence. The computational abilities needed even by the 'agent' in a canonical Arrow–Debreu model were staggering, and the person facing moral problems needs an at least equally complete knowledge of the morally right choice in the face of all moral dilemmas for the axiom of completeness to be a reasonable assumption in the context of moral choice.

Meanwhile, it may be remarked that one can treat the assumption that each agent possesses an ordering as a single axiom, as will sometimes be convenient in this chapter. Or one can spell it out, treating reflexivity, transitivity, and completeness as separate axioms, as will be convenient in Chapters 3 and 4, where we shall want to discuss rankings which violate one or more of the requirements for an ordering, and which are increasingly to be found in current treatments of general equilibrium. It will be useful to have a notation for each of the component parts of what is asserted when one writes 'x_1Rx_2'. One is asserting that, for some agent, either x_1 and x_2 are ranked equally, or x_1 is preferred to x_2. The first case is what is called 'indifference', conventionally written 'x_1Ix_2'. It is defined: x_1Ix_2 if and only if x_1Rx_2 and x_2Rx_1. We shall need a notation for 'preferred to'. This is normally referred to as 'strict preference' and written 'x_1Px_2', and is defined: x_1Px_2 if and only if x_1Rx_2 and not x_2Rx_1.

Once the choices of an agent in a canonical Arrow–Debreu model had been assumed to conform to an ordering, it required essentially the adoption of one more axiom to endow the agent with a 'utility function'. This is a real-valued function which, given certain conditions, can be said to 'represent' the agent's ordering. It is derived from the agent's ordering by means of an axiom of continuity. Choices (or 'plans') ranked equally by an agent are then said to form an indifference class. (The set of points on an indifference curve in elementary micro-economic theory constitute such a class.) The set of alternatives possible for an agent, X, is then partitioned into such indifference classes. Can one then associate with each such indifference class a real number so that, where indifference class I_2 is preferred to indifference class I_1, the number assigned to I_2 will be greater than the number assigned to I_1? (See Debreu 1959: 55–6.)

It will turn out that, very roughly, where an agent's ordering yields the familiar indifference curves, such a real-valued function will exist. But if the agent has a so-called 'lexical' ordering, where there are no indifference curves—indeed no indifference choices at all—such a real-valued function will not exist, although other representations have been found. (Lexical orderings will come up in Chapter 7.) Debreu's axiom of continuity was designed to rule out lexical orderings—in effect, to guarantee the existence of the familiar indifference map.

For any given agent, consider a pair of sets. First the set of all choices which are ranked by the agent as no better than a choice x_1. This is called the lower contour set of x_1. Secondly, the set of all choices which are considered at least as good as x_1, known as the upper contour set of x_1. If I_1 is any indifference curve, and x_1 any point on it, then the lower contour set contains all the points on I_1 plus those lying below it, while the upper contour set contains all the points on I_1 plus those lying above it. The two sets intersect in the points on the indifference curve I_1.[7] Now Debreu's axiom is designed to guarantee that any point like x_1 will lie on an indifference curve, which forms the boundary between points ranked below x_1 and points ranked above x_1. Roughly, Debreu's axiom of continuity requires that:

For all x_1 in X, the upper contour set of x_1 and the lower contour set of x_1 are closed in X.

Crudely, a set is said to be closed if its limit points belong to it. One may visualize the effect of this axiom in the simple case of a two-dimensional indifference map. Sometimes a utility surface is shown in a third dimension, with indifference curves appearing as

---

[7] The properties of upper and lower contour sets play an important role in Chapter 6, where they are discussed and illustrated.

contour lines on a sort of 'hill'. More highly ranked indifference curves lie higher up on the hill—greater or less height representing the preference ranking. This surface, with its third axis designated utility, constitutes a simple model of a real-valued representation of preference, or 'utility function'. It implicitly depends on continuity.

Generalizing earlier work, Debreu proved that any ordering satisfying the continuity axiom is representable by a real-valued function. Actually, if U is a real-valued representation of a given agent's ordering, then any positive monotonic transformation of U is equally a representation of that ordering. It will be seen that, if the utility associated with x_1 is greater than that associated with x_2, then this represents the fact that x_1 is preferred to x_2; but no meaning is attached to saying that (for instance) the agent experienced fifty utils. This is to be expected, since the information conveyed by the utility function was derived from the agent's ordering, plus the axiom of continuity. This is roughly what is intended when such real-valued representations are described as 'ordinal' utility functions.

On the other hand, for all their formal derivation, real-valued representations of orderings are not just uninterpreted real functions possessing certain mathematical properties. They are representing orderings, and not just any ordering relations—say 'at least as soluble as', or 'at least as ugly as'. The binary relation R which is being represented is specified as standing for 'at least as preferred as', 'at least as desired as', or 'at least as good as', which, while far from being equivalent, all have to do with the sort of subject-matter that has been the habitat of utilitarianism. Debreu was entirely consistent with this tradition when he observed that his utility function 'gives a precise content to the intuitive notion of a numerical measure of how satisfied the ith consumer is with x_i' (Debreu 1959: 56).

Nor is the utility maximization garb something tacked onto the theory as an afterthought. It derives from the fundamental assumption of an ordering, together with the assumption of continuity. Nor was it treated as in any sense peripheral to the theory in developments or applications. As for the attitudes of philosophers, well it certainly would not suit Bentham: it represents the lowest octane version of utilitarianism. But 'ordinal' or 'preference function' utilitarians have been able to live with it, and it has been a bracing but hospitable environment for a utilitarian moral philosophy which is consequentialist, welfarist, and ordinal.

The octane level of the utilitarian elements in neo-classical theory had initially been reduced by the work of Hicks and Allen, later formally expressed in canonical Arrow–Debreu models dealing with choice under certainty. But even as the earliest such axiomatic models were appearing, utility was in process of being enriched again (although this was a long time in being recognized) with the gradual absorption by neo-classical theory of the analysis of decision-making under risk by means of the concept of expected utility.

It was really the publication of the work of John von Neumann and Oskar Morgenstern ([1944] 1947) which forced questions concerning utility maximization in risky situations upon the attention of economists. Word spread that Neumann and Morgenstern were using a classical concept of utility, and the reaction of religiously ordinalist economists to this news was at first predictably negative. Calm was restored when the new theory was given an 'ordinalist' interpretation. A few voices were raised in objection to this interpretation, most notably that of Maurice Allais. But until recent years, few paid serious attention to the dissidents.

ORIGINS OF EXPECTED UTILITY THORY

The expected utility hypothesis has a long history, and at least a sketch of this—however elementary it may seem to specialists in decision theory—is necessary if readers who have not studied the area are to follow present-day arguments for and against expected utility theory. The first discussion of the idea seems to have arisen over some problems with the concept of 'expected value'. Discussions of this rule have been found as early as the mid-sixteenth century, as has been noted by Paul Anand (1993: 3). The 'expected value' of an action was seen as the sum of the monetary pay-offs, weighted by their probabilities. Certain paradoxical results of this idea came to be known as the 'St Petersburg Paradox'. Daniel Bernoulli (1700–82) had held a mathematical post at St Petersburg; his cousin Nicholas pointed out the problem, and Daniel and Gabriel Cramer appear to have independently suggested what has become a famous solution. Cramer did this in a letter to Nicholas Bernoulli and Daniel in his famous paper (Bernoulli 1738).

Returning to the St Petersburg Paradox: the expected value rule implies that one should be willing to pay any price to take part in a series of gambles the sum of whose expected values is infinite. What Bernoulli and Cramer saw was that, as an agent's wealth increases, a given addition to the agent's money holdings is valued less than avoiding loss. Their approach to the problem is normally expressed by saying that they argued that the agent should consider the expectation of utility rather than the expectation of monetary gain. Now, as we shall see, it has been argued that Bernoullian 'utility'[8] is the cardinal utility of classical utilitarianism. Maurice Allais always claimed that Bernoulli's concept was in fact cardinal utility of the sort attacked by Hicks & Allen. And several different commentators, over many years and for very different reasons, have been united in insisting that Bernoulli's original hypothesis differed significantly from present-day axiomatic expected utility theory.

Allais claimed from the beginning that, for Bernoulli, cardinal utility existed '*independently of the consideration of random outcomes*' (Allais 1979*a*: 521, emphasis in original). Furthermore, that Bernoulli's purpose was only to offer a model that would explain the St Petersburg Paradox and that he was well aware that his model was not a general one. Thus when Allais launched his critique of twentieth-century axiomatic expected utility theory, he incorporated in his criticism a couple of general claims which were bound to be unpopular at the time: that the original Bernoullian theory rested on classical cardinal utility, and that it was not intended by its author to be a general theory of choice or action under risk or uncertainty.

Up to the publication of the work of John von Neumann and Oskar Morgenstern (1944) there had appeared to economists to be nothing to challenge the fashionable pure ordinalism of Hicks and Allen. Things were to be found in the history of the literature of decision theory, of course. Bernoulli's work was highly relevant, as was Frank Plumpton Ramsey's now celebrated paper, written in 1926 and posthumously published in Ramsey (1931). But this essay,

---

[8] Bernoulli's word was emolumentum, as is noted by Broome (1991*a*: 58 n. 19). He argues that when Bernoulli writes in Latin of the emolumentum of some outcome for a given person, he means 'how good that outcome is for the person' (ibid.).

as William Fellner has remarked, 'was not very widely known and was not even mentioned in the *Theory of Games*' (Fellner 1967: 42). It was thus in Neumann and Morgenstern that economists were first compelled to confront a theory involving cardinal utility again. As has been noted by Ole Hagen, the initial ordinalist reaction was 'to raise doubts about the validity of the theory. The second was to give it an interpretation which did not conflict with ordinalism in general' (Hagen 1979: 17). It is becoming recognized today that, as Robin Pope has recently put it, 'the logical positivist doctrine of revealed preferences contributed to efforts in the early nineteen fifties to disown the utility mapping embedded in the expected utility procedure' (Pope 1994*b*: 6).

This was the situation when Allais launched his now famous critique of what he called the 'American School' at a conference in Paris in 1952, and (although it was not necessary to his critique) insisted on supporting the idea of utility in the classical sense. Hagen has recalled that in the discussion of Allais's critique 'the defenders of the expected utility principle all appeared to be ordinalists, which does not at all follow from the original von Neumann-Morgenstern presentation' (Hagen 1979: 18). Indeed Allais claimed that for Neumann and Morgenstern themselves, utility was cardinal in the sense of the late nineteenth-century neo-classics: 'it represents the intensity of preferences' (Allais 1979*b*: 7). He argued that Neumann and Morgenstern used experiments involving random choice simply as their way of determining actual differences in satisfaction, or utility in the sense of the founders of neo-classical theory. To Allais, it should be stressed, this was not a fault, since he has always believed in utility in this sense himself. (His critique lay quite elsewhere.) But in the climate of the times, what he found acceptable in expected utility theory was as controversial as what he objected to—a strictly ordinalist interpretation had become an item of faith. For Leonard Savage, for instance, cardinal utility in the sense of the early neo-classics was 'undefined, now almost obsolete, completely discredited, and mystical' (Savage 1954, cited by Allais 1979*b*: 7–8).

If Savage's denunciation of classical utility sounds a trifle extreme, the reader must bear in mind the climate of the times. Consider the situation of an economist who proposed (especially in America) to re-examine the validity or usefulness of cardinal utility in the early 1950s. This concept, as we have seen, was associated with writings critical of the distribution of wealth and income such as those of the old welfare economics of Pigou, and the times were not such that ideas potentially critical of the existing social arrangements were looked upon with favour. Then, for good measure, the whole weight of logical empiricist philosophy—not to mention the formalist posture of economic theory—further told on the side of discretion.

It should be noted here that, although Allais consistently supported the old Benthamite concept of utility, he was careful to point out that his critique of the 'American School' could be conducted without introducing this concept at all (Allais 1979c: 133). It should be stressed once more that a theory of expected utility does not have to adopt the classical concept of utility in order to be utilitarian. Recall that a purely ordinal account of choice can retain key utilitarian components.

The critique of expected utility theory begun by Allais many years ago, and now being developed by a growing number of younger theorists, is vital to our appraisal of the constructed concept of rationality in its axiomatic expected utility dress. This critique, however, would be somewhat opaque to readers who have not read the expected utility literature without some sketch of the elements of axiomatic utility theory. I shall therefore make some rather general comments on the most important axioms, deliberately avoiding those matters of formalization which distinguish one celebrated version from another. This procedure is bound to leave the proponents of any given axiomatization dissatisfied, so I crave the patience of professional decision theorists during this section.

SOME AXIOMS OF EXPECTED UTILITY THEORY

In standard versions of expected utility theory the agent is assumed to be able to rank all possible outcomes; the axioms of transitivity and completeness thus play an important role, just as they did in the formal account of choice or action under conditions of certainty. Matters then diverge, however. Various axioms have been used in different formalizations of the theory (part of the difference being due to the manner in which probabilities are handled by different authors). For our purposes the following sketch should, I believe, suffice.

It is usual to adopt an axiom guaranteeing continuity in the following sense. Consider a simple situation where there are just three objects of choice, i.e. 'prospects'. Suppose that an agent prefers x_1 to x_2 and x_2 to x_3. It is argued that, in that event, there must be a 'gamble' or 'lottery', where x_1 and x_3 are the outcomes, such that the agent will be indifferent to having the certainty of x_2 or having this lottery (involving x_1 and x_3). If the chance of getting x_1 in the 'lottery' is great enough, the agent will prefer the 'lottery' to x_2. If the chance of getting x_1 is very small, the agent will prefer the certainty of x_2 to the 'lottery'. Since the agent's preference for the 'lottery' is a function of the probability in this way and the probability of x_1 is assumed to change continuously from 1 to 0, there must be a definite point (i.e. a possible value of the probability) at which the agent's preference for the lottery changes into a preference for the certainty of x_2. It is evident that any triple of cardinal numbers would have done as well if and only if the numerical difference between the utility number given to x_2 and that given to x_3 is twice that between x_1 and x_2. More formally, the expected utility function is unique up to a positive linear transformation.

It should be noted that the procedure just sketched has sometimes been given a heroic interpretation, the idea being that it supposedly enables axiomatic utility theorists to keep their hands free of infection from the grubby old notion of classical cardinal utility. For Allais, however, as we have seen it was simply a procedure for estimating differences in cardinal utility which has to be presupposed anyway. An increasing number of younger theorists born too late to have been deeply affected by logical empiricist scruples concerning cardinal utility, are sympathetic towards Allais today on this as well as other issues. We shall catch a glimpse of this in the next chapter.

It is usual to regard the next (and last) axiom which we will discuss here as the most controversial. This is the 'independence' axiom, or 'sure-thing' principle (in its post-Savage form). There are many versions on offer, the specifics of each depending, of course, on the particular formalizations used in the many axiomatizations of expected utility.[9] One line of approach can be sketched as follows. Consider two prospects facing an agent, x_1 and x_2, and suppose that the agent prefers x_1 to x_2. Now, for any other prospect x_3,

---

[9] Two recent works in which the reader will find discussions from a number of points of view are Gardenfors and Sahlin 1988 and Bacharach and Hurley 1991.

the agent must prefer a given probability mixture of x_1 and x_3 to a similar probability mixture of x_2 and x_3. Likewise, if the agent is indifferent between x_1 and x_2, and x_3 is any other prospect, then the agent must be indifferent between getting a given probability mixture of x_1 and x_3 and getting a similar probability mixture of x_2 and x_3.

Many violations of independence have been pointed out since the pioneering work of Allais in the early 1950s, and some will be discussed in the next chapter. Perhaps some of the most immediately intuitive examples arise over the 'menu dependence' of choice. Menu dependence affects even choices under certainty, and can be illustrated by a simple example where risk is not at issue. Suppose I have been brought up never to take the largest apple when offered a fruit bowl at a children's party, and that I decide always to take the second largest. Let x_1 and x_2 be apples, x_2 being the larger. Then from this 'menu' I shall take x_1. But now suppose that x_3 is larger than x_2. Then from a menu which includes x_3, I shall take x_2. We can easily introduce risk. At Irish race meetings sixty years ago, my parents would place one or two small bets for me. Suppose I had a friend whose parents never placed any bets for her. Now if I have bets on only two horses, Croppy Boy and Tipperary Lass, and I fancy Croppy Boy most, I can give my friend Croppy Boy and keep Tipperary Lass for myself. But if I am given a third bet on Wings of the Morning, now the hot favourite, I can keep Croppy Boy and give her Wings. Instead of the second largest apple, I am taking the second most fancied bet. (Menu-dependent choice and its implications will be discussed in Chapter 4.)

Underlying the various formulations of independence and the sure-thing principle is an important concept: separability. This requires, roughly, that one's preferences about what happens in one state be not affected by what happens in another. Even where the 'states' at issue are states of nature, separability is often violated. Consider Carmen, a single mother living in New York with her daughter Juanita. Carmen works long hours to make the best life possible for Juanita, leaving the child with her grandmother, but she can afford few treats for the little girl. She takes Juanita to the beach as often as possible in the summer for day trips, but they cannot be many. She was planning one for the coming Sunday, but has not yet told Juanita. Now the Weather Channel is showing a

TABLE 2.1

States		States	
good weather	bad weather	good weather	bad weather
works & makes \$	works & makes \$	Juanita happy	Juanita miserable
(x_1) Work		(x_2) Trip	

distinct possibility of bad weather. Consider two possible states of nature, good weather and bad, as shown in Table 2.1.

If she goes ahead with the trip, Juanita will be wildly happy if the weather is good, but miserable if the weather is bad. Whereas if Carmen spends the weekend working, she will earn money which will make more such trips possible later on. This choice gives Carmen the certainty of avoiding disaster, and she simply cannot afford to have one of their days at the beach together be a disaster. But certainty is not a property of any state of nature taken separately. As Broome remarks of a similar example: 'The fact of certainty only appears when you take the states together. So state-by-state comparison is inadequate if you like to be certain. In general, it is inadequate if the value of what happens in one state depends on what happens in another' (Broome 1991a: 23).

So Carmen's ranking, which would ordinarily be said to be eminently rational, violates separability between states—what happens in one state is not, for her, independent of what happens in others. Separability between states of nature has been widely questioned but, as we shall see in the next chapter, separability between *times* looks, if possible, even more doubtful. It requires us to claim that what happens at one time does not affect an agent's preferences at another time. Broome, who shows with pellucid clarity how deeply dependent utilitarianism is upon the concept of separability, is explicit in stating that he is unwilling to defend separability between times, which utilitarianism requires (Broome 1991a: 29).

After the initial qualms concerning the species of 'cardinality' involved, which we have noted, expected utility theory was widely accepted by economists, almost its only severe critic for many years being Allais. The theory rapidly became a standard component of the extension of neo-Walrasian analysis to models where agents faced risk. In 1952 Arrow and Allais had presented independently developed models of neo-Walrasian general equilibrium with risk-bearing. These were published as Arrow 1953 and Allais 1953b.

In the last fifteen years or so, however, growing dissatisfaction has arisen over two distinguishable but related issues. The Expected utility theory can be seen as a formalization of a hypothesis about how people actually choose in risky situations, or as an account of how they would choose if they were rational. The experimental evidence that people do not conform to the axioms of expected utility has by now reached the point that the theory is no longer taken very seriously as an account of how in fact people choose. Since my concern in this book is with constructed concepts of rational choice, I shall not offer another survey of these experimental results.[10]

Before passing to the critique of expected utility as a theory of rational choice or action, it should be noted that persistent failure of the theory as an account of actual choice or action can impinge on its status as an account of rationality. Philosophically, this failure forces the theorist to adopt a radically revisionist concept of rationality. The theorist must say in effect 'if you don't act in conformity with my axioms then you simply are not rational'. Interestingly, while this line has been taken on occasion, the supporters of expected utility theory have also shown a desire to convince their critics that the dictates of the theory as to what was 'rational' would be accepted by reasonable people, once the technicalities of the theory were understood. Thus there has been an argument in defence of axiomatic utility theory which, in philosophical terms, has amounted to an appeal to ordinary language! There has also been a willingness to react to the paradoxes pointed out by critics by attempts to modify the axiomatic structure so as to remove what appeared paradoxical.

The claims of expected utility theory to characterize rationality, and the more general claims of utilitarianism as a whole, will be explored in the light of present-day criticism in the next chapter.

---

[10] An up-to-date evaluation, together with both recent and earlier references will be found in Anand 1993: 17–42. He concludes that, of the evidence reviewed, 'very little seems to validate [expected utility theory]. Rather, the evidence that does exist seems to go against both explicit and implicit assumptions' (ibid. 42).

3

CRITIQUES OF RATIONALITY AS MAXIMIZING UTILITY

ANY discussion of the criticism which has been levelled at expected utility theory, even a brief sketch like the present, must start with the work of Maurice Allais. Only a few of his leading ideas, however, can be noted here. Allais is famous for his examples, which offer us pairs of situations in which a reasonable person, choosing subject to risk, may make what for expected utility theory are conflicting decisions. Thus Allais habitually argued that a rational person might well prefer certainty where this is attainable and important sums of money are at issue, and yet at the very same time when dealing with outcomes which are far from certain, weigh utilities by their probabilities as the theory requires (Allais 1979c: 92). On the other hand, when in the neighbourhood of certain ruin, a rational but prudent person might well follow the dictates of expected utility theory as long as the chances of ruin are small, yet simply stay away from any option where the chances of ruin are greater than some maximum acceptable level.

Consider, to see the point of the concept of certainty, a version of a famous paradox of Allais's (1979c: 89). It is assumed that the outcomes, or prizes, are to be valued simply according to their money value in each case. The agents can choose lotteries A or B in Problem 1, and can choose lotteries A' or B' in Problem 2.

Allais, and many others following him, have argued that a rational person might well choose lottery A in Problem 1 and B' in Problem 2, thereby opting for certainty where it is available, yet choosing the small chance of a very large prize in Problem 2 over the slightly greater chance of a much smaller prize. It will be seen from Table 3.1 that certainty is not a property of any single state of nature alone. This has the consequence that Allais's choice violates the independence axiom. Peter Fishburn, who considers six versions of the independence axiom, offers as his general under-

TABLE 3.1 *States of Nature*

Problem 1	1%	10%	89%
Lottery A	1	1	1
Lottery B	0	5	1
Problem 2			
Lottery A'	1	1	0
Lottery B'	0	5	0

Note: All prizes are in millions of dollars.

standing of Allais's critique that an individual's preference judgement should be based on a comparison of the two relevant prospects 'in their full perspectives and not on a comparison of separate parts' (Fishburn 1979: 249). We may contrast this 'holistic' point of view which Fishburn finds characteristic of Allais and those who have followed him with the belief in separability which is a leading characteristic of the defenders of the independence axiom in its various forms (including the sure-thing principle).

We have already noticed some problems with separability across states of nature in looking at Carmen's problem in Chapter 2. As John Broome is careful to note,[1] when it is legitimate to assume separability 'the metaphor of weighing goods is appropriate; otherwise it is not. When the locations are states of nature, the leading theory about how good should be aggregated across them is *expected utility theory*, and separability is the key assumption of this theory' (Broome 1991*a*: 23–4, emphasis in original). Utilitarianism in its present-day axiomatic expected utility dress is thus deeply involved with separability. As it happens, utilitarianism needs separability in respect of states of nature, persons, and times. Independence axioms in the various versions of expected utility theory can be violated by failures of separability between times—indeed, separability between times is especially crucial for utilitarianism—so this may be conveniently used as an example of what is at issue. Can outcomes, it may be asked, be evaluated separately time by time, or does what happened at a certain time interact with what happens later?

---

[1] The non-economist reader will find an excellent account of separability in Broome 1991*a*: 60–89. The formal theorems underlying this account are owing to Debreu (1954) and W. M. Gorman (1968).

There is a nice illustration of failure of separability between times in the recent work of Mark Machina (1989). His example involves a mother with two children, a son and a daughter. I shall instead consider a situation where Mother has two daughters, Muriel and Gwendolyn, who are identical twins with exactly similar histories, needs, and capabilities (on needs and capabilities, see Sen 1992). A horse-coping friend of Mother's now makes the following offer: either girl may ride a splendid mare, Tempest, in a forthcoming show. Muriel and Gwen are equally good horsewomen, of course, and neither Mother nor Tempest's owners mind which daughter shows the horse. Mother wishes one daughter to have the chance, but sees no argument in favour of choosing between them. She judges that the fairest thing is to let the issue turn on the toss of a coin. So Mother prefers the probabilities $\frac{1}{2}:\frac{1}{2}$ of Muriel or Gwen riding to any other, and prefers this to either of the certain outcomes. Unknown to Mother, there is one difference between the histories of her two daughters, however: Muriel has been secretly seeing a decision theorist (much older). Muriel, keeping quiet about her (to Mother) undesirable connection, now asks for a written confirmation from Mother, before the toss of the coin, that Mother strictly prefers the 50:50 gamble to giving Tempest to Gwen. Notice that Muriel has left herself free to claim Tempest if she wins. In fact, she loses. She now produces Mother's signed note, declaring a preference for tossing the coin over simply giving Gwen the horse to ride. She insists that, on Mother's own stated preferences, she should toss again.

Mother tells Muriel crisply that she has had her chance, and begins to wonder whether it had been wise to choose a school for them near a large research university. Mother, it will be seen, has non-separable preferences with respect to times. Her non-expected utility ordering is depicted in our Figure 3.1 (which is adapted from

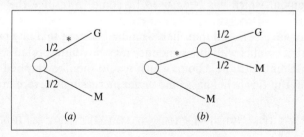

(a)   (b)

Fig. 3.1.

Machina). Mother prefers the 50:50 gamble for Tempest to either sure outcome (M or G) so she chooses the gamble. 'Nature' then chooses the upper branch of the tree in part (*a*) of the Figure. Muriel then tries to talk Mother into snipping off the tree at the point marked by an asterisk, throwing away the tree below the asterisk, and applying her original preference ordering to the remainder of the extended tree in part (*b*) of Figure 3.1.

As we have seen, however, Mother's preferences are not separable as to times. The fact that there was a toss of the coin, and that therefore Gwen took her chances of losing, still matters to Mother. The branch which Muriel wants snipped off and discarded shows precisely this (to Mother) crucial fact. Gwen has already undergone her 50:50 chance of losing. Separability, however, requires that any valid reason for preferring one alternative to another must have to do with what happens in one state of nature on its own—independent of what happens in any other.

Now there is an argument, going back at least to Paul Samuelson (1952), which the Allais tradition including its most recent developers have to meet. It is roughly this: how finely should the different 'consequences' or 'outcomes' be individuated? When Mother is asked to toss again, are the outcomes simply a 50:50 chance of Muriel or Gwen winning, or are they a 50 per cent chance of Gwen winning, and a 50 per cent chance of Muriel winning *unfairly*? Allais individuated outcomes, as a matter of fact, only on the basis of *money* prizes. But Broome claims that the special value of certainty for Allais concerns 'feelings': 'All the rationalizations of Allais' preferences point out a good or bad feeling you may experience. This feeling, they claim, can rationally be taken into account, as well as the money prizes, in determining your preferences' (Broome 1991*a*: 98). This interpretation of Allais has been shown to be wrong (see Allais 1988). But it illustrates a line of argument which has been used by some to resolve the Allais paradox.

Many have believed that there is a danger here that any preferences that conflict with independence may be reinterpreted so as to be consistent with the axiom, which would then be emptied of its content. But this belief has come under increasingly severe fire.[2] So

---

[2] See Pope (1984, 1991, 1994*c*), Harry M. Markowitz (1994), and Bernard R. Munier (1994).

the route to saving the independence axiom by individuating outcomes does not in general work.

INDEPENDENCE VS. ORDERINGS

Meanwhile a number of theorists recently have shown a willingness to contemplate abandoning the independence axiom. It has been suggested that escape from the paradoxes and problems of expected utility may be sought in either of two directions. One may give up the independence axiom, or one may give up the requirement that agents possess rankings which are orderings. Attacks have been mounted against the axiom of transitivity, denying in some cases the transitivity of preference and in others the transitivity of indifference.

Peter Fishburn, for example, tells us that several of his modified axioms have been designed to avoid 'the questionable assertion of transitive indifference' (Fishburn 1979: 244). He points out at the beginning of his analysis, however, that even what he calls his drastic weakening of original expected utility theory does not completely take care of the well-known failures of the independence axiom pointed out by Allais.

An example of work which responds to the Allais critique by relaxing the axiom of transitivity (over consequences too narrowly defined) is that of Graham Loomes and Robert Sugden (1982). They were responding to a paper by Daniel Kahneman and Amos Tversky (1979), whose experimental work offers extensive evidence of violation of the axioms of expected utility. From the point of view of this book, a notable feature of the theory proposed by Loomes and Sugden is their adoption of a concept of cardinal utility in the sense of the early neo-classical economists, defined independently of choice under risk. Their approach is utilitarian in the classical sense. What they understand by 'choiceless utility' is, they tell us, essentially what Bernoulli and, later, early neo-classical economic theorists had in mind when they wrote of utility: 'the psychological experience of pleasure that is associated with the satisfaction of desire' (Loomes and Sugden 1982: 807). Long embraced only by a few daring spirits such as Allais, Bernoullian cardinal utility is to be found reappearing in present-day work by economists and decision theorists critical of standard axiomatic

expected utility theory. It is far from having died out as was predicted by the formalists of the 1950s. Utilitarianisms using utility
concepts of all octane levels are appearing. The ghost of Jeremy
Bentham is beating on the door.

For Loomes and Sugden, an agent maximizes Benthamite utility
modified either by feelings of regret or rejoicing. Where someone has neither feelings of regret nor rejoicing, they will 'simply
maximize expected choiceless utility' (Loomes and Sugden 1982:
809). In this special case their theory becomes identical to that of
Bernoulli, as they interpret him. It is worthy of note that they allow
their agent another degree of freedom: they are perfectly willing to
recognize that maximizing even expected modified utility is not the
only objective 'that is consistent with a person being rational'
(ibid.). They are thus not committed to utilitarianism in the philosophical sense. A theorist can adopt a high octane concept of
utility, but stipulate that its maximization is modified by other
considerations and is not the agent's only goal.

Loomes and Sugden recognize as a controversial feature of their
theory that the relation 'preferred or indifferent to' (which we have
been writing as R) is not necessarily transitive unless the consequences are sufficiently broadly defined. But they are unrepentant,
indeed they argue that orthodox expected utility theory represents
'an unnecessarily restrictive notion of rationality' (Loomes and
Sugden 1982: 820).

In some ways the most dramatic move in the debate which we are
considering, however, came from a theorist who wished to retain
the independence axiom, and instead give up the requirement of
completeness. The striking character of Isaac Levi's (1986) argument arises partly from the fact that it comes as part of a full-dress
endeavour to defend the claim that a rational person may have to
choose in a situation of unresolved moral conflict and, further, that
criteria for choosing rationally in such situations *can* be developed.
These are deep philosophical claims, and Levi's view of the axioms
of expected utility theory comes, as it were, as part of the package.
I shall discuss the arguments of Levi and others concerning the
status of the axiom of completeness for an analysis of rationality
and for moral philosophy in Chapter 4. Here I simply wish to note
that there has been an active discussion of Levi's proposal in the
context of debate on the axioms of expected utility theory, which
has been largely concerned with technical issues of that theory.

Deep moral conflicts within a person's system of values can arise (as we shall see in Chapter 4) even when risk or uncertainty about the outcomes of the choices or actions contemplated is not the issue. Thus only one aspect of Levi's discussion concerns decisions subject to risk or uncertainty. But of course value conflicts of the sort with which he is concerned are more likely to arise, and to be severe, if the actions among which we have to choose have uncertain outcomes.

Teddy Seidenfeld notes the long list of those who have reacted to the paradoxes of expected utility theory by abandoning the independence axiom, and contrasts this with the strategy adopted by Levi: 'There is, however, a persistent underground movement that challenges instead the normative status of the "ordering" postulate for preference' (Seidenfeld 1988: 267). He supports Levi in retaining independence while abandoning completeness.

Why does Levi believe that giving up completeness enables him to escape from the paradoxes of expected utility? Levi argues that, where there is no unresolved conflict among an agent's values, these values will specify a uniquely admissible evaluation of feasible options. His concept of 'admissibility' is still applicable, however, in cases where there is unresolved conflict among values. An option is said to be admissible if it is the optimal choice for one of the ways of evaluation accepted by the agent, even if there are several of these ways of evaluation 'as there will be in cases of unresolved conflict' (Levi 1986: 21).

Now consider a situation where a choice must be made, yet there is a still unresolved conflict. There may be a hierarchy of value structures, so that conflict may be present at the first level yet absent at the second or a higher level. Two life plans may conflict, but one of them may be available in a place where there are people the agent loves. It is a salient feature of Levi's theory, however, that an agent may have to go ahead and make choices with conflict still unresolved. A surgeon, perhaps, must operate *now*: a young person who has been called up must serve or become a conscientious objector. Levi insists that people may have no chance to resolve the issues—he refuses to construe an action taken under such pressure as a commitment to the preference 'revealed' by the action.

His position profoundly affects his interpretation of what happens when an agent faces situations of the type which led to the paradoxes of expected utility theory. It becomes arguable that what seem paradoxes if the agent is assumed to possess an ordering may be accommodated if the agent is acting in a situation of unresolved conflict. It should be noted that Levi's approach explicitly recognizes that simple maximization of expected utility may often fail to render determinate verdicts due to the presence of conflicts of values and of probabilistic beliefs. These are just the conflicts which the orthodox 'wrongly and, indeed, absurdly condemn as manifestations of irrationality' (Levi 1986: 122).

Recall Allais's famous concept of an agent's becoming strongly attached to certainty in one sort of situation and, in another kind of situation, rejecting more than some small given probability of ruin. Now an important characteristic of Levi's approach is that it supports the reasonableness of an agent's becoming concerned with other criteria such as security 'when considerations of expected utility fail to render a verdict' (Levi 1986: 1223). Thus in a sense Levi's analysis of rational choice in the presence of unresolved conflict supports Allais. It would seem, however, that Allais could not use Levi's argument, since he has always insisted that to be rational an agent must possess an ordering.

Levi wishes to represent an agent's value-judgements by a whole value structure, which embodies all the utility functions consistent with that agent's values. He also wants to represent an agent's degrees of belief, not by one single probability function, but by a set of such functions as are consistent with the agent's degrees of belief—what he calls the agent's 'credal state'.

It then follows that an option which maximizes expected utility for some utility function in the agent's value structure and some probability function in the agent's credal state will be an admissible maximization of expected utility for that agent. He calls this 'E-admissibility'. This is a necessary but not sufficient condition of rationality. It is at this point that his concept of the agent's security level enters. If the agent judges a choice as having a security level below that of others in the set of E-admissible options it will then not be what Levi calls 'S-admissible'.

A simple way to give the reader some of the flavour of Levi's approach to expected utility theory is to glance at his reaction to the Allais paradox depicted in Table 2.1. (It should be carefully noted that Levi's interpretation would not be accepted by Allais.) Levi's position involves the possibility that the agent may not possess an ordering, so that both A and B may be E-admissible in the first problem, while both A' and B' may be E-admissible in the second problem. Levi then needs to bring in security considerations. It will then be obvious that A may well be regarded as the only S-admissible choice in Problem 1. In the second problem, both A' and B' are S-admissible. In the case of A', however, the second-worst outcome gives only $1 million, whereas B' gives $5 million as its second-worst outcome, so Levi's agent can choose B'.

Levi's approach has been the subject of active recent debate on several grounds,[3] some of it centred on the specific problems of sequential choice. We caught a slight glimpse of a model involving a simple sequential issue in looking at Mother's problem with Muriel's unsporting proposal. Questions concerning time at a deeper level have emerged as a leading theme in recent work critical of axiomatic expected utility theory. It has been argued that a distinction must be made between a period when the outcome is not yet known, and a subsequent period when the outcome is known:

The single period framework of the expected utility procedure focusses exclusively on the subsequent outcome period when the uncertainty will be past. That is why the expected utility procedure requires people to evaluate outcomes as if they were certain. The single period framework of the expected utility procedure omits the uncertain pre-outcome period. With-

[3] Patrick Maher has constructed some modified examples, intended to illustrate Levi-type choices (Maher 1989: 72–8). Maher claimed that his experimental results did not confirm that agents choosing in the manner characteristic of the Allais paradox (and others) did so for the reasons indicated by Levi's theory. Levi's reply will be found in Levi 1989: 79–90. Teddy Seidenfeld offers a sophisticated defence of Levi's theory in dynamic situations (Seidenfeld 1988). Peter Hammond concedes that a theory like Levi's, which does not assume a preference ordering 'may lead to rather weaker inconsistencies, at worst' (Hammond 1988a: 296). But to avoid inconsistencies altogether, he argues for both ordering and independence. Seidenfeld, in reply to Hammond, opines that difference exists between them is 'over the question of so-called "weaker inconsistencies", which Hammond rightly conjectures may be present in Levi's theory' (Seidenfeld 1988: 309). Edward F. McClennen, on the other hand, is a well-known sceptic about independence; but he is willing to defend the requirement of an ordering as necessary to prevent the incoherent choices which he expects will be the fate of 'those who, like Isaac Levi, are prepared to violate the consistency conditions' (McClennen 1988: 298). Against this Seidenfeld argues that it remains 'unclear how McClennen's program of resolute choice is to avoid the quandary of sequential incoherence that results from denying independence' (Seidenfeld 1988: 314). Even this short sample of views may be enough to suggest that the jury is still out on these issues. A detailed and closely argued critique of the claims of expected utility theory to be a theory of reason, by Jean Hampton (1994), came to my attention at the end of October 1994, too late to be embodied in the present work. I hope to be able to discuss it on a later occasion.

out a pre-outcome period there is never a period when people do not know the outcome, nor a period when there is more than one possible outcome. Hence the expected utility procedure has to omit the *direct* dependence on risk. In omitting the pre-outcome period, von Neumann and Morgenstern could not consistently incorporate the emotional and material utilities and disutilities that arise *directly* from not knowing the outcome, Pope, 1983, 1985, 1986 and 1988. Nor could their numerous successors in the endeavor to model the risk taking considerations arising *directly* from not knowing the outcome. (Pope 1994*a*: 16)

The importance for rational decision of being able to take account of the utilities and disutilities that arise directly from not knowing the outcome has been explored in a series of papers by Robin Pope. Decision theorists, she has argued, have been misled by focusing attention on 'frivolous gambles' (Pope 1983: 138) as their exclusive examples. In fact the addition of a pre-outcome period, which can be lengthy, allows one to see that deep emotional traumas, tragic dilemmas, and financial ruin, are all possible. If individuals are to experience what it is to suffer uncertainty, 'time must elapse during which they are aware that they do not know an aspect of the future. If no such time elapses there is no uncertainty, i.e. uncertainty is a flow. Risk theorists have not appreciated this, and hence the fundamental import of time for uncertainty' (ibid. 137).

Pope, turning her back on gambling casinos, chooses instead to look at the dilemma of Penelope, left alone after the fall of Troy with no news of Ulysses. She divides Penelope's future into three periods: (1) A decision period, during which Penelope must decide whether to wait and hope for Ulysses' return, or to take a lover. (2) A pre-outcome period of hope and fear between her decision and news of Ulysses' fate. (3) An outcome period—from learning of Ulysses' fate until her death (Pope 1983: 141–2; 1994: 11–12).

Penelope's utility after her decision and in the pre-outcome period can well be crucial in determining whether her total utility from both periods is greater or less in the option where she waits or in the option where she takes a lover. For one thing, one can make the pre-outcome period longer or shorter; or one can diminish (or increase) the utility experienced by Penelope in the pre-outcome period. Under the 'wait' option, where her utility in the pre-outcome period is lowest, one would expect her total utility from the two periods together to decline as the pre-outcome period was lengthened. The opposite is true where she decides to take a lover.

There are several important differences between this approach and expected utility theory, but the crucial difference for present purposes arises from the fact that expected utility theory omits the pre-decision period and does not distinguish between the pre-outcome period and the outcome period, so that it leaves out of consideration Penelope's utility *before* Ulysses returns. Pope comments on 'the irony of omitting the uncertain period from an uncertainty model' (Pope 1983: 148). Time appears to have been seen in expected utility theory simply as an added complication, arising when one chooses to treat, for example, problems of sequential choice (such as that posed for Mother over her daughters' respective claims to ride Tempest). But there is a more basic role for time, which has been overlooked: simply that without a specified pre-outcome period, there is no room for uncertainty.

Can one introduce the pre-outcome period into the expected utility formulation? Well, the need for separability between times will demand that Penelope's utility in the period of uncertainty depend *only on her state in that period*. But, of course, her welfare during the pre-outcome period depends crucially on hope and fear as to what the unknown future outcome will bring her. If she has taken a lover, her welfare is diminished by fear of the return of a vengeful Ulysses, if she is still waiting, what little welfare she has 'springs entirely from hope of Ulysses' return' (Pope 1983: 171 n. 7).

Penelope's predicament casts a vivid light on the issue of lack of separability between times. Can one endow her with the utility mapping of expected utility theory? Were there only an outcome period, this would be non-controversial, since by then the decision-maker knows her future. But for the pre-outcome period, expected utility 'would apply only to a few rare souls whose well-being depends solely on their current... situation and who are unaffected by the fact that they face an unknown future' (ibid. 149).

This work has interesting links with some economic theorists, notably with Lord Keynes and Joan Robinson. Pope notes that in Keynes (1921: 322) as in Allais, there is the idea of giving more weight to safety and to the avoidance of dire outcomes than would be done by an agent who followed the rules of expected utility maximization (Pope 1994*b*: 30). Now Robinson never tired of insisting, both in conversation and in print, that it was essential to understand Keynes to see that what he meant by uncertainty could only be experienced by *living in real time*. When, on the other hand, time was modelled, as in Arrow–Debreu theory, as a dimension analogous with space, we only get 'logical time', and not what we live in. In logical time one can go backwards as well as forwards. In the canonical, complete Arrow–Debreu models 'time' was a series of 'elementary time intervals', each of which was a general equilibrium.

As Robinson remarked, in a world which is supposed to be always in equilibrium 'there is no difference between the future and the past, there is no history and there is no need for Keynes' (Robinson [1979] 1980: v. 173). Whereas in the world we live in, in historical time, then as indeed Arrow and Hahn recognized, 'if we take the Keynesian construction seriously, that is, as of a world with a past as well as a future and in which contracts are made in terms of money, no equilibrium may exist' (Arrow and Hahn 1971: 361). This, of course, was commonplace to Robinson.[4] For her, one of the deepest and most pervasive reasons for the failure of attempts to embed Keynes in canonical Arrow–Debreu models arose from the impossibility of treating historical time in them. Likewise, Pope's models require the concept of historical time. The hope and fear involved in looking forward is quite distinct from the regret or rejoicing over what is past. Thus she, like Robinson, needs the irreversibility of real time.

THE EXPECTED UTILITY DEBATE AND THE PROSPECTS FOR UTILITARIANISM

The debate on the merits and defects of axiomatic expected utility theory has brought under a spotlight a number of properties which arguably must characterize a utilitarian theory that addresses choices made in conditions of risk or uncertainty. At first glance it might appear that the works of some of the most dedicated critics of axiomatic expected utility theory in fact offer a preferable model to the utilitarian. This is simply because the works of theorists like

---

[4] For Joan Robinson on historical time versus equilibrium, uncertainty in Keynes, and 'getting into equilibrium' (as well as other related matters), see Gram and Walsh 1983, Gram 1989, and Walsh 1989.

Loomes and Sugden, Pope, and others have brought out vividly the relevance for expected utility theory of the agonizing fears, desperate hopes, and deep regrets and joys, that go with risk and uncertainty. Can a person possibly be said to be more rational, in a morally non-trivial sense, if she is without these fears, hopes, and regrets? Surely on the contrary they are often just what is *reasonable*. For Penelope not to suffer agony at the prospect of never being reunited with Ulysses would turn her from a figure of tragic proportions into what Sen has aptly called a 'rational fool' (Sen [1977] 1982: 317–44). If there was one feature of our moral experience which classical utilitarianism claimed to be able to encompass, it was surely our happiness or misery! Expected utility theory would appear to have severe limitations just where nineteenth-century utilitarianism felt it was at its strongest.

Pope's analysis of Penelope's situation, be it noted, runs strictly in terms of classical cardinal utility, and is thus consistent with the Allais tradition. What is more, the emotional price of living through a period of uncertainty is not the only effect on Penelope's utility left out by expected utility theory's ignoring of the pre-outcome period. In fact, as Pope shows, uncertainty during this period can well alter Penelope's material resources, diminish her entitlements, and impair her capabilities to achieve various functionings. And the longer the pre-outcome period, the more serious this damage will be.

It would seem natural to suggest that the utilitarian abandon axiomatic expected utility theory for the theories of some of its critics in the Allais tradition. Unfortunately for this view, the debate on expected utility shows up deep problems facing a utilitarian who abandons the orthodox ranks.

One branch of the contemporary critique of expected utility theory attacks the axiom of completeness, as we have seen in this chapter. But it is arguable that a utilitarian is of necessity committed to completeness. As Levi, a leading figure among the protagonists of a decision theory without completeness has argued, utilitarians 'typically claim that their doctrine is capable of resolving all conflicts in value' (Levi 1986: 162). Broome (1991*a*) bases his case for the claim that the structure of axiomatic expected utility theory is that required by a utilitarian account of good precisely on the coherence of good. But by this he means, roughly, that the betterness relation satisfies the axioms of symmetry, transitivity, completeness, and the sure-thing principle. It is significant that he has doubts about completeness (Broome 1991a: 7–8, 136–8). He concludes finally that 'one might easily doubt that betterness relations are complete, because there may be incommensurable goods. This is, I think, the most serious gap' (ibid. 238–9). Yet despite these doubts he clearly believes that the utilitarian conception of good *requires* completeness.

Critiques of expected utility theory which attack transitivity are, I believe, also problematic for the utilitarian on grounds similar to those given for completeness. Broome is well aware of critical arguments against the transitivity of preferences, but the transitivity of the betterness relation is for him a necessary part of the coherence of that relation, and thus of utilitarianism. It should be stressed that it is not that he is convinced that utilitarianism is sound, he is convinced about what structure utilitarianism requires. And about this I believe he is right.

Utilitarianism (as formalized by writers like Broome) also requires independence, or the sure-thing principle. Broome states the famous utilitarian principle of distribution thus: 'One alternative is at least as good as another if and only if it has at least as great a total of people's good' (Broome 1991a: 16). This principle, which has deeply inegalitarian implications, has been regarded by many as a serious flaw in utilitarianism. But at the moment I am concerned simply with the point that, as Broome shows, the principle requires separability. He tells the reader explicitly that one of the major aims of his book is to examine how well the utilitarian principle of distribution can be defended by the use of arguments based on separability. He writes: 'I shall be making out the best case I can for the principle. But I think, myself, that the case is ultimately inconclusive. The argument contains gaps . . . its most serious weakness is that it needs in the end to appeal to separability of good in the dimension of time, and this seems to me implausible' (Broome 1991a: 29).

If Broome is correct it would appear to follow that a utilitarian, being in any case deeply committed to completeness, transitivity, and separability, can make no use of the critical developments which carry decision theory beyond the constraints imposed by these axioms.

If, as is often claimed today, these axioms impose an unreasonably narrow view of what counts as rational choice or action in situations involving risk or uncertainty, then the same charge would lie against utilitarianism. And if as a result morally significantly issues are ignored by expected utility theory they would likewise be ignored by a utilitarian moral appraisal.

The philosopher, jurist, social scientist, or simply thoughtful person concerned over the claims of constructed concepts of rationality can also, I believe, learn from the critical debate over expected utility theory. One of the most daunting features of the long period when Allais was almost the only voice challenging the ruling orthodoxy in expected utility theory was the feeling that many would-be critics must have had that Science had discovered that a rational person (one properly instructed in its truths) must choose and act as dictated by expected utility theory or stand condemned for invincible ignorance. And then expected utility theory had been accepted by and formed part of the core of Arrow–Debreu general equilibrium theory. But now instead of the imperial sway of the canonical complete, intertemporal Arrow–Debreu model, there are an ever-growing proliferation of temporary equilibrium models, with sequences of equilibria in which markets may not even clear, and asymmetric information runs rife—something unthinkable in the Augustan calm of the original complete Arrow–Debreu model.

It can also be clearly seen now that utilitarianism was far from being eliminated from the axiomatic utility theory at the core of neo-Walrasian economic theory despite the claims made by economists and decision theorists during the logical empiricist period. Indeed, the orthodox formalization crystallized exactly those limitations upon what is supposed to count as rational choice which would appear on the standard view to be necessities for utilitarianism: completeness, transitivity, and independence. And these are no longer questioned only by people of common sense, but by a whole new group of theorists who acknowledge Allais as their mentor.

UTILITARIANISM, MAXIMIZING MORALITIES, AND ORDINARY LANGUAGE

The questions which I now wish to discuss can be posed with respect to decision-making even under certainty. But they arise, if anything, in a more acute form for decisions under risk or uncertainty, once the severe constraints imposed upon utilitarian moral judgement outside certainty (which have just been noticed) are realized. Utilitarianism, as we have seen, has certain structural needs. I now want to look at a more general structural feature of the theory, which underlies the particular structural properties enshrined in the axioms. Utilitarianism has what has been called a 'consequentialist', or 'teleological', or 'maximizing' structure. This is true of utilitarian theories of all octane levels. We noted this feature of utilitarian theories in Chapter 2, and the time has come to explore it at greater length.

It used to be said that a consequentialist theory judges actions solely by their consequences, whereas a non-consequentialist theory can assign an *intrinsic* value to certain actions, apart from their consequences. But it is now widely acknowledged that if I do an action, any moral quality inherent in that action can itself be included among the action's consequences. This has been discussed, for instance, in Samuel Scheffler (1982, 1988). Broome prefers 'teleological' to 'consequentialist' because he believes that 'teleological theories are not distinguished by any special status they give to consequences' (Broome 1992: 271). But since consequentialists now habitually define consequences so as to include any good inherent in the act itself, Broome's point is normally covered. I shall often use the word 'consequentialist' simply because it is the term used by the authors I happen to be discussing.

Consequentialist, or teleological, moral positions are often contrasted with 'deontological' ones. But alas, nowadays the word deontological covers a multitude of virtues. Traditionally, a deontological moral philosophy was one which stressed duties or obligations. Even within this traditional use of deontological, there are non-trivial differences in the nature of what is being claimed: Sir David Ross (1930) for example, was very different from Kant. But a philosopher may insist on the importance of non-teleological claims of many kinds, some of which are not happily described simply as 'duty'. An essential role may be assigned to the virtues, as is done by Phillipa Foot (1988) and, as has been noted by Samuel Scheffler (1988: 244), many traditional deontological theories do not do this. Or someone may have a personal ideal, and living up to this may lead them to reject certain repugnant acts which appear called for on consequentialist grounds. It is sometimes claimed that this is pure self-indulgence. But the ideals could be those of Mother Theresa: easing the last hours of the destitute could hardly be expected to have a high priority in a consequentialist utopia.

Much of what makes life worth living depends on the sharing of deep love with rather few people. It depends upon lasting bonds. Now, of course, children in the Hitler Youth were taught to put the well-being of Party and Fatherland first, and conscientiously betrayed their parents to the Party on what could well have been consistent consequentialist arguments. Observe, however, that an appeal to pure duty would not necessarily have moved them to reconsider, since they would regard their single overriding duty as being that to the Party. One needs here what Thomas Nagel has called 'agent-relative values'. Broadly, these are reasons which would 'limit what we are obliged to do in the service of impersonal values' (Nagel 1988: 143). Some of these are based on the right of a person to have some autonomy, and have to do with the moral goals, commitments, and loving ties of the person. Others, which he groups under 'deontology' would 'limit what we are *permitted* to do in the service of impersonal values' (ibid., emphasis in original).

Nagel is particularly interesting, I believe, for his defence of the traditional principle of 'double effect', which may be found for example, in Charles Fried (1978). Nagel recognized how much this ground has been worked over in recent years, and that the approach has problems of application. The core idea, however, is quite simple: to violate a deontological constraint it is necessary to maltreat some person or persons intentionally. One need not perform the act oneself—for example, an officer can order soldiers to torture a prisoner, or even simply turn a blind eye to their doing so. What is crucial is intention. To do this is to aim at evil and make it our goal: 'But the essence of evil is that it should *repel* us. If something is evil, our actions should be guided... towards its elimination rather than toward its maintenance. That is what evil *means*. So when we aim at evil we are swimming head-on against the normative current' (Nagel 1988: 163, emphasis in original).

So there are two morally relevant perspectives: a totally detached view which sees the world, as it were, from nowhere within it, and the perspective of a particular person who must choose an action and do it, *and live with it*. To offer someone who faces an agonizing choice a totally detached view of the possible states of the world 'from nowhere within it' (Nagel 1988: 165)[5] is, I believe, to offer moral counsel which—borrowing the vivid term of the French existentialists—can be said to be 'in bad faith'.

It should be remarked at this point that, as is widely recognized, our ordinary moral judgements are to a significant extent non-consequentialist. This has led consequentialists on a number of occasions to adopt a sharply revisionist stance towards natural languages. But it is hardly surprising that the moral discourse in these languages should have evolved so as to bear on the predicaments of human beings facing particular and often acutely personal situations.

It may be well to stress at this point that by 'non-consequentialist' one does not intend to refer to a moral position which denies that consequences have any moral importance. Such positions are very rare in moral theory. Indeed, among the many philosophers who have criticized consequentialism in recent years, I cannot think of any who have denied the moral significance of the consequences of actions. What they have denied was that *only* consequences were of moral significance.[6]

It is also important to distinguish what have been called 'welfarist' consequentialisms, namely, the various versions of utilitarianism, from what might be termed 'pure' consequentialism. One may then immediately claim that recent rights-based arguments are clearly fatal to utilitarian (welfarist) consequentialism. As Sen has remarked:

Indeed, if rights violations are treated as bad things and rights fulfillments as good things, welfarism must be compromised, since welfarism requires that nothing else be intrinsically valued other than utilities. When the different elements of utilitarianism are unpackaged, it is seen that although a rights-based moral theory cannot coexist with 'welfarism' or 'sum-ranking', it can very well do so with consequentialism. (Sen 1987: 74–5)

It would thus be possible, from the point of view of this chapter, to accept the argument based on the moral importance of rights as fatal to the welfarist-consequentialism of axiomatic utility theory, and leave the debate over pure consequentialism alone.

[5] For a lengthier presentation of Nagel's whole position, see his book *The View from Nowhere* (1986).

[6] Commenting on recent critiques of consequentialism, Sen has observed that: 'None of them has, however, argued in favor of ignoring consequences altogether in assessing the rightness of acts' (Sen 1993: 207 n. 7).

This might, however, be a trifle premature. A kind of moral theory is emerging which is certainly about maximizing 'good' in some sense, but which is arguably not welfarist (in the way in which neo-Walrasian theory is welfarist, for example). An extensive and subtle exploration in this direction is the work of James Griffin (1986). There is an element of paradox in the fact that Griffin's title was *Well-Being*. He begins by abandoning the notion that 'utility' is any sort of mental state. Nor does it, for him, reflect the felt intensity of wants. A person's objective can be a state of the whole world. One might be dedicated to bringing the world nearer to a state of Rawlsian justice, for instance. He remarks that: 'An old and potent objection to the utilitarian way of thinking is that it assumes that we value only one kind of thing, whereas we value many irreducibly different kinds of things...But that point counts against certain mental state accounts' (Griffin 1986: 31). He is explicitly defending a new notion of utility, and admits that it is a much less rich notion—lower octane level, as I have been saying.

Griffin admits that: '"Utility", on the old monistic interpretation, was the super, over-arching, substantive value' (ibid.). But now utility is not a substantive value at all, simply a formal analysis of "what it is for something to be prudentially valuable to some person' (Griffin 1986: 31–2).

It will be seen that his concept of utility is explicitly non-reductionist. Maximization stays, but it is a matter of choosing the most valuable life we can—we are comparing ways of living: 'We can never reach final assessment of ways of life by totting up lots of small, short-term utilities...It has to take a global form: this way of living, all in all, is better than that' (Griffin 1986: 34–5). It is a major claim of Griffin that we have not yet worked out, or understood fully, 'how radical the consequences are of the shift to a formal conception of well-being...Thus, there is nothing in the formal conception of well-being that rules out one value's being incommensurable with another' (ibid. 243). Griffin is not supporting incompleteness—he believes that all values can be compared. But he argues that there are values 'such that no amount of one can outweigh a certain amount of the other' (ibid.). In such an ordering it may be that no amount of (say) prosperity can outweigh some vital level of respect for the rights of persons. Respect for personhood may have a status incommensurable with all those things which would have been included in 'welfare' in the neo-Walrasian tradition.

So far this is still teleological, or consequentialist, or maximizing (although Griffin shows that he is not wedded to these concepts, especially when one is concerned with more than one person). But it is further from classical utilitarianism than (for example) Broome seems prepared to go. Broome does mention such 'lexical' orderings; he writes: 'It is consistent with teleology to think that some considerations dominate others lexically. You might think, for instance, that any unjust act is worse than any just one, whatever other features the acts possess' (Broome 1991a: 7). But he does not give such rankings an important place in his model.

Sugden, who characterizes Griffin's book as 'a reformulation of utilitarianism' (Sugden 1989: 103) judges that 'rights have little place in Griffin's system' (ibid. 105). Well, if 'well-being' is interpreted as it habitually has been in neo-Walrasian theory, then this might be true. But given the ways in which Griffin's constructed concept of 'well-being' behaves in his theory, it is not so clear that Sugden's charge is correct. At least on the face of it, it is arguable that Griffin has a teleological moral theory which is both related to utilitarianism and not (in the traditional sense) welfarist. At any rate, even this brief glance at Griffin's position may suggest why the question of 'pure' consequentialism deserves some attention in the present work.

An interesting, and critical, point of view on consequentialism as such is to be found in Robert Nozick (1993). He tells us that:

Many writers assume that *anything* can formally be built into the consequences,[7] for instance, how it *feels* to perform the action, the fact that you have done it, or the fact that it falls under particular deontological principles. But if the *reasons* for doing an act A affect its utility, then attempting to build this utility of A into its *consequences* will thereby alter that act and change the reasons for doing it; but the utility of *that* altered action will depend upon the reasons for doing it, and attempting to build this into its consequences will alter the reasons for doing that now doubly altered act, and so forth. (Nozick 1993: 55, emphasis in original).

Nozick points out that consequentialism has a problem in dealing with issues concerning dynamic consistency. Perhaps having reached a particular subtree of a decision tree gives you information which changes the utility of a future outcome: 'If we attempt to cope with this by insisting that the utilities within the tree always be

---

[7] Nozick here refers the reader to, for example, Hammond 1988b.

fully specified conditional utilities, then we cannot have the *same* outcomes at any two different places in the decision tree' (Nozick 1993: 56, emphasis in original). It may not be the case that there is any description of an act such that, 'for *all* facts about the act, that description incorporates them within the act's consequences' (ibid., emphasis in original).

Nozick's subtle and elegant argument pursues the consequentialist through a thicket of decision and game theoretic issues. No reader of Nozick could deny that the debate between consequentialist or teleological moral philosophies and their opponents must partly be fought today amid a thorny growth of constructed concepts. But there are also issues concerning ordinary moral discourse (as indeed Nozick's treatment shows) which call for recognition. An interesting illustration of this is an analysis by Phillipa Foot, which suggests that any consequentialist position involves a sharply revisionist stance with regard to the conclusions of our ordinary moral language.

Consider a standard example used by anti-consequentialist moral philosophers. Should we torture and kill one wholly innocent person if this will save five other innocent persons from the same fate? A consequentialist will have to say that we are not only justified in doing this, but indeed morally obliged to do it. Foot comments: 'There will in fact be nothing that it will not be right to do to a perfectly innocent individual if that is the only way of preventing another agent from doing more things of the same kind' (Foot 1988: 226).[8] Remarking that she finds this conclusion totally unacceptable, Foot stresses that it is 'a conclusion not of utilitarianism in particular but rather of consequentialism in any form' (ibid.). She thus intends her counter-argument as directed against what I have been calling 'pure' consequentialism, indeed she stresses that the argument leaves 'welfarist' utilitarianism behind.

Foot's argument starts from the claim that the appeal of consequentialism lies in a very simple and apparently innocent idea: namely, that it cannot be right to prefer a worse state of affairs to a better. The rabbit has already gone into the hat once we have gone along with the idea "that there *are* better or worse states of

---

[8] Quoted from the version of Foot's article reprinted in Scheffler 1988. An early version appeared in the *Proceedings and Addresses of the American Philosophical Association* (1983) and was republished with revisions in *Mind* (1985).

affairs in the sense that consequentialism requires' (ibid. 227). This is the claim against which she mounts her ordinary language argument. She argues that within morality there is a particular virtue, benevolence, whose proper end is the good of others. And benevolence enjoins the promotion of such good states of affairs, if you will. But there are other virtues such as justice.

Expressions like 'good state of affairs' and 'good outcome' are used in ordinary language for those objectives which benevolence properly seeks to promote, and not (she might well have argued) for some abstract maximand such as 'greatest total expected utility' satisfying the axioms of transitivity, completeness, and independence. The ordinary concept of good and bad states of affairs is a much more work-a-day and partial one which we learn to use in particular contexts where we recognize a duty to do some good for someone. Our concept, as Foot puts it in a telling phrase 'comes only from the virtues themselves' (Foot 1988: 247). If we accept and adopt the constructed concept of an overarching sense of 'good', such that it is in all situations our unquestionable obligation to maximize this, then we have welcomed a Trojan horse into our midst. The philosopher who accepts the legitimacy of talk about 'good states of affairs' in this sense, 'will be giving the words the sense they have in his opponents theories, and it is not surprising that he should find himself in their hands' (ibid. 238).

The object of the virtue of benevolence, it would ordinarily be said, is to do as much good as possible. But the object of the virtue of justice is to act justly. This simple distinction, and others like it, is of course in origin Aristotelian; but it is also deeply embedded in our language. In this century, however, as we have noted, a view of rationality has moved from economics and decision theory into the writings of philosophers, jurists, social scientists, and others. This is vividly illustrated by Samuel Scheffler's reaction to Foot's argument. We find her position paradoxical, he appears to feel, because 'we are relying on a conception of rationality that seems to lie at the heart of consequentialism' (Scheffler 1988: 251). He describes this as a 'powerful conception of rationality' (ibid.) and tells us that it is 'what we may call *maximizing* rationality' (Scheffler 1988: 252, emphasis in original).

How true. The prestige of the formal concept of rationality, and the appearance of being simply a matter of pure logic which was long an accepted view of the axioms of transitivity, completeness, and (in risky situations) independence, seemed impregnable. But as we have seen each of these axioms is fighting a rearguard action today.

It will be recalled that Mother, in dealing with her rambunctious daughter Muriel, refused to conform to the axiom of independence because of her sense of justice. And it is out of caring for others that we may make menu-dependent choices, thus violating the axiom of transitivity. And consider the moral conflicts dealt with by Levi, which may cause a perfectly *reasonable* person to act in a situation of unresolved conflict with the axiom of completeness unsatisfied. This bears a close resemblance to the plight of an agent who faces the consequentialist conclusion that a certain action will maximize 'good', yet rejects that action because of finding it morally repugnant on other grounds. If Scheffler is right that the strength and persuasive power of consequentialism is founded on its being derived from the formal concept of rationality as a maximizing structure, then its foundations may not be too secure.

Broome's formal model is explicitly consequentialist, or teleological as he prefers to say. But he is fully aware of what it will not cover. Specifically, acting in accordance with a non-consequentialist morality will not be consistent with it: 'If people do *that* it will call for a radical change at the deepest foundation of economics' (Broome 1992: 280, emphasis in original).

Broome remarks that if a *moral* theory tells us to maximize something, 'then what it aims to maximize must be what the theory takes to be good' (ibid. 27). But he opens his book with the clear statement that: '*One part of* ethics is concerned with good' (Broome 1991*a*: 1, emphasis added). This will not serve the pure consequentialist's turn, however. It would readily be admitted, and can perfectly correctly be said in ordinary language, that we ought to do as much good as we can, subject to our not neglecting our duties and obligations, and subject to our not violating other moral principles such as justice and fairness, or engaging in some morally repugnant activity.

The proponent of a maximizing morality, on the contrary, must give the word good (or whatever word is chosen to stand for the objective of the exercise) a set of uses which are not included in the family of its normal uses in a natural language. And when this is done, the result is not just a formal, axiomatic analysis of the logic of a binary relation satisfying the axioms of transitivity, completeness, and independence. A deeply controversial substantive moral claim has slipped in. What is more, in the course of the construction of a formal model using good in this way, good has to do some fast racing changes. In Broome, for instance, a person who is wholly self-interested may be correctly said to be maximizing her own good. Now Mother might well say of the delinquent Muriel, 'She certainly knows what's *good for her*—the little brat.' But good here is not doing the work the formal theory requires, since it is part of a moral condemnation. Again, Mother might well say to Muriel: 'If I allow you to behave badly to your sister, you will acquire the habit of behaving badly and not considering others. And quite apart from the harm you do to them, that habit would not be *for your own good.*'

Consider the nursery word 'goodies'. One could say that Muriel's mother sometimes had to deny Muriel some 'goodies', if this were for her own good. Now good in a formal model supposed to have moral implications cannot slip from standing for good into standing for 'goodies' and back again. (We shall turn to the analysis of rationality as self-interest in Chapter 5.)

The constructed concept of rationality embodied in the axioms of neo-Walrasian theory and decision theory, gave aid and comfort to a revisionist and reductionist moral philosophy. It clothed in what was then a bright new formal dress philosophical positions which have been disputed in a large part of our philosophical heritage, and which have never become accepted and absorbed into the structure of our ordinary moral discourse. Even when shorn of mental state accounts (which, however, are far from dead and gone) the axiomatic expected utility version of the constructed concept of rationality in economic theory and decision theory is far from an ethically neutral piece of formalism.

INDIRECT UTILITARIANISM AND INDIRECT CONSEQUENTIALISM

'Indirect' or 'rule' utilitarian theories are far from new.[9] They experienced a revival during the 1970s and 1980s, however, at the hands of utilitarian philosophers under fire from the then recent

---

[9] Indirect, or rule, utilitarianism has had quite a long history. In his now classic paper on the subject, John Rawls (1955) pointed out instances of rule utilitarian

renaissance of rights-based critiques of utilitarianism. Did this retreat from unqualified (or 'act') utilitarianism enable the defenders of the doctrine to find a defensible line and hold it?

It will be useful to consider an example from the general area of law enforcement and punishment, since this was often in the minds of those who wrote on the issue, as in the now classic paper by John Rawls (1955). Suppose that a population has been the subject of repeated terrorist attacks, and that for a long time none of those who took part in these attacks has been caught. Then the police pick up a suspect who has just the background to make it plausible to them that he might have been involved. In addition it transpires that the suspect has been involved in minor criminal activity. Having launched a prosecution, however, the police discover definitive evidence that their prisoner could not even have been near the scene of the bombing. They are able to suppress this evidence. They argue that the good that will result from the much publicized trial and conviction of a 'terrorist' will outweigh the harm done to the innocent (of terrorism) suspect. The act utilitarian has no argument against the corrupt police.

A rule utilitarian, however, can argue that what must satisfy the utilitarian test of maximizing utility is the underlying rule or practice and not the act. If we adopt into our jurisprudence the practice of punishing the innocent whenever it is expedient to do so, then our whole system of criminal justice will fall into contempt. True, the act of suppressing the evidence would maximize utility on one occasion (if never found out). But the establishment of such a practice would in the end lead to greatly less utility than would our maintaining a just judicial system.

How successful is this attempt to escape the morally repugnant side of utilitarianism, and to defend a modified utilitarianism, where the maximizing is applied to rules or practices rather than to

arguments in the work of classical utilitarians, such as Hume, Hobbes, Bentham, and John Stuart Mill. J. O. Urmsom (1953) had argued in detail for this interpretation in the case of Mill. J. D. Mabbott (1956), on the other hand, is an example of those who have questioned this interpretation of Mill. The twentieth-century discussion of 'indirect' utilitarianism probably began with Sir Roy Harrod (1936), although the actual terms 'act utilitarian' and 'rule utilitarian' are attributed to Richard B. Brandt (1959). Whatever may be the final verdict as to the existence of rule utilitarianism among the classical utilitarians, certainly various versions of this position have been widely adopted by philosophers troubled by some of the implications of act utilitarianism in the last twenty-five years or so.

single acts? Well, I am willing to say straight away that if we had to have judges and senior police officers who were utilitarians of some sort, I should prefer if they were rule utilitarians rather than act utilitarians. Some of the well-recognized uglier consequences of act utilitarianism can perhaps be held in check by this change. But I fear that the utilitarian is now on a slippery slope.

To begin with, it may be remarked that one of the most appealing properties of utilitarianism must surely have always been its appearance of clarity and simplicity: simply maximize good. This shows particularly strongly in Broome's architecturally ambitious study of the weighing of goods. But a two-level theory of acts and practices seriously impairs this simplicity of structure. For Broome, individual acts must be weighed and ordered by their goodness, and he needs separability with respect to states of nature, persons, and times. Perhaps it may be well to recall here that this need for separability is in no sense an eccentric or individual property of Broome's model. It is, as we have noted, a feature of any axiomatic expected utility theory. The agent in this theory must maximize expected utility in each action taken. And from the early work of Allais, critiques of axiomatic expected utility theory were directed to showing that a rational agent might violate the separability requirements of the axiom of independence.

Perhaps it is understandable that, as Sen has pointed out, 'mainstream economics has tended to ignore even the more complex and refined versions of utilitarianism itself... concentrating instead on the simpler—more "direct"—versions' (Sen 1987: 50 n. 21). In the same work he comments on the strategy of the indirect, or rule, utilitarians:

This move has much merit in broadening the scope of utilitarian arguments, and for avoiding some of the special follies of act-based utilitarianism... But some serious problems must also be noted. First, the 'welfarism' implicit in 'rule utilitarianism', which is essentially an amalgam of 'rule consequentialism' and 'welfarism', limits the scope of this extension, since individuals may not, in fact, assess states of affairs in terms of utility information only. Second, 'rule utilitarianism' of any kind can sometimes produce *worse* states than would have emerged from act-based reasoning (the 'rule' acting as an inefficient constraint). (Sen 1987: 88 n. 27, emphasis in original).

Within a few years of the work in which he gave a classic exposition of rule utilitarianism (Rawls 1955), Rawls made it clear that he did not believe that utilitarianism could be made consistent with the requirements of justice (Rawls 1958). And indeed a number of philosophers would appear to have adopted a view that indirect utilitarianism does not offer a strongly defensible line.

To see some of the reasons why this is so, let us return to our example of the prisoner who turned out to be only the shadow of a gunman. Suppose that the few police officers who know that the captured 'terrorist' is not the real perpetrator of the bombing could successfully suppress this information. If these officials were *act* utilitarians, how does a rule utilitarian go about countering their claim to have done the utility maximizing act? Remember that the only ultimate moral principle that any sort of utilitarian has is the principle of maximizing utility. It is therefore to this principle that the defenders of a particular rule or practice must in the end appeal if the practice is violated. The rule utilitarians either had all along a principle of justice which could dominate the principle of utility, in which case they are not bona fide utilitarians, or they have only the principle of maximizing expected utility to fall back on. And the police can now say that they truly believed that (given the high probability of getting away with it) their suppression of the truth (and the travesty of justice which resulted) would maximize expected utility for the society.

By retreating from act utilitarianism, the indirect utilitarian, it should be observed, has admitted the force of objections to the simple utilitarian principle of maximizing utility in the case of each act. But when the supporter of the moral claims of justice, personal integrity, duty, or any other moral principle discovers what indirect utilitarians now offer in support of their rules or practices, the result is liable to be disappointment. It is no support of a principle like justice (to anyone not already a convinced utilitarian) to say that justice should be upheld because of a probability judgement that this is likely to maximize utility in the long run.

The problems of utilitarianism go quite some way towards explaining why some theorists should have sought for a minimalist account of rationality. This has led to the development, of a number of more or less austerely formal accounts of rationality simply in terms of consistency. Economic theorists have been notable contributors to this development, which surely has among its ancestors the work of Robbins, Hicks, and Allen at the London School of Economics in the 1930s. Hicks and Allen, as we have seen, failed to produce an account of rational choice or action wholly free from utilitarian elements. But as we shall see in the next chapter, the attempts that have been made to distil a concept of rationality purely from the logical implications of consistency have run into serious problems of their own.

4

RATIONALITY AS CONSISTENCY

CAN one distil a concept of rationality from the idea of consistent choice or action? This, if it could be done, might be supposed to give economic theory a minimalist and formal concept of rationality which would provide a firm axiomatic foundation. This approach has in fact been popular with economists and (even before the later axiomatic developments) can arguably be said to have inspired thinkers like Robbins, as well as Hicks and Allen.

Aside from the numerous different formalizations used, the object in view can be significantly different: at least two versions of the concept of consistent choice need to be distinguished. The first, and most ambitious—which here means the most minimalist—seeks to derive rationality properties from the internal consistency of an agent's choices or actions. The second approach explicitly considers the consistency of an agent's choices or actions with that agent's goals.

Concepts of 'internal' consistency are characterized by requiring correspondence between different choices made by an agent 'without invoking anything *outside* choice (such as motivations, objectives, and substantive principles)'[1] (Sen 1993*b*: 495, emphasis in original). Concepts of consistency with a goal, on the other hand, are concerned with making the very different claim that rationality lies in the correspondence of our agent's choices with some goal or objective.

INTERNAL CONSISTENCY

The concept of rationality as internally consistent choice was long believed to rest on secure logical foundations. It depended on axioms like transitivity, which were regarded as logically necessary.

---

[1] Sen refers the reader at this point to Richter 1971.

In recent years, however, this confidence has been severely shaken.[2] We can see part of the reason why this decline in confidence has occurred by returning to the concept of menu-dependent choice. Two well-known basic conditions for internal consistency may be termed 'contraction consistency' and 'expansion consistency'. Contraction consistency requires that, if an alternative x_1 is chosen from a set X, and if x_1 is an element of a subset A of X, then x_1 must still be chosen when the attainable set of options for the agent is *contracted*: if x_1 is in any attainable set A, it must still be chosen. If you drink claret when you could have drunk claret, burgundy, or champagne, then you must drink claret when you could have claret or burgundy. *Expansion* consistency, on the other hand, requires that if an alternative x_1 is chosen from every set in a particular class, then x_1 must be chosen from the union of all these sets.

Now consider two 'menus' or attainable sets A_1 and A_2, and suppose that A_1 is the set of options $\{x_1, x_2, x_3\}$, while A_2 is the set $\{x_1, x_2\}$. If x_2 is chosen from A_1, and x_1 is chosen from A_2 this violates contraction consistency. Yet it has been seen that reasonable people might make such choices in a number of situations. Suppose once more that I was taught never to take the largest piece of cake available, and so I always took the second largest, at a children's party. Then if x_1, x_2, x_3 are slices of cake in increasing order of size, I would take slice x_2 when offered A_1, but take x_1 when offered A_2. As Sen has noted: 'The ordering of the alternatives...varies with the menu, but this does not deny that for *each menu* there is a clear and cogent ordering' (Sen 1993*b*: 501, emphasis in original). But to see this ordering we had to have information about what the agent is trying to achieve—we needed to know something 'external to the choice itself' (ibid.).

It should be noted that menu-dependent choice does not resist formalization. Indeed, an axiomatization of the decision rule 'never choose the uniquely largest' is to be found in the recent work of Nick Baigent and Wulf Gaertner (1993).

In order to pursue the implications of menu-dependent choice for the structure of traditional formalizations of rationality as internal consistency, we need a brief sketch of the concept of a choice function. Let X be any set of outcomes or alternatives, here

---

[2] See, for instance, Sen 1985, 1987, 1993*b*, 1994, and the references given there.

assumed for simplicity to be finite. Let A be any non-empty subset of X (an attainable set, or menu taken from X). The statement that a choice function defined over X exists, is then in effect the claim that there is at least one 'best element' in each non-empty subset of X. The choice function $C(A)$ then specifies, for any particular set A, a non-empty subset $C(A)$, known as the 'choice set' of A. Since the choice set from any particular attainable set or menu A is not required to be unique, it is actually more correct to interpret $C(A)$ as the set of 'choosable' elements from A.

Now it has been shown that a choice function is binary if and only if contraction consistency and expansion consistency hold.[3] But we have seen reasons for rejecting contraction consistency. Hence if contraction consistency is rejected, so must the usual concept of the 'binariness' of preference. However, if binariness over sets of outcomes is violated, then, as Sen has noted: 'With that would go real-valued representations of preference orderings over the outcomes. This does not, however, require abandoning *maximization* as an operation. Instead the function to be maximized would have to be defined over the pair (x, S) of outcomes and menus, rather than over outcomes x only' (Sen 1994: 385, emphasis in original).

It will be recalled that axiomatic utility theory was constructed using a binary relation, 'at least as preferred as' or 'at least as good as' (which we have been writing as $x_1 R x_2$ where x_1 and x_2 are outcomes). A choice function derived from R, it should be noted, required reflexivity and completeness, but a weaker property than transitivity is sufficient.[4] The fact that a choice function with respect to R requires completeness is of some importance to the discussion in this book, given the controversial role of that axiom. It is also easy to see: let there be a single pair of alternatives x_1 and x_2 in X, such that neither $x_1 R x_2$ nor $x_2 R x_1$; then the choice set of this pair of alternatives will be empty. To see that the choice function for our example of menu-dependent choice cannot be derived from the binary relation R, consider the choice sets involved in the example. The choice set from $C(\{x_1, x_2, x_3\})$ is $\{x_2\}$ while the choice set from $C(\{x_1, x_2\})$ is $\{x_1\}$.

It will be seen that the treatment of rational choice in Arrow–Debreu theory and in axiomatic expected utility theory embedded

---

[3] See Sen 1971 and Herzberger 1973.
[4] See Sen 1971: 14–20 for a thoroughgoing discussion of these and related matters.

properties like contraction consistency deeply in the structure of the formalized context in which what counted as rational choice was discussed. Within such a conceptual scheme, it was only natural for theorists to believe that a delicate structure of formal internal consistency properties could be found, sufficient for the characterization of rational choice or action.

Add to this the fact that economic theorists had a strong desire (by now rather familiar to us) to explain rationality, if at all possible, in terms of some consistency properties exhibited by choices or actions themselves, and thus hopefully to avoid dependence on a concept like utility. Hicks, for example, had reached the high-water mark of his project to free economic theory from utilitarian concepts in a work which Sen (1993*b*: 497) quotes. Hicks had become persuaded that economics should endorse the study of human beings 'only as entities having certain patterns of market behavior; it makes no claim, no pretense, to be able to see inside their heads' (Hicks 1956: 6).

There are some ironies in this. Logical positivism, which had captured the hearts and minds of economists in its original strong and clear-cut form was by the time Hicks wrote this passage retreating from its original strongholds under the banner of logical empiricism. But even in its gilded youth, positivism could not have afforded to take the position on the philosophy of mind vividly evoked by Hicks's remark. Positivists needed to construe our ordinary talk about other minds as expressing perfectly reasonable empirical claims, which could be shown to be true or false, as we shall see in Chapter 7. So economists never needed to take vows of epistemological chastity and write only about actions on markets.

Theorists who had got hold of the idea that bringing in references to preferences, goals, or objectives was taboo, however, may often have felt obliged to express consistency claims as claims about internal consistency among actions, even when their own theory would be more naturally articulated as involving claims about the requirement that choices be consistent with the agent's goal. This is not to deny that a theorist might want to see how far one could go with the concept of internal consistency, even if quite free from influence by the ghosts of logical positivism. A fine example of this latter position, I believe, would be a well-known paper by Marcel K. Richter (1971), which is cited by Sen as an example of work in which consistency is given a central role in the analysis of rational choice.

Richter's paper is indeed focused on consistency, and notable for its systematic development of a formal treatment of rational choice from elegantly minimal assumptions. But how 'internal' is the consistency depicted by Richter? In fact, he is quite explicit right at the beginning of his paper. He wishes to formalize 'a useful intuitive notion of rational behavior' (Richter 1971: 30). His approach is in effect an appeal to ordinary language: 'We often hear it said, "I would act differently, but his behavior is rational from his own point of view"' (ibid.). He spells it out by arguing that, 'if we start with observations of choices, it would be etymologically proper to call them rational if there were *some* preference ranking ("point of view") which rationalized them' (Ibid., emphasis in original).

He will thus accept any point of view, or goal or ranking, as long as it 'rationalizes' the choices. So his concept of rationality is value neutral and simply instrumental. This limitation, however, does not render his concept of consistency a purely internal one: he explicitly looks beyond the choices to some 'point of view' to rationalize them.

It is therefore remarkable to find that Richter's formal conditions are all internal.[5] But if one were not thinking of problems like menu dependency, these 'internal' conditions might well have seemed sufficient to pick out just those patterns of choices which are consistent with the pursuit of a goal. Consider his theorem one: that not all choices can be rationalized. His set of alternatives X consists of three possible choices, say x_1, x_2, and x_3. There are two budgets, or attainable sets, A_1, and A_2. The first of these, A_1, consists of $\{x_1, x_2, x_3\}$, while the second, A_2, consists of $\{x_1, x_2\}$. Consider the following choices made by an agent: x_2 from A_1 and x_1 from A_2. Richter concludes that this pattern of choices cannot be rationalized. But if the agent is making menu-dependent choices, and x_1, x_2, and x_3 are pieces of cake of increasing size, we can well understand the choice of x_2 from A_1 and x_1 from A_2. Richter's development of rational choice in this paper, however, is from a binary preference relation on the set X, so contraction consistency is embedded in the formal structure.

---

[5] As was pointed out to me by Sen in conversation.

RATIONALITY AS CONSISTENCY WITH A GOAL

It should be noted that neither the argument of the last section, nor that of Sen (1993: 499 n. 11), is an argument against consistency. It is solely intended to support the claim that one cannot determine whether or not choices are consistent on purely internal grounds, without reference to the goals or objectives of the chooser.

It will, of course, be argued throughout this book that the consistency of a person's choices with some goal (however misguided, wicked, or frivolous) has always been correctly regarded by the common moral consciousness as far from being a sufficient condition for regarding that person as rational. But such consistency with a goal or objective is surely a necessary condition for calling choices rational.

When economists speak of 'purely consistent' or 'simply consistent' choice I think they often have in mind the willingness to put all values aside and accept indifferently the choices of the saint and of the sinner as 'rational' if they fit the respective agent's goal. I think they were mistaken in calling this internal consistency. I shall, however, accept consistency with some goal as a necessary but not sufficient condition for rationality.

Consistency in this sense has until recently been habitually seen as entailing that the choices of an agent conform to a number of axioms, of which transitivity, completeness, and the various independence axioms of expected utility theory are leading examples. We have already seen how recent work has cast doubt on the status of these axioms. This chapter will further consider their reasonableness as putative requirements for choice to be regarded as consistent with some goal. We may begin with the axiom of transitivity.

TRANSITIVITY

During the ascendancy of the canonical complete, intertemporal Arrow–Debreu models, the axiom of transitivity (as well as the axiom of completeness) could draw great strength from these models. On the one hand, these axioms shared the wide fame of the models of which they were a central part; on the other hand, the whole neo-Walrasian account of general equilibrium could be said to depend on them. But with the proliferation of general equilibrium models which did not require transitivity and/or completeness, this source of strength was withdrawn.[6]

Paul Anand has recently noted that the axiom of transitivity was formerly crucial for the construction of 'interesting mathematical theories of economic behaviour' (Anand 1993: 54) Now, however, all this is changed: 'Insisting on transitivity would rule out many of the new theories of utility maximization that decision theorists have shown to exist. From a technical viewpoint, it is anything but the progressive assumption it once was.' (Ibid.)

Anand is quick to stress the connection between the fall of transitivity and deep disruption of the internal consistency view of rationality. Theorists had earlier been tempted to see the absence of transitivity as amounting to logical inconsistency. He draws the reader's attention to the implications of the title of Georg von Wright's well-known work *The Logic of Preference* (1963) and to a paper of Gordon Tulloch, which was actually called 'The Irrationality of Intransitivity' (1964). Again, Broome claimed that the reflexivity and transitivity of his betterness relation 'are both necessary truths. Indeed, I take them to be truths of logic' (Broome 1991a: 11).

Tulloch had offered an explicit argument in proof of his claim. Suppose someone prefers x_1 to x_2 and x_2 to x_3 and x_3 to x_1. Tulloch wanted to ask the agent what she prefers from the whole attainable set, $\{x_1, x_2, x_3\}$, and expected to catch her in a contradiction. But Anand argues, correctly I believe, that Tulloch was confounding two-place and three-place predicates. Tulloch needed to claim that a *ternary* preference ranking (over the three elements in the attainable set) 'contradicts i.e. is the negation of a statement in the set of possible binary preference rankings' (Anand 1993: 56). But a statement involving a ternary preference relation cannot, strictly, be the negation of a statement from Tulloch's set of binary preference relations.

Transitivity, as we know, has habitually been expressed in terms of *binary* strict preference relations, indifference relations, and relations like R, where some x_1 is preferred or indifferent to some x_2. Yet Anand suggests that a link may exist, and have been left

---

[6] See, for example, Mas-Collel 1974, Shafer 1976, Gale and Mas-Collel 1975, Kim and Richter 1986.

implicit in Tulloch's argument: perhaps the proof might be completed if we brought in contraction consistency. Writing binary preferences as before, but adding the ternary relation '$Tx_1x_2x_3$' which may be read as 'x_1 is preferred to x_2 is preferred to x_3', we may express his proposed assumption as follows:

For all x_1, x_2, x_3 in X: if $Tx_1x_2x_3$, then x_1Px_2 & x_2Px_3 & x_1Px_3.

Anand concludes that: 'If we force preferences to be bound by the contraction constraint, intransitivities are logically impossible' (Anand 1993: 57). Clearly, however, as we already know, people can make perfectly reasonable choices which violate contraction consistency. Anand is far from suggesting that choices which do not conform to the above axiom are irrational. He may well be right, however, that the imposition of some additional assumption is necessary on the part of those who wish, for one reason or another, to be able to retain transitivity.

It might be thought that for moral philosophy, good—or rather betterness—ought to yield transitive relations. Broome seems drawn to this view (see, for example, Broome 1991*a*: 119 n. 20). But surely there is no reason to suppose that the pursuit of good would always satisfy contraction consistency. Our poor single mother, Carmen, may deny herself something she needs so that Juanita may have it. Were she a little more in funds, she might better fulfil her own need as well as the child's. This is another model for the now familiar violation of contraction consistency.

It seems to me that an important part of what is going on here has to do with differences between the logical family of legitimate uses of the verb to prefer in English and the technically prescribed uses of the binary relations 'P' and 'R' in axiomatic choice theory. It is a property of the constructed concept (misleadingly) known as 'preference' in the axiomatic theory, that one cannot be said to have chosen what one does not prefer. (Sen, most notably, has been insisting on the importance of counter-preferential choice over a number of years now.)

In a natural language like English, a very large part of the actions done by a responsible person are not correctly described as 'preferred'. Indeed, the requirements of the moral distinctions crucial for the expression of the insights of the common moral consciousness depend for their accurate linguistic expression on such discriminations. The simplest and most obvious example is of course all those actions done because they are our duty.

It would be perfectly correct English, for example, to say of Carmen: 'It was a rare occasion when a little extra money enabled her to consult her own preferences and indulge one of them.' As we have seen, it would be absurd to expect her choices to exhibit contraction consistency, and it certainly would not endow her choices with a higher rationality if she did exhibit it.

It is sometimes claimed that an agent whose actions cannot be 'rationalized' in terms of a binary preference relation will (or should?) feel regret: her choices are not 'ratifiable'. But as Anand has remarked, 'there is no logical reason why a person choosing from three items should see their binary preferences as relevant' (Anand 1993: 66). I profoundly doubt whether Carmen, if asked about these matters, would show any regret over the choices she has made, to favour her little girl at the cost of violating contraction consistency.

It may be noted here that it has been known for some time that an agent may violate transitivity when ranking alternatives in terms of several criteria. It was pointed out many years ago by Kenneth May (1954) that analogies exist between the paradox of voting (noted in Chapter 1 above) and the problem of a single person ranking in terms of several criteria. Suppose that I can live in any one of three cities, and assume (for simplicity) that I am ranking them in terms of just three criteria: freedom from pollution, freedom from violent crime, and quality of musical offering. I may then find that one city ranks highest in terms of two of the criteria, another in terms of a different combination of criteria—so that again one finds the transitivity of the strict ranking relation violated.

In the context of the theory of consumer's choice it was argued by Kelvin Lancaster (1966) and others that we can avoid such problems by regarding a good such as an automobile or a place of residence as a bundle of characteristics. In the familiar indifference curve construction of elementary microtheory, we may then let each axis measure, not different amounts of a commodity, but different degrees of some characteristic desired by the agent. In such a space of characteristics, given divisibility assumptions, each point in the space would represent a bundle (or vector) of characteristics, and one might perhaps expect the agent to have a ranking of all such points which was transitive (and complete).

But this conclusion crucially depends on the assumption of divisibility: each characteristic was assumed to be available in any non-negative amount (or degree) within the agent's budget. In the problem of choosing which of three cities to live in, however, each characteristic is supposed to be available in just three alternative degrees. When this is the case, multiple criteria may certainly lead to intransitivity. And human experience abounds in situations where a choice must be made from only a few alternatives.

Something needs to be said concerning a compromise position which is, I believe, gaining in popularity. In the canonical axiomatizations of Arrow–Debreu theory, transitivity was assumed to hold for the relation R. But of course this can be factored into the assumption that strict preference, P, is transitive and the assumption that indifference, I, is transitive. Now in a number of situations in recent axiomatic work it has seemed useful to demand transitivity for preference, but not for indifference: one then gets what is known as 'quasi-transitivity'. The case of quasi-transitive rankings has turned out to have some highly important implications. Arrow's famous proof of the impossibility of finding a social ordering, for example, has been shown to depend on full transitivity by Sen (Sen [1969] 1982: 128).

The concept of quasi-transitivity does not arise only in the context of social choice, however. A homely and familiar example will illustrate a case of a quasi-transitive ranking on the part of an individual agent. This arises over what are often called 'threshold' effects. A small difference in temperature, for instance, may not be noticed, and so may not matter. Thus I might not distinguish between 66° Fahrenheit and 68°. So, writing x_1 for 66° and x_2 for 68°, I may say that for me $x_1 I x_2$. Again I may not notice any difference between 68° and 70°. Writing x_3 for 70°, I may then say that $x_2 I x_3$. So, on the assumption that indifference is a transitive relation, one would infer that for me, if $x_1 I x_2$ and $x_2 I x_3$, then $x_1 I x_3$. But I may very well be able to distinguish between 70° (x_3) and 66° (x_1), and prefer x_3 to x_1, thus violating the transitivity of indifference.

We have looked at some violations of the axiom of transitivity which would appear to be rational. A number of others could have been mentioned.[7] Instead of offering such counter-arguments to transitivity, however, a more sweeping line of attack has on oc-

---

[7] Readers who would like to see many more counter-examples to transitivity will find plenty of these in Sugden 1985, Schumm 1987, Anand 1987, 1993, Bar-Hillel and Margalit 1988, and Pettit 1991.

casion been adopted: it has been argued that transitivity claims are, in the end, empty.

This argument employs a strategy which we have seen tried in the debate over the independence axiom, where its use goes back at least to Samuelson (1952). In that case it was supposed to be possible to individuate the outcomes more finely until a violation of independence could be made to 'disappear'. Here one individuates the alternatives more finely until (it is argued) the violation of transitivity melts away. One of the problems with this is that it is equally possible to give any apparently transitive choices a new description, under which they are *intransitive*.[8]

Broome has a nice illustration of a type of situation where this kind of reinterpretation can easily be made to appear plausible: the story of his character Maurice. The predicament faced by Jeremy, which I am about to describe, has a roughly similar structure to that of Broome's example. Jeremy is in love with Gillian, who is presently away for the summer in the United States. Given her absence, Jeremy would like most to spend August quietly at home in Devon. He has been invited to visit friends in Scotland, but does not like the damp mists. Now Gillian's father, the Brigadier, asks Jeremy to crew for him on the Fastnet race. (One of the Brigadier's regular crew has had a bad accident and is not available.) Gillian's father, who has recently met Jeremy, turns to him now in his need. Jeremy is quite a decent offshore cruising sailor, but he has no ocean racing experience and has a distinct fear of the Fastnet, especially in one of the smallest boats entered.

So: Jeremy prefers staying in Devon to Scotland, and Scotland to the Fastnet, so he should prefer staying at home in Devon to the Fastnet. But now that he has been explicitly asked by Gillian's father, he is afraid that the Brigadier (and what is worse, Gillian!) will think him cowardly if he refuses. Does Jeremy have intransitive preferences? As the case is constructed the finer individuation needed to restore the transitivity of Jeremy's ranking rather leaps to mind. Staying in Devon quietly when the issue of crewing had not come up, and skulking at home after Gillian's father has asked for his help, do indeed seem different. Granted true love, it is not unreasonable that Jeremy might prefer even the prospect of the Fastnet to skulking.

---

[8] But see the critical literature cited in Ch. 3 n. 2.

Here transitivity seems to win the day, but as Broome remarks, 'where will it all end?' (Broome 1991*a*: 101) If someone appears to have intransitive preferences, is one allowed to individuate away until they turn transitive? The concept of transitivity would then become empty. Indeed Anand goes so far as to offer a proof of what he calls the Translation Theorem (Anand 1993: 103–5). The idea is that, confronted with any apparently intransitive behaviour, this can simply be redescribed so that, under the new description, transitivity will not be violated. But by the same token, any apparently transitive behaviour can be given a new description under which it is intransitive. He remarks that: 'Without prior agreement on the linguistic conventions that will be used to say what counts as a particular choice primitive, we can choose, *ex post facto*, some convention (richness of language permitting) in such a way that an observation (set) can be counted, either as a violation of transitivity…or not, depending on choice' (Anand 1993: 105).

What is more, for transitivity to have normative content, i.e. for the axiom to tell us something about what we ought to count as rational choice or action, 'The linguistic conventions would have to be the conventions of a rational language' (ibid.: 109). Anand expresses reasonable doubts that this notion of a rational language is philosophically coherent. In any case, as he observes, one is unlikely to find a *unique* rational language.

I might remark here that the quest for an ideally rational language had in effect the status of a search for the holy grail for the logical positivists, and was undertaken with truly Arthurian dedication. This pursuit was closely linked to their belief in the unity of science, and thus to their acceptance of reductionism with regard to the languages of special sciences. It also underlay their belief in the desirability of translating things said in natural languages (seen as full of confusions and of primitive 'metaphysical' notions) into the supposedly pellucid logical clarity of the constructed language whose chaste perfections were their goal.

Surveying the debate on transitivity among economists, decision theorists, and philosophers, I believe that, even on the most favourable interpretation of the debate, one cannot present the axiom of transitivity as one of the unshakable twin pillars of rationality as consistency. The condition of the other pillar, namely the axiom of completeness, must now once again occupy our attention.

COMPLETENESS

Rankings which are reflexive and transitive but not complete, which will be referred to here as 'quasi-orderings', have been increasingly used in special branches of economic theory. At the purely formal level, then, the decision to do without the axiom of completeness is separable from the decision to do without transitivity. This, of course, does not imply that the reasons why theorists have questioned completeness are totally unrelated to the reasons why they have questioned transitivity. Once again it should be noted that, as in the case of transitivity, completeness has been shown to be unnecessary for the proof of many of the key theorems of present day neo-Walrasian general equilibrium theory.

It will be recalled that completeness was characterized in Chapter 2 as follows:

For all x_1, x_2 in X: either $x_1 R x_2$ or $x_2 R x_1$

One must carefully differentiate indifference from incomparability (incompleteness). If a ranking is not complete, if it is a quasi-ordering, then there will exist alternatives such that the agent cannot compare them—can neither rank one higher nor give them equal ranking. One may then say that x_1 is incomparable with x_2, if and only if, neither $x_1 R x_2$ nor $x_2 R x_1$. Contrast the case where $x_1 R x_2$ and $x_2 R x_1$, which as we know from Chapter 2 is equivalent to $x_1 I x_2$.

For many years now critics of the concept of completeness have been pointing out that it is rather a tall order to require that a rational agent be able to compare and rank every pair of conceivable alternatives.[9] Models constructed without the completeness

---

[9] The literature is extensive, and goes back to a period when the axiomatization of economic theory was in its infancy. It is also widespread, and includes the work of scholars working outside economics proper. However, I shall offer here no more than a sampling of contributions which had the development of economic theory explicitly in mind. Nicholas Georgescu-Roegen ([1936] 1966) had shown many years ago that neither completeness nor transitivity are necessary assumptions for the theory of consumer's behaviour. A selection of his papers has been reprinted (Georgescu-Roegen 1966). John von Neumann and Oskar Morgenstern (1944: 19) consider the matter briefly. Aumann (1962, 1964a) showed that the completeness axiom could be dispensed with for certain purposes. Richter (1971) and other contributors to Chipman, Hurwicz, Richter, and Sonnenschein 1971 also addressed the dispensability of assumptions of completeness and transitivity. Sen (1982, 1987) has offered a number of discussions of these and related matters, and gives extensive references. Recall also the authors already cited in n. 6 above.

axiom (and/or that of transitivity) appeared with sharply accelerating frequency in the 1970s and 1980s, as we have seen in the last chapter, in both neo-Walrasian economics and in decision theory.

The implications of all this for philosophy, and specifically for moral philosophy, are I believe far from trivial. It is an important virtue of Isaac Levi's (1986) work on choice without completeness that the importance of the issue for moral philosophy takes centre stage from the beginning. It is necessary to start by contrasting two broad views of our moral predicament. According to one of these 'there are no gaps in our moral knowledge requiring completion through inquiry as there are gaps in our scientific knowledge' (Levi 1986: 1). Levi supports the opposite view, as I did in several early works.[10] This is the view that our knowledge of good and evil, and our grasp of what we ought to do in a given situation, are radically incomplete. As Levi puts it, 'our wickedness is often the product of our ignorance and not our perversity' (ibid.). Indeed this was precisely the theme of my first book (Walsh 1961). It is an old theme, prominent in ancient Greek philosophy, and redeveloped by successive thinkers ever since.

The insights which we acquire through knowledge of the ordinary uses of moral language, vital though they are, do not turn us into moral supercomputers, nor endow us with the ability to calculate the moral implications of every feasible choice or action. On the contrary, with the best will in the world, we may still face moral dilemmas of truly tragic proportions.

Levi begins with a distinction which was very clearly made in a work of J. Dewey and J. H. Tufts (1932). They distinguish between two kinds of moral struggle; one of these, which they believe is most frequently the subject of moral exhortations, 'is the conflict which takes place when an individual is tempted to do something which he is convinced is wrong' (Dewey and Tufts 1932: 174–5). However important in a person's life such struggles may be, as Dewey and Tufts note, they are not strictly speaking the occasion of moral theory. To illustrate the other kind of moral struggle, which is the kind which calls out for moral theory, they use an example that is as fresh today as when it was written. Someone's country has just declared war: 'One side of his nature, one set of

[10] See Walsh 1958a, 1958b, and 1961.

convictions and habits, leads him to acquiesce in war: another deep part of his being protests. He is torn between two duties: he experiences a conflict between the incompatible values presented to him' (ibid.). He is not struggling between a clear duty and a temptation to do what he knows to be wrong: 'Moral theory is a generalized extension of the kind of thinking in which he now engages' (ibid.).

Now anyone who wishes, as Levi assuredly does, to emphasize the vital role of moral enquiry must resist efforts by philosophers and others to suppress or leave unacknowledged this moral struggle of the second kind. Unaware of the work of Dewey and Tufts, I had come to a position closely related to Levi in the 1950s, writing of situations 'when we feel, as we sometimes do, that we are faced with a choice between two whole patterns of life, and the cost of choosing one is giving up the other' (Walsh 1958*a*: 253).

If we understand only moral struggle of the first kind, where someone is struggling to carry out a crystal clear duty where there are no impediments or doubts, then the whole nature of tragic dilemmas will be obscure to us. These dilemmas inhabit areas where the moral issues are deeply complex and involve a whole web of intricate considerations.

The ability to remain in some degree in suspense, torn by the incompatible claims of irreconcilable values, is a necessary condition for experiencing moral struggle of the second kind. As Levi remarks, the importance attached by Dewey and Tufts to this second kind of struggle 'will seem untenable to anyone who doubts the feasibility or, perhaps, the intelligibility of remaining in suspense among rival value commitments and rival ways of evaluating feasible options licensed by such commitments' (Levi 1986: 14).

Levi clearly sees it as evidence of strength of character, not weakness, that someone should be able to hold conflicting claims in suspense while using every effort to resolve them, and I agree. It is noteworthy that he insists that one can reasonably act while this conflict is unresolved, and what is more, that one can deny that one's action implies that one has resolved the conflict in favour of one of the conflicted values.

Jeremy, a few years older than when we first met him, has just returned from some harrowing 'peace-keeping' duties in Bosnia. He is dining with the Brigadier (for whom he now sails, as mate of the starboard watch). Someone asks Tommy, another dinner guest

and an old sailing friend of the Brigadier's, 'are you going to
Scotland for the grouse?'. 'Oh, no,' replies Tommy, 'I don't like
killing, you know'. There are smiles from the group of old friends,
who know that Tommy (to use the Brigadier's phrase) was 'one of
Dicky's cloak and dagger boys' in World War II. 'Oh well,' Tommy
concedes 'I was a murderer during the war, but I don't have to be
any more.' Having a last brandy after the guests have gone, Jeremy
says, 'That was a touch awkward for a moment.' The Brigadier
snorts: 'Tommy's such a donnish old thing, you wouldn't think
butter would melt in his mouth. But he was a bloody hero, you
know.' He thinks for a moment, then adds, 'I don't think he's ever
been happy about it. I think he felt that the country's peril forced
him to put aside some of what he most valued. Make any sense?'
Jeremy sighs. 'It does to me—now,' he says. 'It wouldn't have
before I saw a few things.'

It is commonly assumed that when a choice is made, then a
rational agent must have resolved the conflict—indeed is clearly
signalling this by the very act of choosing. Perhaps if we buy a
packet of margarine rather than a packet of butter we have revealed a preference for margarine. But if someone does an act
because (for example) they feel bound by an inexorable duty, does
this allow us to infer that all moral conflict is forthwith resolved?
Should moral philosophy probe no further than a concept of revealed preference appropriate in a grocer's shop?

Surely, rather, we may counter any such facile dismissal of a
tragic situation as Levi does: 'Precisely because he is compelled to
choose, he does choose; but he refuses to consider the conflict in
value commitments to be settled' (Levi 1986: 15–16). Hence the
need for analysis of decision-making under unresolved conflict, and
for insisting that a rational person may face this necessity.

Now classical utilitarianism, it is arguable, must reject this idea.
Levi cites a passage from John Stuart Mill (1806–73) which makes
the utilitarian position vividly clear: 'There must be some standard
by which to determine the goodness or badness, absolute and com-
parative, of ends or objects of desire. And whatever that standard
is, there can be but one; for if there were several ultimate principles
of conduct, the same conduct might be approved by one of these
principles and condemned by another. And there would be needed
some more general principle as umpire between them' (Mill 1949:
620–1, cited by Levi 1986: 15).

Mill, of course, was leading up to his claim that 'the promotion of happiness is the ultimate principle of teleology' (Mill 1949: 621). Whether or not utilitarians use this concept of happiness, however, they would appear to be bound by Mill's argument. Broome, as we have seen, takes a position similar to Mill's, though in Broome's case it is about the maximization of good. We have seen Broome express uneasiness about the axiom of completeness. But any version of utilitarianism arguably needs it, and a formalization which uses axiomatic expected utility theory would appear to have an extra reason for needing it. If it comes to that, it is certainly arguable that any teleological moral philosophy is committed to completeness; however, since the teleological moral philosophy which I am concerned with in this book is utilitarianism, I shall not pursue this question here.

Levi argues that for Kant a conflict of duties is inconceivable. But of course Kant has no need to deny that duty can conflict with the promotion of good things, like happiness. With his duty-dominated moral philosophy, Kant is in a sense at the opposite extreme from the utilitarians, who see the only ethical concern as that of maximizing good (to use Broome's term). Many have held that Kant's moral philosophy is too duty dominated. Kant, it could be said, has obtained completeness by giving this one principle absolute sway. He did make an exception to this iron rule of duty for the hypothetical case of a perfectly good will, on which see, for instance, Walsh 1954*b*.

Kant's reputed effort to derive moral obligation from the form of practical reason alone suggests a question: could one argue that completeness is logically required of rational choice? This can be seen as a question concerning deontic logic, which is often interpreted as the logic of obligation and permission. Some theorists would appear to have believed that a 'classical' principle of deontic logic forbade the existence of unresolved conflict.[11] B. van Frassen, on the other hand, took the view that this was so much the worse for deontic logic. Defending the possibility of unresolved conflict, he comments that he can only conjecture 'that the original devisers of deontic axioms had a certain ethical bias; perhaps they were utilitarians, or accepted some other axiological creed' (Frassen 1973: 12).

[11] The reader interested in deontic logic might begin with G. K. von Wright's well-known work (Wright 1951) and go on to Follesdal and Hilpinen 1970.

Levi, however, does not believe that the principle of deontic logic at issue in any way rules out the existence of unresolved conflict. This is because in his work, the two conflicted obligations are *suspended*—neither is binding while a solution to the moral dilemmas is being sought.[12]

In Levi, the conflicting obligations are in abeyance in somewhat the way in which two conflicting scientific hypotheses are. One is not obliged to believe both: they are in suspension pending further enquiry. (Levi intends his analysis to apply to conflicted goals in whatever context.) The believer in such dilemmas is as we know accepting the view that moral knowledge, as well as other kinds of knowledge, is difficult to acquire, and that moral issues may thus be complex and baffling. So with the best will in the world, a human being may lack the requirements to solve her moral problems. Her attainment of good may be stunted, not by imperfections of will, but by lacking the capabilities needed. Even Kant was well aware that we may lack the means to implement what we will. But we may also lack the prerequisites for seeing what, exactly, we ought to will.

CAPABILITIES AND COMPLETENESS

Aristotle, perhaps as different a moral philosopher from Kant as one could find, nevertheless also recognized that one may be prevented by the lack of various external necessities, or possessions, from leading what he regarded as the best kind of human life. In a later period of history, medieval philosophers were to recognize that much of what we call evil is more properly described as a privation of good. They were well aware that such deprivation could come from the lack of anything necessary to the flowering of our capabilities, whether or not what was needful was a physical object, or possession. Many years ago I began to explore this in a series of works.[13] Kenneth Arrow later summed up what I was trying to explore, namely the 'moral implications of the position

---

[12] Contrast with this some recent work of Robin P. Cubitt, who offers an axiomatization which yields three conceptions of rationality, the 'weakest' of which allows there to be conflicting obligations which stay binding (unlike Levi's suspended obligations). Cubitt comments on Levi's treatment: 'This ingenious suggestion cannot be captured in the simple framework considered here' (Cubitt 1993: 15 n. 19).

[13] See Walsh 1954*a*, 1958*a*, 1958*b*, 1961 for a discussion of some of the issues involved.

that many attributes of the individual are similar in nature to external possessions' (Arrow 1967: 21 n. 10).

I was attempting to formulate, in place of Kant's niggardliness of nature, a more subtle concept of every sort of deprivation which might prevent the attainment, even by a fundamentally moral person, of any achievements adequately reflecting what Kant would have called the person's moral will. For this I turned to the neo-classical concept of scarcity. This was certainly the most revisionist position which I ever adopted on a question of moral philosophy, but even so it was only intended to clarify some insights which are to be found in natural languages, and to extend them in a systematic way.[14]

As I remarked then: 'Moral philosophers have often felt the need of a concept which would cover all those cases where we are prevented from achieving our ends through no fault of our own: a criterion for saying when failure is not blameworthy. The deontologists thought we were not to blame for actions done in genuine ignorance of the facts. Kant declared in a famous passage that we were not morally responsible for failures due to the "niggardliness of stepmother nature"' (Walsh 1958*a*: 249).

Any lack, any deficiency, whether of technical means in our possession, of knowledge, or abilities, or of the means to fulfil what are today called our 'capabilities', is clearly a legitimate excuse for what I referred to as our attainments falling short of what we willed. Scarcity of the necessary means to function could prevent the attainment of our goals, but should not destroy the moral worth of our intentions. I tried to express this by distinguishing between

---

[14] The concept of scarcity lies at the very core of neo-classical theory, where its significance is no less than that of the concept of rationality. In models of the reproduction of capital derived from the classical economists, scarcity is not centre stage. In simple reproduction models, with no non-reproducible inputs, what have been called scarcity prices (prices reflecting relative scarcity) are replaced by prices consistent with continued reproduction of the capital stock. Once more than one non-reproducible input is introduced into a classical model, however, complexities arise. Even within a pure reproduction model, once the harvest is in we know how much corn (say) will be available till the next harvest. If it will not feed all those who depend on it then, as the original classics knew well, some people will die. In that sense, it is scarce. In moral philosophy, if some deprivation impoverishes what I can attain, or destroys some innocence (recall Tommy) it may never be replenished. This is best modelled as the using up of some non-renewable resource. The appropriate metaphor is the destruction of a rain forest, or of some wild creatures, rather than the using up of this year's corn crop. (Present-day classical models are discussed in Chapters 8 and 9.)

two different kinds of ethical claims: ascriptions (of responsibility, praise, blame, condemnation) and appraisals (of good or bad states of affairs, attainments, realization of capabilities) (Walsh 1958*b*: 1063).

I argued that ordinary language seeks to make distinctions of this kind, and that the interplay between philosophical ideas which bear on these issues and ordinary speech is an ancient and persistent one. Thus: 'A putative ascription will always be *withdrawn* upon a certain sort of factual evidence being produced. If an ethical judgement is held in abeyance pending the production of this sort of evidence, then it is not an appraisal, for an appraisal is not concerned with *how* any state of affairs came about or with who is responsible—if anyone' (Walsh 1958*b*: 1064, emphasis in original).

I knew, however, that this conclusion is not as consoling as it might seem at first. This is simply because there is not one of our finest potentialities which cannot be withered by the cold blast of some fatal deprivation: 'Whatever properties a person has that we could do without, there must be some which we could not give up without giving up most of what he or she means to us. There is no property except blamelessness that the effects of scarcity cannot destroy, and blamelessness is a bodiless thing for a human being to love' (Walsh 1961: 71).

The recognition that we may be deprived of the ability to resolve fundamental moral conflicts, and nevertheless must act in that state, drives home this point. If our obligations were always simple and clear cut, it would still be logically inappropriate to ascribe moral failure, where what existed were tragically stunted attainments. But, once recognize the existence of genuine moral conflicts together with the human necessity often to act with these conflicts unresolved, and the picture grows vastly darker. It grows darker, that is, in respect of what one can expect human beings to attain. It does not grow darker in respect of how worthy of blame these failures are.

A humane moral philosophy, which recognizes fully the tragic nature of life, lies nearer to being within our grasp once we accept the idea that choices must be made and actions taken in many situations where deep and agonizing moral conflicts remain unresolved by the best efforts of our variously hindered capabilities.

I have been using this term 'capabilities' (which of course I did not use in the 1950s and early 1960s) because it is so well fitted to capture some of the ancient moral themes which I have been discussing. This concept, whose recent development is of course the work of Sen (1980), is found by him in Aristotle, Smith, and Marx (Sen 1987: 46 n. 16) and extended into the analysis of inequality in recent work (Sen 1992, on which see Walsh 1995).

Once one sees, what indeed great literatures have typically shown, namely the intricate and delicate web of needs whose fulfilment would alone release a person's latent capabilities into full flower, the plausibility of requiring the satisfaction of an axiom of completeness by human beings placed as they are is surely all but gone. All that remains is to try to limit the incomparabilities which are virtually bound to arise wherever this is possible.

Levi marshals an intricate apparatus of analytical distinctions in order to enable an agent to minimize the effects of value conflict. Thus he introduces a hierarchy of value structures, arguing that conflict at one level may be surmountable at a higher level. Suppose there are two patients, each of whom will die without a kidney transplant, and there is only one kidney available to the hospital in time. At this level there is no resolution of the dilemma. But suppose, to borrow an idea of Sen's, one of them has struggled against some other handicap all her life, while the other has had a life of enjoyment and fulfilment. Valuing equality could then tell in favour of the patient who has suffered more.

This is a very simple case, where the conflict might be resolved at the very next level in the hierarchy of values. Clearly resolution, even where it is possible, may involve much more complex evaluations at yet higher levels. On the other hand it would be a mistake to imagine that where a value structure is conflicted, the conflict is necessarily total. Ranking of alternatives may be possible within each of several parts of a person's whole structure of values. Structures may be discoverable, and significant, even if no one of them yields completeness. The recognition of the necessity for choice in the presence of unresolved conflict is not, therefore, a carte blanche licence for anarchy.

DISASTERS, DILEMMAS, AND DIAMONDS

The search for what might be called damage control strategies in the face of moral dilemmas is a notable feature of the work of

Adam Morton (1991), who incidentally tells the reader that he regards Levi (1986) as the work whose ideas are most closely connected with his. Morton's book, however, seems to me to be distinctly further removed from conventional decision theory than is Levi's. Levi, as we have seen, is a severe critic of axiomatic expected utility theory, and specifically of that theory's dependence on the assumption of ordering. Morton's work, however, goes beyond this in distancing itself somewhat from decision theory as such. As he remarks, 'it does not bear a simple relation to what is usually called "decision theory". Decision theory tries to give precise procedures by which, given a fixed list of options and relatively clear beliefs and desires (or probabilities and utilities), one can choose a single "best"action to perform' (Morton 1991: p. xi). His book has a somewhat different emphasis. He is concerned, rather, with 'strategies for getting complex, vague, incomparable or otherwise recalcitrant beliefs and desires into a form in which one could apply the procedures of decision theory. I am interested in an earlier state of the process.' (Ibid.)

He is particularly interested in developing what he calls non-balancing strategies. These are strategies designed to avoid forcing the choosing agent to achieve a balance, or trade-off, between incomparable goals or desires. These strategies are explicitly intended to apply to both moral and non-moral dilemmas. It is, I think, significant that like Levi he finds the distinction between moral and non-moral dilemmas 'a very unclear one' (Morton 1991: pp. x–xi).

Observe that an incomparability may arise where the obvious moral value at issue is one about which the agent has no doubts. A surgeon may have no doubt about the duty to save a patient's life. The dilemma arises over whether a major operation is too dangerous in the patient's very weakened condition. There are technical issues here, but there are also values—they simply happen to be scientific values: how vital is the surgery? How long could it be postponed? A surgeon who has had brilliant successes with the operation may have one point of view, a physician sensitive to the patient's total state may propose another. If the surgeon is open-minded enough to see the other side of the issue, an acute dilemma has arisen.

Morton does not neglect the issues involved in hunting for a solution to such dilemmas. But he is notable for his efforts to find strategies which enable the choosing agent to act but allow 'incomparables to be left incomparable' (Morton 1991: 13).

If finding an injured child forces you to choose between abandoning it and missing an appointment crucial to a friend's future, he suggests choosing the action which, if undone, cannot be made up later. You could find the friend another job; the child needs hospital now. Rather endearingly, he is against compromise—the economist's favourite lore of nicely calculated less or more.

Jeremy and Gillian are visiting New York (they are now engaged, with the Brigadier's blessing). They are staying with people they met at Cowes before a Fastnet, and saw again later. They are being generously, but a trifle overwhelmingly entertained. Jeremy wants to take Gillian and their hosts to something special: he can (just!) afford good seats at the Met, *or* a really first-class French restaurant, but not both. Rather than a combination of lesser options, Jeremy decides on the Met. He would have Morton's approval.

The notion of the limits of compromise is an important one in this area. Neo-classical economic theory standardly assumes that every good is as divisible as could be wished (available in all non-negative quantities within some constraint). It has also, as we have seen, a deep-seated utilitarian belief that all choice is ultimately an effort to maximize expected utility. Even Broome, with all his philosophical subtlety, tells us firmly that 'a *rational* agent will have coherent preferences' (Broome 1992: 277, emphasis in original). And what is more: 'The axioms of expected utility theory are requirements of rationality' (ibid.).

As Morton notes, it is not that our desires or goals are usually incomparable in a truly simple and total way, so that there is some objective which cannot be compared to anything else. Rather, an objective or desire 'will be comparable to some others and incomparable to others' (Morton 1991: 34). As a simple example of this he offers what he calls a diamond pattern, which is reproduced as Figure 4.1.

Morton's agent prefers the tour of Japan to any other option in the diamond. Skiing in Switzerland is ranked above skiing in Andorra, but the agent cannot compare either skiing option with the week in Vienna. The wretched weekend in Brighton is ranked below all other options! Morton writes that one could simplify the diamond by removing one of the skiing options. But he wants two

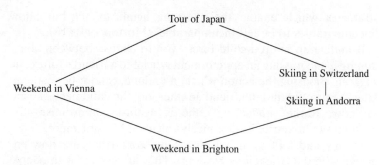

Fɪɢ. 4.1.

options to illustrate the difference between incomparability and indifference, which it does rather well. Switzerland and Andorra are both incomparable to Vienna, but Switzerland is *preferred* to Andorra. The simple diamond shown is far from exhausting the possible complexities of patterns of choice. As Morton notes: 'The overall structure of most people's preferences must contain diamonds within diamonds' (Morton 1991: 35).

One can use a construction of this type to study some of the most acute cases where compromise between goals, possible at certain levels, ultimately fails. Indeed the incomparability may even show in the physical development of the body. A child may begin to study classical ballet, and dance very nicely while at the same time taking riding lessons and developing quite a decent seat. But the more she goes deeply into the dedicated training of a classical dancer the less she will develop in the ways most suitable to a truly high level of equestrian performance.

Many years ago I used a few elementary ideas from lattice theory (Walsh 1967) to express some situations strikingly like those depicted in Morton's diamonds.[15] Consider the situation of Luigi. As a boy, Luigi was torn between two great longings and by his devotion to mentors from two equally powerful callings. He was good enough, it seems, for a brilliant future to be promised him in either music or mathematical physics. His situation, like many of those

[15] When I wrote the paper just cited (Walsh 1967) Putnam and I had been having long discussions of incomparability, and planned a joint paper on it, of which a first draft was written but which was never published. The use of lattice notation was suggested by Martin Davis, with whom we had also discussed these matters.

considered by Morton, was a mixture of comparable and incomparable options. He might well be able to compare and rank the options he might be offered if he devoted himself to becoming a concert pianist. Indeed he already knew where and with whom he most wanted to study. And we may suppose that likewise he could rank the options within physics. But how to compare winning *this* prize for piano with acceptance by *that* great centre of research?

Write X for the set of all musical options (Julliard versus the Eastman School, etc.) It could sometimes be difficult to rank even some of these, but we may suppose that it would be possible. The elements of X, the individual options, are then written x_0, x_1, x_2 and so on. For simplicity, consider only a few alternatives. We assume that these alternatives could be ranked, so one has the music chain x_0, x_1, x_2, etc.

We may now write Y for the set of physics options and, assuming Luigi can also rank these, we have the physics chain y_0, y_1, y_2, etc. Let $\{x_0, y_0\}$ be a point before either career is seriously embarked upon. We may then treat $\{x_0, y_0\}$ as the greatest lower bound of a partial lower lattice, as in Figure 4.2. In this figure one has comparability along a chain, but incomparability between chains. But there may be an upper bound to the two chains—as Morton has correctly suggested with the uppermost point of his diamond. Consider Figure 4.3. As I remarked of a similar figure, here 'there is a complete lattice (omitting x_3 and y_3), whose least upper bound is $\{x_2, y_2\}$. But if the development of incomparabilities is not *seen* in

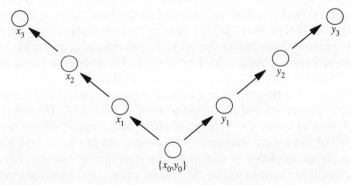

F IG. 4.2.

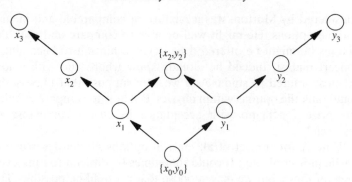

FIG. 4.3.

the system, and either x_2 or y_2 is passed, this possibility is ruled out'
(Walsh 1967: 248, emphasis in original).

A possibility of compromise like $\{x_2, y_2\}$, if it exists, may only be
a cause of suffering in a case like Luigi's. It would enable him to put
off taking the final plunge into one or the other life. As it happened,
he did in the end reject physics, and is now a world famous pianist.
But not without desperate and deeply painful struggle, which the
significance of options like $\{x_2, y_2\}$ may illuminate.

On the other hand, one could get a case where the existence of a
compromise like $\{x_2, y_2\}$ was a blessing. In the old article, I considered a case where military strategists are reacting to a situation.
Is there a compromise between being a pure dove and being a pure
hawk? In a world with the appalling means of destruction which we
possess, it is only too evident that strategies for limiting and containing conflicts are vital. Could the awful tragedy of Bosnia have
been averted if it had been nipped in the bud? Morton is surely
right to stress that one of the most important things about
incomparabilities lies in the intricate patterns of comparable and
incomparable choices. As I remarked: 'Obviously, if incomparabilities be admitted, the concept of rational choice needs to be
restated in terms of a new notation, with strikingly more complicated properties and implications' (Walsh 1967: 248). I noted that
all this had implications for moral philosophy, remarking that 'ana-
lysts of the logical structure of language who are concerned with
the meaningful use of ascriptions of responsibility cannot fail to
notice that the criteria for the use or withdrawal of these words
must be different' (ibid).

Now in recent years a wave of writers in philosophy, economics, and decision theory, some of whom we have discussed, have been facing head on the moral implications of tragic choices. They are confronting the deep fact of human life that someone may have 'only two alternatives, both equally horrible' (Walsh 1967: 250) or be forced to 'regard...two ways of life as incomparable' (Putnam [1986] 1989: 22), or be 'faced with an irreducible conflict of compelling principles' (Sen 1987: 66).

One can construct a tragic moral dilemma without having to involve any uncertainty concerning the facts of the situation or concerning the factual consequences of the possible choices. But there can be no question that the profound uncertainty which perplexes us in real life plays a major part in the complexity and doubtfulness of our moral judgements. Add to our uncertainty concerning matters of fact the deep gaps in our moral knowledge which Levi rightly stresses, and matters become dark indeed. Recent work specifically in economic theory has shed fresh light on a distinction which is highly relevant here.

INCOMPLETENESS AND UNCERTAINTY

An old distinction, with roots going back into the nineteenth century at least, has received a notable revival of interest in the last fifteen years or so. This is the distinction which has been known in economics since Frank H. Knight (1885–1972) as that between 'risk' and 'uncertainty' (Knight 1921). As Margaret Bray has noted, Knight confined the term 'risk' to certain situations where probabilities could be inferred from the results of repeated observations or where, for instance, a coin was flipped. For Knight, 'uncertainty' applied to 'unique events where there is no such basis for numerical probability assessments. It is a matter of some philosophical debate whether it is in fact possible to interpret probability numerically in situations which Knight calls uncertainty; subjectivists claim that it is possible, but make no claim that different people will make the same probability assessments' (Bray 1987: iii. 835). Knight, as Bray notes, had drawn the highly interesting conclusion that economic models where the agents face only risk are in effect identical to models with perfect foresight. Not so, however, with a model where agents face uncertainty—which Knight believed was rife in the real world. This suggests an important connection between uncertainty and incompleteness: if, as is clearly the case, one of the reasons why an agent may be unable to compare two alternatives lies in total uncertainty as to the outcomes, then perhaps in models which contain only risk the axiom of completeness has whatever appropriateness it has under certainty, whereas in models with uncertainty it is simply inappropriate.

Despite certain technical flaws in Knight's argument, Bray finds that he 'anticipates recent developments in a fascinating way' (ibid.). Mark J. Machina and Michael Rothschild also find Knight's distinction between risk and uncertainty 'the most fundamental distinction in this branch of economic theory' (Machina and Rothschild 1987: iv. 201). On the other hand, S. F. LeRoy and L. D. Singell (1987) argue that Knight can be seen as a supporter of subjective probability.

Remarkably, the very year 1921 which saw the publication of Knight's work on this question was also the date of Lord Keynes's *Treatise on Probability*. This early work has been the subject of considerable recent attention from theorists interested in the significance of uncertainty, and Paul Anand, for example, has suggested that 'the conceptual basis for behaviour under uncertainty seems to owe rather more to a brief but intriguing chapter in Keynes's (1921) *Treatise on Probability*, on weight of evidence, than it does to Knight's risk-uncertainty distinction' (Anand 1993: 113).

The central importance of the concept of uncertainty in Keynes's economics has had varying recognition from neo-classical interpreters of Keynes, but has always been stressed by those influenced by Joan Robinson and the Cambridge Post-Keynesians. As Jochen Runde has noted, however, it is only recently that economists have 'begun seriously to investigate Keynes' later views in the light of his earlier work on probability' (Runde 1990: 275). There has now been a flurry of new work on these matters.[16]

The recent tendency to wish to anchor Keynes's views on the economic significance of uncertainty to his early philosophical work on probability has not been without its critics: Allin Cottrell

---

[16] See, for example, Tony Lawson (1985, 1987, 1988) as well as the papers in Lawson and Pesaran 1985, Bateman 1987, and also the essays in Bateman and Davis 1991. Keynes's philosophical ideas are further explored in Carabelli 1988 and in O'Donnell 1989.

(1993) is an example. What is of most interest for present purposes, however, is that even though critical of Keynes's early theory of probability, Cottrell does not dispute Keynes's 'notion of incalculable uncertainty' (Cottrell 1993: 42), but simply argues that this can be found, shorn of certain aspects of Keynes's early probability theory which he finds problematical, appearing 'prominently in *The General Theory* and with even greater emphasis in Keynes' 1937 *Quarterly Journal of Economics* article' (ibid.). He considers the question how much this later argument relies on concepts specific to Keynes's early *Treatise on Probability*. He comes to the conclusion that what in fact remains from the early work in Keynes's later writings on economics is his 'general skepticism regarding the measurability of probabilities and his insistence that well-defined subjective probability distributions do not exist in all cases, or even typically. But a rigorous frequentist need have no difficulty accepting these ideas; indeed, paradoxically perhaps, a rigorous frequency theorist would arguably have to work less hard to establish them.' (Ibid.)

For frequency theorists, an unrepeatable event cannot properly be the subject of a probability statement, and Keynes was essentially concerned with such events. As he himself put it in the (1937) article, 'the hypothesis of a calculable future leads to a wrong interpretation of the principles of behaviour which the need for action compels us to adopt, and to an underestimation of the concealed factors of *utter doubt, precariousness, hope and fear*' (Keynes [1937] 1973: xiv. 121, emphasis added).

Keynes's vivid phrase summons up before one a natural breeding ground for incomparabilities. It can hardly be doubted that 'incalculable uncertainty' is another reason, once its ubiquitous presence in life is recognized, for rejecting the axiom of completeness. Such uncertainty is clearly at the root of many of our disasters and responsible for many of our deepest dilemmas. As has already been noted, however, it should not be assumed that uncertainty is an essential ingredient in incomparability. We could be well aware of the outcomes resulting from a pair of alternatives and yet unable to rank them due to a deep conflict of values.

A number of recent developments in the analysis and criticism of Arrow–Debreu models have an interesting bearing upon the implications of uncertainty. To approach this, we need to distinguish between the incalculable uncertainty of Keynes (and perhaps

Knight) on the one hand, and being uncertain which of a finite number of known alternatives will occur. The latter idea was described by Debreu, who pioneered the concept, as originating 'in the choice that nature makes among a finite number of alternatives' (Debreu 1959: 98).

To take the simplest possible case, we may be interested in just two possible states of nature tomorrow: either it is fine, or it is raining. We make a plan for each state. If it is fine, we shall dine at Anton's (he has a patio, with a fine view of the harbour); if it is raining we shall dine at Bruno's (he has a cozy inn, and a fireplace if it's chilly). Anton and Bruno, when marketing, also allow for the same two states of nature. In addition we suppose that everyone, innkeeper or customer, shares the same information and the same subjective probabilities. (We can add any finite number of states of nature, of successive time intervals, and of agents, if we wish). We may call this 'state of nature uncertainty'—or 'state uncertainty' for short. Obviously it has nothing in common with the incalculable uncertainty of our previous discussion. These placid agents have calculated the probabilities and made plans on day one of the model for every contingency that can arise over the whole set of 'days' for which it runs.

This model has been modified in the years since Debreu first presented it in a number of ways, but I want to consider here just one line of development. Suppose we relax our assumption that all the agents share the same information and probability judgements. Now the agents no longer just make their plans to cover each state 'which is chosen passively by "nature" who, one presumes, has no objectives of her own', as Peter J. Hammond has put it (Hammond 1987a: 732–3). Now there is uncertainty about the strategic choices made by the other agents in pursuit of their own special objectives. As Hammond remarks, 'Such uncertainty is much better able to justify Knight's (1921) claim that "risk" offers no profit opportunities whereas "uncertainty" does' (Hammond 1987a: 733). The introduction of 'asymmetric' information has precipitated this change.

By the 1970s it had been seen that key parts of the Arrow–Debreu formulation require the (explicit or implicit) assumption that all agents in a model possess the same information. If they do not, the general equilibrium may lack the prized 'optimality' or 'efficiency' properties. The present-day literature on asymmetric information began with George Akerlof (1970). If some sellers know that they possess a superior product, but buyers do not, problems of asymmetric information arise. Sellers of the superior product may then look for a means of 'signalling' this superiority. For instance the sellers may charge a price which no one would think reasonable if the product were not in fact superior. Such 'market signalling' was investigated by Michael Spence (1973a, 1973b). Workers and employers, again, may have notably asymmetric information, and a literature developed on 'implicit contracts' and on 'principal and agent' problems. The invasion of asymmetric information spread rapidly, affecting numerous aspects of neo-Walrasian theory.[17]

These (and other) invaders of the austere calm of the original Arrow–Debreu models, many of them inspired by the desire to bring these models closer to the real world, took the models beyond the relative straightforwardness of 'state uncertainty' and somewhat nearer to the incalculable uncertainty of Keynes. They thus added their force to the accumulating considerations which are making more and more theorists sceptical about the axioms which characterized the original canonical Arrow–Debreu formalizations, and in particular the axioms of completeness and transitivity. The newer theorists, as we have noted, did not have the same stake in defending these axioms. It is important for philosophers, decision theorists, and others who adopted the constructed concept of rationality under the influence, direct or indirect, of the Augustan age of Arrow–Debreu to be clearly aware that the old legions are withdrawing. Diluted by all the infusions of new and troublesome developments, the old empire is breaking up into clusters of more or less closely allied positions.

When, as often happens today, neo-classical economists find the austere concept of rationality as consistency a rather thin soup (and as we have seen it has lost some of its richer ingredients in recent years) they frequently seek to give it body by adding the claim that the rationality they are concerned with lies in the consistent pursuit of self-interest. We shall explore the significance of this added ingredient in the next chapter.

---

[17] See, for instance, Grossman and Hart 1983, and Rosen 1985. This widening interest in different aspects of the problems concerning rational responses to asymmetric information spread into a number of research areas. The reader might see, for example, Stiglitz 1983 and Hölmstrom 1987.

5

RATIONALITY AS THE PURSUIT OF SELF-INTEREST

WHEN economic theorists have come to regard purely formal, or instrumental, accounts of rational choice as insufficient, they have frequently added substance to their account of rationality by arguing that a rational agent is one who maximizes the attainment of self-interested aims. It may be observed right away that this move is not one which is likely to appeal strongly to moral philosophers. From the work of the ancient Greeks on, the mainstream tradition in moral philosophy would have rejected both the claim that rationality lay in mere consistency of choice or action with any goal, however wicked or foolish, and the claim that the pursuit of self-interest could be the whole goal of rationality. Ordinary language, it may be added, here conforms to the dominant philosophical tradition. Utilitarianism, it should also be remembered, is fully in line with this tradition: it proposes a moral goal, and judges a person or society as rational in so far as these approximate to that goal. Whatever the shortcomings of utilitarianism, they do not lie in this direction. Hume who, as we have seen, pursues a strictly instrumental rationality to the point of paradox, stands out among philosophers for precisely this reason.

It follows that there is a sense in which the debate concerning rationality as self-interest will be of somewhat less interest to philosophers than to economists or decision theorists. Some economic theorists, rightly critical of the self-interest theory, are seen valiantly defending positions which the philosopher would grant them without argument. But the sad truth is that the labours of these economists were far from being unnecessary. They were attacking errors widely present in their own field.

There is also, however, a sense in which the debate over the self-interest theory is very salutary reading for philosophers and other scholars who happen to be non-economists. This is because it casts a cold and unflattering light on some of the consequences that have resulted from the hegemony of a constructed concept of rationality derived from economic theory.

THE STATUS OF THE SELF-INTEREST THEORY

It should be observed to begin with that the claim that rationality lies in the single-minded pursuit of self-interest does not normally appear among the axioms of Arrow–Debreu theory and its successors: self-interest, unlike consistency, is normally an added characterization of an agent who has already been formally characterized as choosing in accordance with some ranking. Robbins, who anticipated in the 1930s much of the spirit of the later formalization of the concept of rationality, took a strictly and austerely instrumental view of rational choice or action: it simply had to maximize the attainment of the agent's goal, given the scarcity of means. The goal could be that of a saint as well as of a sinner.

The idea that the canonical Arrow–Debreu axiomatizations simply formalized this vision is intellectually appealing. It would go along with the philosophically and ethically minimalist claims of that tradition. Unfortunately, as in the case of the claim to have eliminated all vestiges of utilitarianism which we discussed earlier in this book, the claim that the Arrow–Debreu structure as a whole does not depend on an implicit assumption of self-interest maximization on the part of all agents does not stand up to scrutiny.

True, the assumption of self-interest is not presented as a formal axiom—it does not come in, as it were, by the front door. It gets in, however, as is well known to theorists trained in this tradition, through the requirements necessary for the proofs that any perfectly competitive equilibrium in a canonical Arrow–Debreu model will have a property called 'optimality'. Very crudely, when all the agents in such a model are in equilibrium (i.e. do not wish to change their chosen plan of action) then the model's equilibrium cannot be altered so as to make one agent 'better off' without making some other agent or agents 'worse off'. But it is well known to theorists that such proofs depend upon the assumed absence of 'external effects' or 'externalities'. If the ordinal utility achieved by an agent depends positively or negatively upon the consumption bundles of other agents, in other words if the agent is benevolent or malevolent or envious, then this counts as an externality. So the proofs of the 'optimality' of general equilibrium have had to rule out benevolence, malevolence, envy, etc., from the preference rankings allowed to their agents. It will be seen by moral philosophers that this is arguably a high price to pay for proofs of the existence of an 'optimality' which can encompass neither human nobility nor human baseness.

The role played by such optimality concepts (known in the literature of economic theory as Pareto optimality) is deep and important for the general appraisal of the constructed concept of rationality which has been developed by neo-classical economic theory. To discuss it further, however, we need a sketch of a simple general equilibrium model, and this necessary setting will be provided in Chapters 6 and 7.

Meanwhile, it should be stressed here that it is not the axiomatic utilitarianism which is embedded in Arrow–Debreu theory which compels it to embrace self-interest maximization. The most uncompromising critic of utilitarianism could not accuse that philosophical tradition of wishing to narrow the concept of rational choice or action down to the pursuit of self-interest. Nor, on the other hand, need self-interest be aimed at the maximization of utility. A self-interested agent might pursue a goal which it would be very odd to treat as the maximization of utility.

A DISTINGUISHED ANCESTOR FOR THE SELF-INTEREST THEORY?

The concept of rationality as the pursuit of self-interest in present-day neo-Walrasian theory is sometimes given an aura of distinction by the claim that it is the legitimate descendent of an old line which can be traced back to Adam Smith. Consider, for example, the following passage by Kenneth Arrow and Frank Hahn:

There is by now a long and fairly imposing line of economists from Adam Smith to the present who have sought to show that a decentralized economy motivated by self-interest and guided by price signals would be compatible with a coherent disposition of economic resources that could be regarded, in a well defined sense, as superior to a large class of possible alternative dispositions. (Arrow and Hahn 1971: pp. vi–vii)

They argue quite correctly that from Adam Smith to the present day, what has been important to economists about self-interest has been a claim concerning its results. This is the claim that the pursuit of self-interest by individual agents brings about a 'superior' disposition of economic resources. It will prove helpful to consider this claim first in the specific historical context of Adam Smith, especially since his great authority is customarily cited in support of this use of the assumption of self-interest even by present-day economists.

Among those popular misconceptions about Adam Smith, which generations of scholars seem to have been unable to kill off, will be found the notion that Smith paid lip service to the ideas of 'sympathy' and 'benevolence' in his *Theory of Moral Sentiments* but showed his true colours in the *Wealth of Nations* by making self-interest the whole basis of social interaction. We shall have to unpack this claim at length, but we may begin by disposing summarily of any idea that Smith regarded his *Moral Sentiments* as less important than, or superseded by his *Wealth of Nations*. In his treatment of these matters, D. D. Raphael remarks that 'Certainly Smith himself never thought that he had abandoned philosophy, and according to Sir Samuel Romilly he "always considered his *Theory of Moral Sentiments* a much superior work to his *Wealth of Nations*". He spent his last years revising and expanding the *Moral Sentiments* to such an extent that the resulting sixth edition, published shortly before his death, was virtually a new book' (Raphael 1975: 85). Granting, then, Smith's deep and lifelong preoccupation with moral concepts, and especially with 'sympathy' and 'benevolence', those great themes of his *Moral Sentiments*, why are these ideas not prominent in the *Wealth of Nations*? Especially since it has always been granted that this work is characterized by a sweeping moral claim: that a natural harmony exists between the interest of the individual and that of society.

I shall argue that the belief that Smith was claiming the existence of a natural harmony is perfectly correct, but that it was a harmony whose demonstration rested for Smith jointly upon his moral philosophy and upon his classical economic analysis. Smith was not engaging in the so-called 'value-free' economics beloved of modern economists: 'His object, on the contrary, was to demonstrate that the natural economic harmony owed nothing to *human* benevolence, and everything to the workings of the Divine Plan' (Walsh 1987*b*: 865, emphasis in original).

It was by no means that Smith had forgotten the capacity of perfectly ordinary people for human sympathy in private affairs.

Let a man be never so selfish, Smith argues that 'there are evidently some principles in his nature, which interest him in the fortune of others, and render their happiness necessary to him, though he derives nothing from it except the pleasure of seeing it' (Smith [1790] 1976: 1). But as was quite reasonable in his period of history, Smith believed (with the Earl of Shaftesbury and Francis Hutchison) that the mass of mankind were simply not so placed as to be able to feel sympathy for, or act on behalf of, mankind as a whole. The masses were perfectly capable of benevolence towards family and friends, but not that disinterested benevolence in public affairs which could only be expected from a cultivated minority.

It was now up to Smith's economics to show that, despite the limits of public sympathy in mankind as a whole, a natural harmony could be detected in economic life, and attributed (by his moral philosophy) to the workings of the Divine Plan. Observe that Smith's economics is thus carrying out a task defined for it by his moral philosophy, and that he is in this following an example set by his 'tutelary deity', namely Newton, whose natural philosophy exhibited what was seen as an aspect of the Divine Plan. (As to how much Smith fully understood Newton, the interested reader may begin with W. P. D. Wightman 1975: 59–64.)

What is vital for our purpose is to see that Smith's celebrated assumption of self-interest in the *Wealth of Nations*, and its role in his economics, are part of a closely knit intellectual system. His assumption of self-interest cannot be simply cut out of this whole system, and pasted onto a modern general equilibrium model, without doing violence to the integrity of the argument. Nor can Smith's system as a whole be adopted lock stock and barrel by a modern economist without some embarrassment.

Leaving the philosophical aspects of Smith's argument aside, his economic analysis has some things in common with any classic (see Walsh and Gram 1980: 48–81, 269–316), and some which were appropriate to the period in which he wrote. Smith, like any classic, ancient or modern, stressed the long-period reproduction of the economy's capital stock and its growth—the accumulation of capital. To this was to be attributed the growth of the wealth of nations. The industrial transformation of society depended upon the use of the 'net product' or 'surplus' for accumulation rather than for luxury consumption (as will be explored at length in Chapters 8 and

9). How would the great driving force of self-interest affect this accumulation?

He assumed that the overwhelming majority, who worked for wages, would receive simply a customary subsistence. Benevolence could therefore be expected of them only (at most) toward their extended families. As Hiroshi Mizuta has put it, Smith followed Hutchison in accepting the idea that 'self-preservation and self-love are allowed to exist at the level of subsistence' (Mizuta 1975: 117). The class whose role was crucial to Smith's argument was, of course, the emerging industrial capitalist class. He did not see the small capitalist of his day as the 'perfect competitor' of modern microtheory. But he did see this small owner-manager as living and struggling in strongly competitive conditions. And in such conditions self-interest would, on the whole, lead those small capitalists to do what was needed from them for the progress of society: to accumulate capital, providing the machines and the subsistence for an ever-larger number of productive labourers.

The reader of Adam Smith can hardly fail to remark, however, that when Smith's attention passes from the labourers and small competitive capitalists of his period to light upon the 'slothful and oppressive profusion of the great' (Smith [1937] 1978: 566) his praise of self-interest abruptly stops: 'The monied man indulges himself in every sort of ignoble and sordid sensuality, at the expense of the merchant and the trades man to whom he lends out his stock at interest' (Smith [1937] 1978: 563). For Smith, as for any classical economist, devoting the net product of society to luxury consumption was the ultimate irresponsibility. Smith never accepted luxurious waste, and tolerated it (if at all) only because it was an unavoidable cost of that very system of natural liberty which he was convinced was necessary to the greatest accumulation of capital, and thus to the greatest ultimate prosperity. (See Chapters 8 and 9 below.)

Given his historical period, it can be claimed that Smith's assumptions served him well. But today his little struggling capitalist has been more and more replaced by the giant corporation, the multinational, the polluter, and the 'defence' contractor—upon whom one can imagine Smith's comments. As we have seen, there is in Smith the recognition of a healthy self-interest—that of the labouring masses and the small capitalists—which is a potent engine of progress. But, as Skinner and Wilson have pointed out, there is in Smith

another unfailing principle, man's desire to dominate others and enforce his will, which brings it about that the progress of opulence will not diminish but tend to increase and worsen slavery. Man's arrogance is a very conspicuous feature of Smith's science of man,...it overrides considerations of real self-interest and prudence; for example, the fact that slavery is uneconomical, wasteful and inefficient. (Skinner and Wilson 1975: 199)

To the serious reader of Adam Smith there can be little doubt under what principle of his science of man Smith would have construed today's unbridled self-interest, linked to the enormous economic power of the multinational corporation, and no longer operating in the historical conditions of Smith's small-scale competitive capitalist industry. It has been noted that there is a belief among economists that an assumption of self-interest, when embedded in a present-day model, can be regarded as a legitimate descendent of that used by Smith. This belief is surely unwarranted. As I have remarked elsewhere, Smith's argument 'rests upon a philosophical position of which Smith's assumption of self-interest is a component, which is simply not available to a present-day general equilibrium theorist...Smith's political economy applies his philosophical position to the analysis and appraisal of a particular phase in the early development of capitalist production relations, now long gone' (Walsh 1987*b*: 866).

I shall therefore argue that the concept of 'rationality as self-interest', if it is to play a role in contemporary general equilibrium theory, must be constructed afresh in contemporary terms.[1] To a sketch of this project and its problems we now turn.

IS 'SELF-INTEREST' DIRECTLY COLLECTIVELY SELF-DEFEATING?

Consider two distinct senses in which a theory as to what constitutes the substance of rational action may be self-defeating. The self-interest theory is a theory which tells us that the substance of rational action is to act always in our own interest. Now suppose that, if I successfully carry this out, my very own self-interested

---

[1] For a discussion of re-evaluations of Adam Smith in recent years, and for references to the extensive literature, see for example Sen 1986, 1987, 1994, Skinner and Wilson 1975, Raphael 1985, Khalil 1990, Brown 1991, Werhane 1991 and Rothschild 1992.

aims will be worse achieved than if I had not successfully followed self-interest. If this were the case, then the self-interest theory would be what Derek Parfit has called 'directly individually self-defeating' (Parfit 1984: 55).

Parfit offers several arguments concerning the claim that the self-interest theory may be directly individually self-defeating. This claim has great interest for philosophers, but I shall not give it priority in this book. This is because it can be argued that for economic theory a somewhat weaker claim, which is easier to establish, is seriously (if not fatally) damaging to the self-interest theory. This is the claim that self-interest is directly collectively self-defeating. Suppose that when I successfully follow self-interest this does not prove directly individually self-defeating. However, it turns out that if we (a society or group) all successfully follow self-interest, we shall cause the self-interested aims of each to be worse achieved than if we had none of us followed self-interest. A theory of rationality which led to this result would be directly collectively self-defeating.

Now as we have seen by glancing at the claims made by economists concerning the significance of Smith's use of self-interest, economists are interested in the effects of the actions of individuals upon society as a whole. Even the micro theorist today constructs micro agents with a view to their playing the required role in a model of their general equilibrium. Thus, for economists, if self-interest should prove to be directly collectively self-defeating, this would be enough to discredit it as a general substantive account of rationality, without considering the further possibility that self-interest may also be directly individually self-defeating as well.

Consider, then, a case where self-interested action may prove directly collectively self-defeating. It is unquestionably in the self-interest of each deep sea fishing vessel's skipper to maximize his catch. But it can be worse for all if all skippers do so. An important species of fish—such as the herring—may be virtually fished out of existence. This kind of problem is becoming all pervasive as our natural environment is more and more encroached upon and threatened by human activity. But it arises also in many other areas—it is rampant, for example, in the area of public goods. Since, by definition, a public good may be enjoyed by anyone, it may be better for each agent to follow self-interest and not contribute to the provision of the good. But it will be worse for each if few or no agents contribute to the provision of the good.

As Parfit has observed, 'These cases have a misleading name taken from one example. This is the Prisoner's Dilemma' (Parfit 1984: 56). This is illustrated in a familiar diagram, presented as Table 5.1. Tom and Dick are suspected of a crime. Aside from what the other prisoner does, it will be in the self-interest of either Tom or Dick to confess, since this will save him two years in jail. But if Tom and Dick both confess, as self-interest would appear to dictate, it will be worse for each of them than if both had kept silent. Thus the self-interested choice is directly collectively self-defeating.

This example presents a concept of very wide application in terms of a very special model. For one thing, as Parfit notes, 'The rare Two-Person Case is important only as a model for the Many-Person Versions' (Parfit 1984: 59). In fact the original name for this class of games, namely Prisoner's Dilemma, gives the reader no hint of the vast range of models for this kind of game-theoretic structure. As Robert J. Aumann has recently commented 'it is said that in the social psychology literature alone, over a thousand papers have been devoted to it' (Aumann 1987: 468). He adds: 'The universal fascination with this game is due to its representing, in very stark and transparent form, the bitter fact that when individuals act for their own benefit, the result may well be disaster for all' (ibid.).

Recently Anatol Rapoport has argued that models of this kind, where individual and collective rationality conflict 'cast doubt on the very meaningfulness of the facile definition of "rationality" as effective maximization of one's own expected gains' (Rapoport 1987: 975). He concludes that such models 'point to a clear refutation of a basic assumption of classical economics, according to

TABLE 5.1 *The prisoner's dilemma*

	Tom	
	Confesses	Keeps silent
Dick		
Confesses	Each gets 8 years	Tom gets 10 years, Dick goes free
Keeps silent	Dick gets 10 years, Tom goes free	Each gets 2 years

which pursuit of self-interest under free competition results in collectively optimal equilibria' (ibid.).

SELF-INTERESTED CHOICE VS. SELF-GOAL CHOICE

Unfortunately, the problems which we have been glancing at in the last section infect a much wider class of choices than may at first be apparent. So far we have been considering the damaging implications of the widespread prevalence of prisoner's dilemma type situations for the theory of rationality as self-interest. Now it is important to point out that these situations are equally damaging for another class of choices which are not self-*interested*, but are what have been called 'self-*goal*' choices.

To see what is at issue, it is helpful to start with the most narrowly 'selfish' choices, and then extended the range of the agent's interest as far as possible while remaining, in the broadest sense, 'self-interested'. Lying beyond the range of self-interested choice in this broadest sense, we shall find the area of 'self-goal' choice.

Take first the case of an agent, whom we may call Harry, who is assumed to begin with to be 'selfish' or 'self-centred' in the narrowest sense. Stipulate that Harry is solely concerned to maximize utility, that he derives utility solely from his own consumption bundle, and, further, that he consumes all of his own consumption bundle himself. Harry is without either sympathy, malevolence, or envy towards any other person. A general equilibrium model which assumes that there are no externalities ought in logical consistency to be entirely composed of agents like our Harry. As we saw in Chapter 1, however, the 'agents' in such models are often left as unexplored 'black boxes', which whether called 'households' or simply 'consumers' nevertheless are allowed to stand for a person or a family or other group. If we now supposed that our Harry is looking after such a group, then of course he would appear to be exercising benevolence within the privacy of a black box he inhabits.

Now let us set aside any black box around Harry and modify our assumptions about him by supposing that he is motivated to some extent in his choices by sympathy for other people at large. Harry can still be treated as 'maximizing utility' in a perfectly standard way, where it is simply recognized that the welfare of others is one of the things from which Harry derives utility. All this is familiar. What I want noticed at this point is that one can still call Harry's choices self-interested, since his objective can still be characterized as the maximization of his own utility (some of which is derived, certainly, from the prospect of others' welfare). This 'self-interested' choice does not necessarily entail 'crass selfishness'! The trawler skipper, maximizing his catch, may (besides looking after his family) be a generous giver to worthy charities. Alas, this does not save him from the prisoner's dilemma. A tragic possibility now looms on the horizon.

To see it with stark clarity, suppose that an agent, Tom, is wholly preoccupied with some goal. To this goal he will, when necessary, sacrifice what he counts as utility (his own and that of those around him). His goal, dominating his choice, thus takes him out of the logical terrain of self-interest even on the broadest definition. Now suppose there is another agent, Dick, who is likewise possessed of an altruistic goal, but a different one. Tom and Dick act on the basis of what has been called 'self-goal' choice: Tom chooses on the basis of his (altruistic) goal, and Dick on the basis of his different (altruistic) goal. The essence is that neither considers the dependence of his success upon the action chosen by the other. When we last met Tom and Dick together they were self-interested, and prisoners of the law. Now they are altruistic, and prisoners of fate.

The structure of dilemmas where the agents have 'moral' goals (as distinct from self-interested goals) has been examined at length. (See Parfit 1984: 95–114.) For such dilemmas to arise, self-interested choice, though sufficient, is not necessary. Any kind of 'self-goal' choice can give rise to a model for the theory. Sen, who has written upon several occasions on these matters (Sen 1985, 1987, 1994), points out that these results do *not* entail 'that there is no moral solution to the Prisoners' Dilemma, since morality is not merely a matter of having one set of goals rather than another, but also of the relation between action and conduct, on the one hand, and goals, aims, values, etc. on the other' (Sen 1987: 82 n. 22). Clearly self-goal choice dilemmas are an instance of the kind of situation where an agent needs to consider carefully the meta-ranking of possible different moral rankings or goals, in the light of the goals of others.

An interesting conclusion thus confronts us: what makes self-goal choice turn out to be directly collectively self-defeating need by no means be the possession of 'basely selfish' interests on the part of the agents. Tom can be the very model of a modern social activist, and Dick can be a dedicated scientific administrator. It is a kind of situation made of the very stuff of ancient tragedy: it is Creon's duty to uphold the laws of the city, but it is Antigone's duty to bury her brother.

Self-goal choice, however, is not confined to the idealist (however misguided). One can sacrifice one's self-interest out of pure malevolence! As Sen has recently remarked: 'Some of the nastiest things in the world happen as a result of "selfless" pursuit of objectives far removed from one's own well-being but also from the well-being and freedoms of others' (Sen 1994: 389). Actions prompted by hatred and the desire for revenge are clear departures from self-interest. But malevolence will be the topic of a later section of this chapter.

In classical tragedy, a dilemma arises in some fatal form—the protagonists are typically given no second or third chance. In life, fortunately, we are often faced with situations which, because they keep recurring, offer us, at least in principle, the opportunity to modify our strategy. It is thus natural to ask at this point whether co-operative solutions can be found by 'rational' agents, where a dilemma is repeated.

As it happens, repeated games became prominent in the game theory literature in the 1960s. In such games, as Robert J. Aumann has observed, 'phenomena like cooperation, altruism, trust, punishment, and revenge are predicted by the theory' (Aumann 1987: 468). Suggested 'resolutions' of the one-shot (or non-repeated) prisoner's dilemma get no support from Aumann: 'Worse than just nonsense, this is actually vicious, since it suggests that the prisoner's dilemma does not represent a real social problem that must be dealt with' (ibid. 469). In the case of repeated games, on the other hand, there is some evidence pointing to the possibility of co-operation. Here 'the friendly outcome is perfectly consonant with theory' (ibid.).

In repeated situations, methods may be found for enforcing or encouraging co-operation. A player or players defecting from co-operation to the 'greedy' move can then expect retaliation—the so-called 'Tit for Tat' strategy. Of course, if it is known to all players that a game will be played a certain definite number of times, say ten times, then on the tenth play the threat of Tit for Tat will be ineffective, since a future reprisal is impossible. It has then been argued that the same reasoning now applies to the ninth play—and so on. It would appear to follow that the 'greedy' move is the 'rational' choice throughout the ten iterations. This conclusion does not follow, however, if the number of plays is not known to the players, or is determined probabilistically, or is infinite.

An empirical investigation of such iterated dilemmas was undertaken by R. Axelrod (1984). In his experiments, 'Tit for Tat' came out as most successful. Now, as Anatol Rapoport has remarked, these results can be seen as 'further evidence of the deficiency of strategies based on attempts to maximize one's individual gains in situations where both cooperative and competitive strategies are possible' (Rapoport 1987: 975). He notes that the advantages of cooperative strategies do not depend on the existence of explicit agreements among the participants. This is borne out by some findings from an area where game theoretic models are being actively applied, namely theoretical biology. Fights between two members of one species can be modelled game-theoretically: consider a simple model where fighting can be either lethal or non-lethal. A lethal attack will, of course, defeat a non-lethal, but two lethal attacks may be devastating for both animals.

Evolutionary development of certain non-lethal weapons, for example backward curving horns, or the development of behavioural inhibitions regarding lethal forms of attack, 'may have been results of natural selection which made lethal combats between members of the same species rare' (ibid.). The human species in its conduct both of war and of corporate and industrial conflict would appear to have some catching up to do on other animals. These matters cannot be pursued further here, but the interested reader will find them discussed in Rapoport (1985), and in J. Maynard Smith (1982). Rapoport concludes that these developments and applications of game theory 'provide a rigorous rationale for Kant's Categorical Imperative; act in the way you wish others to act. Acting on this principle reflects more than altruism. It reflects a form of rationality' (ibid.).

Two elements of this last claim are highly significant. First, that more than altruism is needed. We have seen that an agent may pursue a goal which, while wholly altruistic, is nevertheless solely that agent's goal, and that a set of such self-goal dominated agents forms a model for the theory of the prisoner's dilemma. Fanatical idealisms and religious wars are bitter illustrations of this. Secondly, it is highly significant that Rapoport claims that the seeking of a co-operative strategy by an agent is a form of rationality.

Hence it would appear that a 'rationality' which is confined to the promotion of the agent's self-goals, whether these be self-interested or altruistic, can hardly pass muster as a complete or adequate characterization of the concept of 'rational' choice. 'Selfish' choice lies under condemnation, and so does 'self-interested' choice (which need not be 'selfish'); but so also does the most altruistic self-goal choice. As Rapoport claims, the evidence from game theory and its applications supports the fine old Kantian idea that 'rationality' (or what Kant called 'practical reason') requires that all agents take into account the interdependence of their actions.

If we fail to see the fatal shortcomings of purely self-goal choice, we may fall into the error of thinking that the only morally significant element missing from self-interest is altruism. But, as we have seen, choices can be purely altruistic and yet be irrational and deeply flawed morally.

Adam Morton describes what is in fact a case of obsessive self-goal choice and judges, I believe correctly, that when the protagonist of his tale is freed from obsession with his goal he 'becomes a better person as he becomes more self-centered' (Morton 1991: 166). Consider a story resembling yet differing in the end from Morton's. A poor Irish American boy grew up in New York in the early part of the twentieth century. In later life he liked to regale his cronies at the bar at 21 with tales of how as a child he went to school barefoot. This may have been a trifle overdone, but clearly he knew bitter hardship as a boy. He worked his way through college, and tried various jobs. Then he married a beautiful young woman who had enough money to launch his career on Wall Street. It was not an enormous sum, but its effect was as if one had given the young Napoleon a brigade. He always claimed afterwards to be a self-made man, and she never challenged this. In a way, it was true. They had one child, a daughter, and he set out to conquer the world for her. For her he would do virtually anything to anyone who stood in the way of his financial conquests (some would call them swindles).

His darling little girl, however, had his blood: she was as passionate and as obsessive as he. And she saw his mounting fortune only as what made him neglect her, what stole him away, and (incorrectly at least at first) what he really cared for rather than her. She came to hate it, and in the end him, quite as much as she loved him. She could see clearly how a hard ugliness of expression and manner was beginning to mar his once handsome face. This story did not end happily, like that told by Morton, and the reason is significant. Unlike Morton's goal-obsessed protagonist, who becomes less obsessed and a better person (ibid.) through acquiring a little healthy self-interest, age made the tycoon and his daughter grow only more deeply entrenched and obsessive. They were both, in short, utterly unable to examine and strive to change their values. But since its earliest beginnings an essential component of both moral life and moral philosophy has been the critical examination of values. We have already discussed some implications of this in the context of completeness, and specifically of Levi's work on conflicted value structures. Now we must look at some others.

It was clearly seen by Aristotle that moral character is a cluster of dispositions, formed over years, and not open to change all at once. Yet the willingness to scrutinize our values, and to undertake the laborious task of changing those practices and attitudes which we come to see are wrong, is an absolutely essential component of serious moral thought and practice. Given the destructive force at our command today, such a capacity for change is quite simply necessary for the survival of the human species. The fact that the extremist could even in principle be free from any element of self-interest, and willing to die for the goal, does not make the situation any less potentially fatal.

In the last twenty years or so economists have begun to discuss these issues, and efforts to form rankings of goals themselves are known in the literature as 'meta-rankings', 'meta-preferences', or 'second-order preferences'. I shall stick to the term 'meta-rankings'. A meta-ranking then, as the name implies, is a ranking of rankings. The alternatives which are ranked by the meta-ranking are not goods, or states of nature, or experiences of any kind, rather the alternatives are themselves different rankings. The idea is of course an ancient one, being implicit in the work of any moral philosopher who discusses and ranks different moral positions. And indeed recent discussion of the concept seems to begin with the work of philosophers, Harry Frankfurt (1971) and Richard Jeffrey (1974), and Amartya Sen appears to have first developed the idea in the context of economic choice theory.[2]

The struggle to form a meta-ranking can be the stuff of tragedy, and involve deep and complex issues. But the phenomenon of meta-ranking can be found exemplified in quite everyday situations. Thus Clarissa had never much enjoyed her mother's company, and had no sympathy[3] for the older woman's perpetual complaints over imagined social slights and insults. Clarissa did not have much time for the standards once cherished by old guard New York: 'We don't crawl out of the woodwork often nowadays', she would remark to friends. But in any case, the irony was that (for what it was worth) her mother was in fact the very model of the breed. However, Clarissa was a very well brought up young woman, so she had agreed to dine with her mother on the coming Friday. Now an English friend called to offer her tickets to a concert he was giving on that night. Clarissa knew her mother would never agree to an evening of solo harpsichord with little time for complaints and gossip. With genuine regret (and some annoyance) she declined the invitation to the concert and dined with her mother.

Lest a horrible suspicion arise that Clarissa had secret financial motives, it may be pointed out that her income from work (augmented by a small trust fund) and her mother's relative poverty, rule out such considerations. (In fact she suspected that, besides being lonely in her widowhood, her mother was in financial need again.)

Formally, we have thus a set of alternatives X, which in our simple example has only two elements, dining with mother, x_1, and the concert, x_2. Writing Z for the set of different rankings being considered, we have in our example just two, R^1 a ranking accord-

---

[2] See Sen 1982 for references to his own part in the philosophical debate, as well as for references to the literature as a whole (Sen 1982: 7 n. 18, and p. 100; also Sen 1987: 82–3 n. 22, for further sources). See also Hirschman 1982, McPherson 1984, Schelling 1984, Schick 1984, and George 1984, 1989, 1993. George has extended the concept of meta-rankings beyond fundamental choice theoretic questions into the basis for a detailed critique of certain market phenomena in his more resent work.

[3] As Sen notes: 'In the terminology of modern economic theory, sympathy is a case of "externality"...On the other hand commitment does involve, in a real sense, counterpreferential choice' (Sen 1982: 93). So it will not do to allow Clarissa to feel sympathy for her mother, since then dining with her and giving her pleasure will arguably increase Clarissa's utility, thus removing the necessity for a second ranking besides that in terms of utility. This kind of issue, concerning the differing significance of sympathy and commitment (or duty) will concern us again when we are discussing benevolent and malevolent choice.

TABLE 5.2

R^1 (Duty)	R^2 (Pleasure)
x_1	x_2
x_2	x_1

ing to duty and R^2 a ranking according to pleasure. A meta-ranking is then a ranking of these different rankings R in Z, and may be written Q. The choice of the letter Q for the meta-ranking relation reflects the fact that this relation may be a quasi-ordering, i.e. may not be *complete* (Sen 1982: 80).

Clarissa's situation is illustrated in this notation in Table 5.2. The elementary nature of the example prevents the introduction of incompleteness. But there is no reason why the rankings R need be few. There might be a large number, representing rival goals, aspirations, or obligations. There could be rankings representing the recognition of differing spheres of responsibility: to family, community, class, country, environment, etc. up to the most global. The possibility that the meta-ranking relation Q may be a quasi-ordering in such complicated situations should be evident.

Finally, it should be remembered that the meta-ranking which an agent strives to follow need not be a moral improvement. One must not forget the bitter fact that children are taught to hate or despise certain other children, and thus learn to suppress their natural friendliness. People can be persuaded to adopt new values for better or worse.

SELF-INTEREST VS. PRESENT AIMS

I now wish to leave aside the problems of self-goal choice, and return to self-interest. It is important to observe that self-interest is often confused with something quite different and much less worthy of respect—although of more vulgar appeal. A philosophical argument which goes back at least to Henry Sidgwick (1838–1900) can be used to make the claim that much of the appeal of the self-interest theory to those who like to fancy themselves 'hard headed' is due to the confusion of choice aimed at the maximization of self-interest with choice which has quite a different aim in view. Parfit, who offers a present-day version of Sidgwick's argument, refers to this second sort of choice as being devoted to the maximization of one's 'present aims'. Sidgwick had countered the proponents of self-interest by asking, 'Why should I concern myself about my own future feelings any more than about the feelings of other persons?' (Sidgwick 1907, cited by Parfit 1984: 138). This, in a nutshell, is what Parfit calls the 'present-aims' theory of rationality.

The present-aims theorist can readily admit that a set of aims might well be inconsistent, and thus irrational. Suppose, however, that I am well aware of the facts and that I am thinking correctly about them, so that my set of present desires is not irrational, in the sense of being either misinformed or confused. Then, if I am a present-aims theorist, 'what I have most reason to do is what would best fulfill those of my present desires that are not irrational' (Parfit 1984: 119).

Parfit calls this the 'critical' version of the present-aims theory (the reader will see that he has stated it so as to eliminate momentary whims, fads, and infatuations based on misinformation). He observes that this view of what is rational is strangely neglected. Yet the critical present-aims theory is important for an account of rational agents because it happens to be the case that the self-interest theory of rationality and the critical present-aims theory can be shown to conflict. Parfit argues that the self-interest theory in fact lies between the present-aims theory (which is on one flank, as it were) and an account of rationality which recognizes moral obligation as interwoven with rationality (which is on the other flank). The self-interest theory is thus exposed to attack simultaneously on two fronts. What is worse, the self-interest theory is forced to defend itself against the rational claims of morality by adopting assumptions which lay it open to the present-aims theory, and vice versa.

From the point of view of the economist, I think that perhaps the most diverting part of this argument is that concerning the exposure of the self-interest theory to attack from the present-aims theory. Despite the unreality of certain well-known properties of general equilibrium models, and of the micro agents which compose them, economists seem to enjoy wearing the garb of the 'hard-headed realist'. It is just here that the proponent of the present-aims theory can steal their clothes.

The essence of the present-aims theory is that it rejects the claims of impartiality between the desires of our present selves and our (possibly utterly different) future selves, just as the self-interest theory rejects the claims of impartiality between our selves and others. As Parfit remarks, 'What would best fulfill our various desires, at the time of acting, often fails to coincide with what would most effectively promote our own long-term self-interest' (Parfit 1984: 129). The theory of intertemporal decisions which emerged in the literature of economics in the 1950s in fact formalizes rather well what Parfit is calling 'long-term self-interest'. An agent in a canonical Arrow–Debreu model was typically assumed to have a given ordering over all relevant alternative plans covering a complete future. State-of-nature uncertainty was taken into account fairly early in the development of models for this theory, as we saw in discussing Debreu's work in earlier chapters. It was, of course, recognized that agents might have a marked preference for present consumption. This concession, however, is not nearly enough to satisfy the present-aims theorist. The latter refuses to see the future simply in terms of agents discounting the value to themselves as they are now of commodities delivered later. Rather, the young poet of today is totally uninterested in the needs of the middle-aged advertising copywriter which it is her destiny to become, the dashing young subaltern cannot be bothered with the needs of the ageing major general which is his future self. Only those who have never come to regret bitterly some of the choices of their youth may reject out of hand the claims of the present-aims theorist: that what people are often actually following when they claim to be pursuing self-interest are in fact simply their present aims. Yet self-interest is often presented in a cozy, down-to-earth way, as if it were what everyone is really pursuing, would they but own up! But self-interest is something much more austere and calculating, and concerned with even the distant future. It is not 'eat, drink, and be merry, for tomorrow we die'. But now that complete, intertemporal neo-Walrasian models are giving way before a tide of temporary equilibria, with rationing, asymmetric information, and so on, the present-aims theorist can press the attack. Could economists settle for present aims? Given the recent proliferation of temporary equilibrium models, this move does not, on the face of it, look totally unfeasible. It might, however, have a certain lack of appeal.

The goddess Reason has been accorded much public worship by the economics profession in the present century. But if she were to be dressed in the trendy and often changing garb of the present-aims theory, Reason might be felt to have lost too much of that austere calm and long-period detachment which she has hitherto been able to retain since the Enlightenment. The careful reader of works on economic theory will have seen that the historic dignity of the appeal to Reason remains as an unspoken background to the economist's appeal to 'rationality' (with a small 'r'). It would be natural for the non-economist to feel that the dignity of reason can best be claimed by the economist who recognizes that rationality has always ordinarily implied the absence of both temporal and personal bias. But unfortunately most (though not all) economists are only now beginning to recover from a long love affair, which began in the 1930s, with the claim that scientific statements are morally neutral (see Walsh 1987b: 861–3). Their belief in the 'value-free' character of economics (seen as a science) led economists to the conviction that the statement 'agents act rationally' could have no moral implications. On the other hand, an equilibrium which resulted from the 'rational' choices of all agents was claimed to lead to a 'coherent disposition of economic resources that could be regarded, in a well defined sense, *as superior* to a large class of possible alternative dispositions' (Arrow and Hahn 1971: p. vii, emphasis added). Not a position whose consistency is exactly evident.

Economic theory thus faces a dilemma: if the down-to-earth, 'everyone's doing it' appeal of self-interest is stolen by present-aims, how should self-interest be presented? If poor humanity, gifted with none of the vast computational abilities of the rational agent in the old complete intertemporal neo-Walrasian models, and thus possessing rankings which are probably neither complete nor transitive, can seldom live up to self-interest, must this latter then be presented as an ideal? A worthy object of aspiration? Then how are other moral goals to be held at bay? If economic theory can be nudged in the direction of a morally non-trivial concept of rationality by the present-aims theory, there is another challenge which may reinforce this effect.

SELF-INTEREST VS. MALEVOLENCE

Self-interest is commonly contrasted with benevolence. But some benevolent actions may be undertaken in the pursuit of self-interest itself. It has been argued that if, for example, the sight of desperate poverty makes you ill or depressed, then your efforts to relieve it can be construed as self-interest. I do not wish to deny this out of hand. But there is an old philosophical reply: you feel sick, this argument runs, because you were antecedently a morally responsible person. An amoral person would not have felt sick. Your feeling sick is not the reason why you wanted to relieve the poverty, simply a natural concomitant reaction of a morally responsible person.

However, this debate—important as it is in moral philosophy— can be sidestepped for present purposes by assuming that you relieve poverty simply because you regard this as your duty. Actions on behalf of others, done from duty, clearly created a problem for the self-interest theory. This, of course, is the direction from which supporters of an account of rationality in terms of the maximization of self-interest expect to be challenged.

It seems to be less often noticed that supporters of self-interest are equally exposed to challenge for ignoring malevolent choices or actions. But the fact that human beings will turn aside from what is in their own interest to undertake actions, from hatred or spite or the desire for revenge, aimed specifically at damaging others, is surely one of the most widely recorded facts of our history. Critics of the self-interest theory who concentrate on that theory's inability to handle morally superior choices give their arguments an unnecessary appearance of naïve optimism about human nature. In fact the self-interest theory can be charged with being as naïve about the human capacity for evil as it is about the human capacity for good. It wholly ignores the dark side of human nature. As Kenneth Boulding tellingly remarked, self-interest is 'a knife-edge between benevolence on the one side and malevolence on the other. It is something that is very rare' (Boulding 1970: 126). These matters will be carried further in the next two chapters, when we have developed models of exchange between agents.

Like the attack by the present-aims theory, this challenge comes from a direction which lies morally 'below' self-interest's position. The self-interest theorist must now claim that malevolent choices cannot be rational. Surely one would not ordinarily say that a consistently malevolent person was rational. However, the appeal to ordinary language is not open to the self-interest theorist, since the latter is advocating a severely revisionist concept of rationality. Thus the self-interest theorist cannot take the high ground, now embracing the moral implications of words like 'rational' in natural language, and look down on malevolence. Self-interest theory has eliminated recognition of all those claims concerning responsibility to other persons and to the community which are inextricably interwoven with the family of uses of words like 'rational', 'reasonable,' 'sensible', 'wise', 'prudent', and so on in ordinary discourse.

The malevolent agent can certainly exhibit consistency, the formal component of the self-interest theory. Economists have been telling people for years that internal consistency can cover the choices of anyone from Jack the Ripper to Mother Theresa. So this component will not keep out malevolent agents. If malevolence is to be resisted, it must be because malevolence is incompatible with something else about self-interest: something which makes self-interest's pursuit worthy of being called rational.

The moral philosopher can hold out a hand to the self-interest theorist, agreeing that long-term enlightened self-interest (absent prisoner's dilemmas) has moral value. Indeed this has been recognized by moral philosophers, at least since Aristotle. But, for well over two thousand years, this qualified approval would be withdrawn whenever the pursuit of self-interest was transformed from a component of a healthy, balanced and wise character, into an obsessive and exclusive preoccupation. Self-interest is entitled to the honourable place which it has always held in the common moral consciousness; but it is not entitled to be transformed into the sole or dominant principle of human rationality.

ARE SOME GOALS RATIONALLY REQUIRED?

Leaving the present-aims theory aside, I now turn to a view of 'rationality' which is, in a sense, at the opposite pole from the self-interest theory. This is the view that there are some goals which are 'rationally required'. It is of some importance to stress right at the beginning that this theory can acknowledge freely that a person does have some perfectly legitimate present-aims, as well as perfectly legitimate long-term self-interested aims. The theory simply insists that persons cannot correctly be said to be rational unless they *also* have some strictly moral aims. This is in effect the claim that if a person's aims were wholly untouched by moral responsibility, then we would not call that person rational.

If someone denies this claim then they are adopting what has been called a wholly 'instrumental' view of 'rationality'. This is of course our old acquaintance, the theory of 'rationality as consistency', which, as Frank Hahn and Martin Hollis have remarked, 'rules out neither the saint nor Genghis Khan' (Hahn and Hollis 1979: 4). Economists often lay claims to this theory of rationality, but in fact, as we have seen, it is an idea with an older ancestry. David Hume's telling passage now needs to be quoted in full: "'Tis not contrary to reason to prefer the destruction of the whole world to the scratching of my finger. 'Tis not contrary to reason to choose my total ruin to prevent the least uneasiness of an Indian, or person wholly unknown to me. 'Tis as little contrary to reason to prefer even my own lesser good to my greater...' (Hume [1739–40] 1978, Book II, Part III, Section III, cited by Parfit 1984: 117–18).

I think it is fair to say that all three of the 'rational' preferences instanced by Hume would ordinarily be judged to be irrational. Economists tempted by Hume need to pause here and consider a concept to which they ordinarily pay much attention—namely the market. I have in mind here, however, the market for economic theory. Part of that market consists of theorists reading each other's work, and of students who have no choice. But if it is hoped to influence a wider public, it needs to be kept in mind that this wider public consists of social scientists, lawyers, civil servants, professionals of all kinds, officers of corporations and of labour unions, representatives of various special interest groups, and others, all of whom need to use the word rational in a number of contexts which imply that the rational choice is the one which a jury of informed and reasonable people would approve of.

When such people hear an economist make the claim that rational agents, acting in a free market, can bring about an allocation of resources which will in turn have certain rational features, they are likely to be initially impressed. But were all those who read such claims to see quite clearly that a rational disposition of resources can be any consistent disposition, from one approved by a saint to one approved by Genghis Kahn, then I fear that they might somewhat lose interest in the economist's claims.

The economist is thus in something of a dilemma. For contemporary general equilibrium theory to gain the sort of prestige among the educated public which was once bestowed upon the classical economists, it is necessary to appeal to a concept of rationality which has existed at least since the ancient Greeks, and which was notably present in the works of the Enlightenment authors. But on the other hand economists since the 1930s have felt obliged to deny the moral implications of the appeal to reason, for fear of violating the early twentieth-century logical positivist fact/value distinction, which as we know made its last stand in philosophy with the logical empiricists of the 1950s.

One cannot have it both ways, however. Trivialize rationality and you trivialize neo-classical general equilibrium theory which, after all, is entirely about rational agents. General equilibrium theory then reduces to a game, like chess: of great interest to the players, no doubt, but of rather less interest to the non-economist (who may, as well, be a highly significant policy-maker).

Economists, of course, have seen this danger, which is why the formal concept of consistency with some ranking is often fleshed out either with a concept of utility, or of self-interest, or (rather inconsistently) of both. But, as we have seen, the concepts of utility and of self-interest, as concepts which might give substantive content to rationality, have serious drawbacks. And, besides, they lead the economist into deep waters conceptually.

The natural way to escape from the inadequacies of utility and self-interest, and at the same time to return to a tradition about rationality which is at least as old as Aristotle, and which certainly acknowledges that some goals are 'rationally required', has recently been well expressed by Parfit. He notes that one must distinguish between two kinds of reasons: explanatory reasons and good reasons: 'If someone acts in a certain way, we may know what his reason was. By describing this reason, we explain why this person acted as he did. But we may believe that this reason was a very bad reason. By "reason" I shall mean "good reason"' (Parfit 1984: 118).

Why is it imagined that, if a choice does not rest on mistaken beliefs about matters of fact or involve inconsistency with the agent's ordering, it cannot be irrational? Economists hold this view in principle (their practice is not consistent with it) because of the residual influence of logical empiricism. But recall the argument's more distinguished ancestor, Hume. As Parfit notes, Hume assumed that reasoning is concerned only with our beliefs, and thus only with truth and falsity. A desire, after all, cannot be said to be 'false'. So a desire can be rejected as being unreasonable (accord-

ing to Hume's argument) only if it involves some theoretical irrationality. To this Parfit, correctly I believe, replies that reasoning
does not have to do only with beliefs: 'Besides theoretical there is
practical rationality. There is thus a different and simpler way in
which a desire may be irrational. It may be a desire that does not
provide a reason for acting' (Parfit 1984: 120).

This idea, which is at the core of the concept of practical reason,
is well conveyed by our simple expression 'good reasons'. It is so
deeply embedded in the whole structure of our ordinary talk about
action that we scarcely notice it. It is also deeply embedded in our
jurisprudence. It surfaces in such concepts as that of the 'reasonable person'. If we adopt this idea, then some goals can be said to
be 'inherently irrational', since they are not based on good reasons,
while some other goals may be 'rationally required'—required of a
reasonable being. Could economists adopt this ancient usage which
is embedded in our language, and in our whole conceptual system?
Notice right away that economists in fact do so in their ordinary
speech, since this is a deep characteristic of the ordinary use of
'rational'. And they depend upon other people interpreting them
in this way whenever they want their policy prescriptions to be
listened to as rational in the sense of based on good reasons. As
Putnam has argued,

If we find that we must take a certain point of view, use a certain 'conceptual system' when we are engaged in practical activity, in the widest sense
of 'practical activity', then we must not simultaneously advance the claim
that it is not really 'the way things are in themselves'. Although philosophers have traditionally allowed themselves to keep a double set of books
in this way, the effect is to perpetuate at least two intellectualist errors: it
leads one to debase the notion of *belief*... and it leads one to indulge in the
fiction that there is a God's Eye point of view that we can usefully imagine.
Our *lives* show that we believe that there are more or less warranted beliefs about political contingencies, about historical interpretations, etc.
(Putnam 1987: 70, emphasis in original).

Putnam's deceptively simple argument has deep roots in meta-
mathematics, logic, and the philosophy of science, which cannot be
explored here.[4]

For many years it was taken for granted by economists that the
old fact/value distinction was a rock-solid implication of the very

---

[4] See Putnam 1978, 1981, 1985, 1987, 1988, 1990.

nature of science. The belief that a science was composed wholly of factual and conventional (mathematical) ingredients, and contained no value-judgements, was (as already noted) an integral part of the logical positivist philosophy of science in the 1930s, and remained a part of the later logical empiricism. With the defeat of logical empiricism, this fact/value distinction lost its logical underpinnings and was abandoned by philosophers. Its long survival in economics is a striking example of the effects of the lack of needed interdisciplinary communication.

Today there are many signs that the old rigid views are being increasingly challenged within economic theory itself. As Sen has recently observed, it is possible to argue that, besides consistency, 'what we aim to achieve should also satisfy some criteria of rational assessment...so that a purely "instrumental" concept of rationality may be quite inadequate.' (Sen 1987: 13 n. 9).

Partly as a result of the game-theoretic literature, partly because of the ever-growing research devoted to social choice and the literature on public goods (among other special areas), economists have in recent years been investigating what have been called 'altruistic preferences'. This is a truly praiseworthy sign that the grip of the old iron-clad fact/value distinction is losing its hold over economists. A limitation, however, upon some of this literature arises from the fact that it confines itself to altruistic preferences (given an ordinal utility interpretation). 'Altruistic' choices are then ordinal utility maximizing choices, and the 'altruism' which can be handled has all the limitations imposed by ordinal utilitarianism. What would be called 'self-sacrificing' choice in ordinary speech is counter-preferential choice, and, as we have seen, results from a person having a meta-ranking which rejects some preference ordering R^1, for some other ordering R^2.

Again, in this literature altruism is, as Peter J. Hammond puts it, a 'regard for other's *welfare*' (Hammond 1987*b*: 85), emphasis in original). It is not a regard for the rights, goals, agency, or achievements of these other persons. It thus perpetuates the welfarist reduction involved in utilitarianism which we have discussed at length in Chapters 2 and 3. Much interesting and thought-provoking work has been done despite these limitations, but the limitations make it less surprising than it would otherwise be that some economists have questioned whether the concept of altruism is even relevant to economic theory (see Hammond 1987*b*: 86, and the references cited there). What may well be questioned is whether an ordinal utilitarian concept of altruism is to the point at this juncture.

This concludes our general discussion of the formalizations of rationality which arose out of neo-classical theory. In Chapter 6 I shall turn to the examination of claims concerning the rationality of allocations resulting from the actions of individual agents who engage in exchange with each other. It is time for this, since, for example, any further exploration of some of the implications of benevolent and malevolent choices and actions requires that readers have before them at least a sketch of a simple model of general equilibrium in which the relationships which can arise between agents who engage in exchange can be studied. An elementary version of such a model will be offered in the next chapter, and its implications further developed in Chapter 7.

6

THE RATIONALITY
(OR OPTIMALITY)
OF ALLOCATIONS

THE rationality of individual economic agents is, as has been seen, a continually recurring theme in neo-classical theory; but it is not studied simply or solely in response to some deep interest in the nature of human individuals, as might be the case with a philosopher studying the nature of persons. This can be seen from the fact that methodological individualism is paid only lip service, when supposedly a fundamental assumption. Rather, economic theorists are interested in the rationality of individual economic agents because it is believed that, if all the agents in a model are rational in the required sense (and given certain other assumptions), it can then be shown that the model will have an equilibrium (not necessarily unique) and that any such equilibrium will possess certain properties believed to be desirable. A key concept in such arguments is that of an 'allocation' of the goods which are available in the model (whether through production or as an initial endowment) to the agents appearing in the model. Certain closely connected classes of allocations have then proved to be of especial interest to neo-classical theory, namely those known as 'perfectly competitive' allocations, and those called 'Pareto optimal' allocations.

We thus now focus our attention upon the 'equilibrium allocations' which arise when rational agents (in the neo-classical sense) engage in exchange of their initial endowments. This requires an elementary development of the theory of general equilibrium in the exchange of commodities. Unavoidably, this account will be trying for non-economist readers, and boringly elementary for the specialist (in Edgeworth economies). Fortunately the points which I wish to make in this chapter and the next can be sketched informally within the confines of very simple models. It should be noted, however, that the states of affairs which can be treated by these models are more varied than might at first be obvious. The goods traded need not be physical: I might offer you sailing lessons in return for your teaching me Italian. A philosopher and an economic theorist may bring their respective talents to a joint work (it has happened several times!).

Physical commodities, and also skills, normally have to be produced. In this chapter and the next, however, it will be assumed that the goods whose allocation among agents is being considered have either been produced using an efficient (i.e. cost minimizing) combination of inputs, or else are present, in a form which needs no productive activity, as part of the initial endowment of an agent or agents. The whole focus of the models in this chapter and the next, in other words, will be upon the allocation of a set of goods, which, within the confines of the model, will be assumed to be fixed in quantity and quality.

Such models are often referred to as models of 'pure exchange'. I have no objection to the term, as long as it is understood that they need not be interpreted as applying only to some strange economy in which no production is in fact going on. Sometimes exchange models are presented as being about a very primitive economy in which nothing has to be produced. One then writes of the imagined trading activities of Adam and Eve, or of simple islanders, or of British officers in a prisoner of war camp who get Red Cross packages and exchange the contents. But in fact just about all of these examples break down—some production is actually going on, even if it is only a matter of shaking a palm tree to make the coconuts fall down. In R. A. Radford's well-known article (Radford 1945), capitalist production relations and the sale of labour power arose among the imprisoned officers!

So in the models about to be discussed, production will have been going on. The focus of these models will simply not be on their production relations. Production, if you like, will not be the action on which the models concentrate—it will be, as it were, off stage, as violence is in classical Greek tragedy and in the tragedies of Racine.

It will also be unnecessary in this chapter and the next to be concerned with an intertemporal version of the models. However, just as production is off stage, so will be the ability of these model economies to reproduce themselves (a matter dependent upon certain conditions which will be discussed in Chapters 8 and 9 of this work). Furthermore, since the passage of time is not involved crucially in our present models, they may be referred to as atemporal allocation (or exchange) models. And since these models will not encompass a series of elementary time intervals, or time periods, it will be unnecessary to distinguish between stocks and flows of goods. It will be convenient to speak of the total initial endowment of a good in such a model as the 'given stock' of that good in the model irrespective of how that stock is divided initially among the agents.

In any such model with which we deal, it will be assumed that there is a set of (two or more) agents, who will be called traders, each of whom has an initial endowment of one or more goods. It will be further assumed, as is standardly done, that each trader has an ordering, and trades only to obtain a basket of goods which is more highly ranked by that trader than the endowment basket originally possessed.[1] A further simplification will be useful: the restriction of our discussion to the simple case where the given stocks are of only two different goods will make possible the use of the rather widely familiar Edgeworth box diagram, which may be recalled by those readers who were exposed to undergraduate micro-economics. Some readers, however, may not be familiar with it, so it will be necessary to give a sketch of the more important features of the Edgeworth box here. This will make it possible to express a number of key points concerning allocation rather clearly and with fairly minimal conceptual outlay.

It is customary to begin with the case where there are supposed to be only two traders, say Trader A and Trader B (the case of bilateral exchange). The given stocks, which will be the subject of exchange, are then supposed to be initially in the hands of the two traders. A trader's initial endowment is then assumed to comprise as much or as little of either commodity as is appropriate to the special purposes of a particular model, and it is often tacitly assumed that any trader can if necessary survive without trade. This is no trivial matter, as will emerge in due course. For the moment it will be convenient to begin with the case where each trader

---

[1] As we know, the assumption that each agent in a model possesses an ordering has been substantially weakened in recent general equilibrium models. In this chapter and the next, however, I am concerned with other issues, and the simplest exchange models in which orderings are standardly assumed (and thus indifference curves are available) will turn out to be sufficient for present purposes.

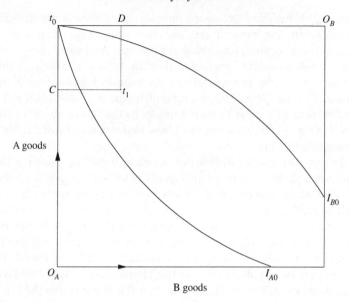

F<small>IG</small>. 6.1.

possesses (before trade) the model's entire stock of just one good. One may then refer to the stock which is initially in the hands of A, as 'A goods', and likewise to B's endowment as 'B goods'.

Now consider the box diagram in Figure 6.1. If we assume that trader A is initially endowed with the whole stock of A goods, we may represent A's initial endowment by $O_A t_0$. If trader B is likewise initially endowed with all the B goods, and has the origin O_B, we may represent B's initial endowment by $O_B t_0$. Then the point t_O represents the allocation of the two goods *before* any trade—sometimes referred to as 'the point of zero trade'. Any other point t, such as t_1, then represents a reallocation of the initial stocks, in other words, a trade. At t_1, for example, trader A has given up $t_0 C$ of A goods in order to acquire $t_0 D$ of B goods, while trader B has traded $t_0 D$ of B goods in order to acquire $t_0 C$ of A goods.

Indifference curves for A and B are then customarily introduced, based on assumptions standardly adopted in neo-classical microtheory. (Such assumptions include: the existence of an ordering, in the case of each trader, over all commodity bundles in the

Edgeworth box, the assumption that each trader's indifference curves are convex to that trader's origin, the assumption that each trader would prefer to have more of each good, etc.)

It is then possible to identify a pair of important indifference curves, one of which curves belongs to each trader. These are the curves I_{A0} for trader A and I_{B0} for trader B, which pass through the initial endowment point t_0, as shown in Figure 6.1. Since the point t_0 on I_{A0} is available to trader A without trading, clearly I_{A0} is the locus of all points (representing possible trades) which trader A ranks as highly as not trading. Likewise I_{B0} is the locus of all points ranked by trader B as highly as not trading. We are now in a position to characterize the set of points (trades) which a trader, say A, will rank at least as highly as not trading. This is the horizontally shaded area in Figure 6.2(a). Its lower boundary, as we have seen, is a set of points ranked equally with not trading, while a point like t_1 or t_2 will be ranked above not trading, since it will be on a 'higher' indifference curve for trader A. This shaded area (including its boundaries) is known as A's 'upper contour set' of t_0, and may be written K_{A0}. This is the set of points (trades) which are ranked by A at least as highly as not trading. Likewise, K_{B0} is the upper contour set for B associated with the point t_0. This is shown in Figure 6.2(b) as the vertically shaded area.

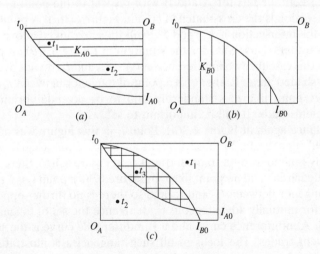

Fig. 6.2.

Clearly A and B will agree to trade only if their respective upper contour sets have an intersection such as that shown in Figure 6.2(c), as the cross-hatched area. Trader A would wish to trade at t_1 in that Figure, but for B this trade is ranked below not trading (it is on a lower indifference curve than I_{B0}, of which a point, t_0, can be obtained without trade). Likewise A would not trade at t_2, while t_3, on the other hand, is clearly a possible trade; it is in the intersection of the respective upper contour sets of zero trade, and thus ranked above not trading by both agents. Will these upper contour sets always have an intersection? Will there always be the possibility of 'gain' from trade? The answer is no. The traders might be initially endowed with stocks of goods which, given their orderings, left one or both with no wish to trade with the other. This fact finds its expression in the Edgeworth box, where, given initial endowments and the indifference curves of the traders, trade will take place if and only if the upper contour sets of A and B with respect to t_0 have an intersection. The set of points in this intersection of K_{A0} and K_{B0} are thus referred to as the trading set associated with t_0.

Now consider point t_1 in Figure 6.3(a). Since it is in the interior of the trading set associated with t_0, it will be more highly ranked by both traders than t_0. Could t_1 be an 'equilibrium' trade? It will be seen from the Figure that I_{A1} and I_{B1} cross at t_1. Consider the new upper contour sets for A and B with respect to the point t_1: their intersection is the cross-hatched area in Figure 6.3(a). A point like t_2 in the intersection if K_{A1} and K_{B1} will thus be ranked above t_1 by both traders. Now consider the situation in Figure 6.3(b), at point t_n. In this case the two indifference curves, I_{A2} and I_{B2} do not overlap in a 'shaded area'. Rather, t_n is a point of tangency between I_{A2} and I_{B2}. A point like t_n is standardly said to be an 'equilibrium' or 'efficient' trade. It will be important to see why.

Glance again at Figure 6.3(a). Point t_1 in this Figure was not an equilibrium trade, because a point such as t_2, was clearly more highly ranked by both traders. But at t_n, in Figure 6.3(b), there is no 'shaded area', and no point like t_2 in Figure 6.3(a); point t_n is a point of tangency between I_{A2} and I_{B2} and so there is no further opportunity for mutually advantageous trade. Hence the set of tangencies of an A indifference curve and a B indifference curve is the set of efficient trades. The locus of all such tangencies is illustrated in Figure 6.4, where it is the curving line running from O_A to O_B. This

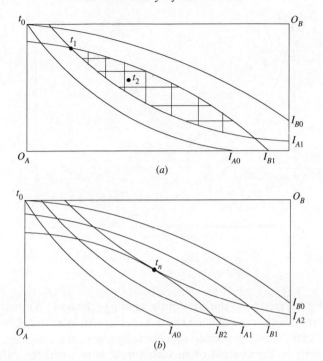

FIG. 6.3.

locus is the set of efficient trades, or efficiency locus. Actual trades, however, as we already know, will not take place outside the area defined by the respective indifference curves through the initial endowment point, here t_0. So we shall normally be interested only in the part of the efficiency locus lying between point C on I_{A0} and point C' on I_{B0}. Points t_3 and t_4 are examples of such points, while trade would not take place at points such as t_1 or t_6 (only small sections of the indifference curves, close to tangency, have been shown to avoid clutter). The part of the efficiency locus lying within the trading set, CC', has been called the 'contract curve'. Usage, however, is not uniform, and the entire efficiency locus (or set of efficient trades) is sometimes referred to as the contract curve. I think this is a confusing usage, since trade (or contract) would never take place at a point outside CC'.

The part of the efficiency locus labelled CC' in Figure 6.4 is

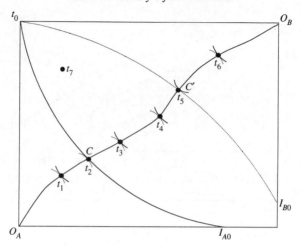

Fig. 6.4.

usually referred to as the core of the trading economy. We shall be concerned with some of what the use of this term 'core' implies, but the reader should be warned that the full powers of the concept are seen only in the context of specialist models of exchange, whose technical apparatus will not be developed here. For the moment it will be enough to note that the core consists of all allocations, or trades, which lie on the efficiency locus and which in addition 'do not make either [trader] worse off than if it were to consume only its endowment' (Arrow and Hahn 1971: 185).

The reader should note the two requirements for an allocation or trade to be in the core of the exchange economy: (1) the allocation must be on the efficiency locus (in the set of efficient trades) and (2) the allocation must be at least as highly ranked by each trader as the trader's initial endowment. Thus, in Figure 6.4, trades such as t_2, t_3, t_4, and t_5 are in the core, while trades such as t_1 and t_6 are not. Allocations t_1 and t_6 satisfy requirement 1 but not requirement 2—they are efficient trades, but not ranked as highly by each trader as that trader's initial endowment. Thus t_1 fails because trader A ranks it below t_0 (the initial endowment) while t_6 fails because trader B ranks it below t_0. Now consider t_7. This allocation satisfies requirement 2 but violates requirement 1. The Allocation t_7 is more highly ranked by both traders than is the initial endowment, t_0 (glance back at Figure 6.4). On the other hand t_7 is not an efficient trade, since it is not on the contract curve (*CC'* in Figure 6.4).

The spotlight, in exchange models, tends naturally to fall on those allocations which satisfy both of these requirements, thus constituting the core of the economy, *CC'*. There is, however, a concept to which great consequence has been accorded, which can be derived from the notion of the efficiency locus as a whole, rather than from that of the core of an economy. This is the concept of 'Pareto optimality' (or 'Pareto efficiency'). A detailed critique of this concept will be offered in the next chapter, but we are now in a position to use the Edgeworth box model just outlined in order to give a simple account of Pareto optimal, versus non-Pareto optimal, positions.

A 'Pareto optimal' equilibrium, in general, is an equilibrium such that any one agent A cannot be moved to a position more highly ranked by A without some other agent B being placed in a position less highly ranked by B. To see what this amounts to in terms of the Edgeworth model we have been discussing, consider the efficiency locus (as shown in Figure 6.5) as a whole. The allocations labelled t_1, t_2, and t_3 shown there all have in common the property of being off the efficiency locus, while the allocations t_4, t_5, and t_6 are all on the efficiency locus. It will be seen that both traders will rank t_4

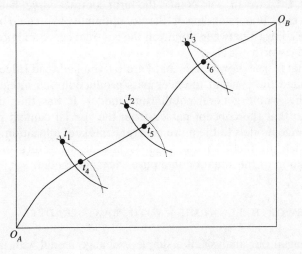

Fig. 6.5.

above t_1, t_5 above t_2, and t_6 above t_3. If one compares any two trades both of which are on the efficiency locus, on the other hand, such as t_4 and t_5, there will be conflict: A will rank t_5 above t_4 and B will rank t_4 above t_5.

The concept of 'Pareto optimality' can thus be given a simple interpretation pertinent to a wide class of models of allocation. At a point off the efficiency locus such as t_1, at least one trader could be in a position more highly ranked by that trader, without the other (or with many traders, any other trader) being in a position less highly ranked by that trader (or traders). Whereas at any point on the efficiency locus there is no other point which is ranked as highly (or more highly) by both (or all) traders. The set of efficient trades is therefore also known as the set of Pareto optimal allocations.

Despite the simplicity of this idea (in our Edgeworth models at any rate) its implications have not been a matter of universal agreement and, as will appear at length in the next chapter, are today increasingly a subject of controversy. Even the origins of the concept have been somewhat cloudy. Its name implies that it is due to Vilfredo Pareto (1848–1923) the famous general equilibrium theorist and sociologist. But, as is now recognized, this is somewhat unjust to the brilliant and fascinating Anglo-Irish mathematical economist and philosopher, Francis Ysidro Edgeworth (1845–1926). Edgeworth, who coined the term contract curve, had a perfectly clear understanding of 'Pareto' optimality expressed in terms of the contrast between points on the contract curve and points off it (Edgeworth 1881).

What is true, however, is that Pareto (who had read Edgeworth) extended the concept to encompass production and integrated it into his whole general equilibrium model. It was thus through Pareto that the concept passed from the special context of pure exchange models to the more general context of allocation models in which production is on stage. Meanwhile we return to a consideration of the situation in a pure exchange model.

EDGEWORTH ECONOMIES WITH MANY TRADERS

We began our analysis of a simple exchange model with the case where there are assumed to be only two traders. Further progress, however, requires us to relax that assumption. We have seen that an equilibrium trade must be on the contract curve, and lie between C and C' in Figure 6.4. Edgeworth was well aware, however, that in the case of bilateral trade equilibrium could lie anywhere between C and C', for example, at t_2, t_3, t_4, or t_5 in Figure 6.4. There was thus an indeterminacy in bilateral exchange. Edgeworth himself stressed this indeterminacy, but he was by no means the first to point it out—the nineteenth-century classical school had been familiar with the problem. The point is that where you have only two traders you have bilateral monopoly, and so the terms of an equilibrium trade will depend very much on the relative bargaining strengths of the two monopolists. This bargaining strength, and the resultant indeterminacy, Edgeworth argued, would grow less as the number of traders grew—one would move in the direction of increasingly competitive conditions.

Edgeworth approached competition by increasing the number of traders in his model in a rather special way. This enabled him to launch the brilliant idea that, with enough traders (and given certain additional assumptions) the set of core allocations comes arbitrarily close to the set of perfectly competitive equilibrium allocations. Consider a model where (to begin with) there are four traders, but they are of only two kinds. In other words, we clone trader A so that we have two As, and we also clone trader B. This device of a replica economy greatly simplified Edgeworth's problems, and makes it possible to continue to use the same box diagram. In Figure 6.6, O_A is the origin for a single trader of type A, $O_A t_0$ is the initial endowment of a single type A trader, and I_{A0} is an indifference curve of a type A trader. Similar remarks apply to a B trader's origin, endowment, and indifference curves. As the replica economy is enlarged, for each trader of type A added, a trader of type B is also added.

In a trading economy with four traders (two of each type) it might be thought that one pair (an A and a B) could trade on different terms from the other pair. But, as Edgeworth (who called his traders X and Y) remarked: '(1) if possible let one couple be at one point, and another couple at another point. It will generally be the interest of the X of one couple and the Y of the other to rush together, leaving their partners in the lurch. And (2) if the common point is not on the contract-curve, it will be in the interest of *all*

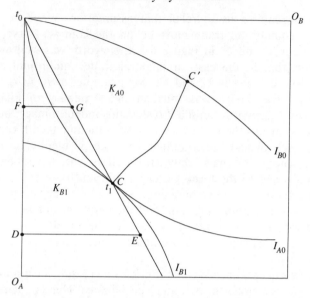

FIG. 6.6.

parties to descend to the contract curve' (Edgeworth 1881: 35, emphasis in original).

Somewhat deeper is Edgeworth's argument that, once there are four traders, the contract curve is only a segment of that applying to bilateral exchange—the 'ends' of the previous contract curve 'drop off', as it were. Consider one end of the contract curve for two traders, say point C. Is this a possible trade with four traders? No, because it will be to the advantage of either B trader—say B_1—to enter into a coalition with the two A traders, in order to block an allocation at C. To see this, draw the straight line in Figure 6.6 from t_0 through C, and note the point E on this line, which is in the interior of B's upper contour set K_{B1} with respect to t_1 (on B's indifference curve I_{B1} through C). Given the assumption that a trader's indifference curves are convex, points such as E will exist. Draw the horizontal line DE. Now bisect the line t_0 D at F, and draw FG parallel to DE. Again, given the assumption of convexity, point G will be in the interior of A's upper contour set K_{A0} with respect to t_0. We are now ready for four traders.

B_1 now offers the two As the following terms: each of the A traders is to supply B_1 with t_0F of A goods (so, in total, B_1 now has t_0D of A goods). Each A trader receives FG of B goods in return (so, in total, B_1 gives up DE—twice FG). As a result of this the A traders are each in a more highly ranked position than if they had accepted the trade t_1 at C (or if they had stayed at t_0). But B_1 is also in a more highly ranked position than t_1, as a result of the coalition with the two A traders.

Meanwhile trader B_2, as Edgeworth puts it, has 'been left out in the cold' (Edgeworth 1881: 37). He argues that this trader 'will now strike in, with the result that the system will be worked down to the contract curve again; to a point at least as favourable' (ibid.) for the A traders as G. A similar argument, using a coalition composed of the two B traders and either of the As can be used to show that, with four traders, point C' at the other end of the contract curve is likewise no longer a possible equilibrium trade. Edgeworth concludes by considering the implications of there being larger and larger numbers of traders (with equal numbers of both types). He argues that, in general, 'for any number short of the *practically infinite* (if such a term be allowed) there is a finite length of contract curve . . . at any point of which if the system is placed, it cannot by contract or recontract be displaced; that there are an *indefinite number of final settlements*, a quantity continually diminishing as we approach a perfect market' (Edgeworth 1881: 38–9, emphasis in original).

Edgeworth's work on the core was neglected for many years, the modern discussion probably beginning with Martin Shubik (1959). Important contributions then rapidly appeared.[2] Commenting on the work of Robert J. Aumann (1964*a*), Roy Weintraub notes: 'As the number of traders in an exchange economy increases, the core "shrinks" to a limit, the set of competitive allocations. If we model the economy *ab initio* with an uncountably infinite set of traders (each trader indexed, say, by a point in the interval (0, I) then the core coincides with the competitive allocations for the model' (Weintraub 1979: 133).

This way of characterizing perfect competition may be somewhat

[2] Following the work of Martin Shubik just cited, came Herbert Scarf (1962), Debreu and Scarf (1963), Robert J. Aumann (1964*a*), Karl Vind (1964), and a growing number of others. Readers wishing to explore the very extensive literature which now exists on approaches to perfect competition might well begin with Mas-Colell 1982, 1985.

unfamiliar to any non-economist readers whose acquaintance with neo-classical theory has been confined to the undergraduate texts. But if so it is all the more important to stress that Edgeworth's approach was in no way eccentric (despite the fey qualities of his Anglo-Irish prose style) nor was his work peripheral to the development of the concept of perfect competition. As George J. Stigler has observed, 'Edgeworth was the first economist to attempt a systematic rigorous definition of perfect competition . . . His exposition was the most influential in the entire literature' (Stigler 1987: 533). The concept, of course, did not spring fully armed from the head of Edgeworth—he was building on the contributions of earlier theorists.[3]

Edgeworth was clear that perfect competition required a 'large' number of traders, and that his concept of the core would come closer to perfect competition as the numbers of agents of each type grew. But the two concepts, though intimately related, nevertheless differ in rather deep ways, some of whose implications have only been understood in our own time. As Leonard J. Mirman has put it:

The core is a cooperative game with complete information. Since the idea of a core involves coalitional or cooperative behaviour the core and competitive equilibria are quite different. In particular the price taking assumption is incompatible with cooperative behaviour . . . The surprising result is that for economies with a continuum of players the set of core allocations coincide with the set of competitive allocations. The use of a continuum of agents is a natural way to model price taking behaviour since no individual agent has power to affect prices . . . However the relationship between competitive equilibrium and the core does show that prices are implicitly contained in the idea of a core. (Mirman 1987: 837)

The concept of a continuum of agents certainly does consistently model a fundamental property of 'perfect' competition in formal neo-classical theory: only here can one contend that the individual agent has no influence on prices. Hence the appeal of what are referred to (with striking understatement) as 'large economies'. The somewhat sweeping character of the assumption of a continuum of agents has been seen, however, to have its costs. In these models, as John Roberts has remarked, the individual agent

---

[3] Edgeworth had among his predecessors, for example, Antoine Augustin Cournot (1801–77) (notably Cournot [1838] 1929), and of course, Jevons (1871).

'formally disappears. Instead one has coalitions (measurable sets of agents), and an individual is formally indistinguishable from any set of measure zero. The irrelevance of individuals is made very clear in the model in Vind (1964), where only coalitions are defined and individual agents play no part. Debreu (1967) showed the equivalence of Vind's and Aumann's approaches' (Roberts 1987: 132). As Roberts is quick to note, the disappearance of the individual agent is embarrassing: 'economists are used to thinking about individual agents being negligible, but not about individuals having no existence whatsoever' (ibid.).

Since perfect competition is a typical assumption in much of neoclassical theory, it is important to see whether the very nature of perfect competition, once the concept is fully explored, defeats the equally pervasive, though usually tacit, assumption of methodological individualism. At first sight this might appear to be so. Part of the reason why theorists have not seen the two assumptions as irreconcilable, however, is contained in the last quotation from Roberts above: economists are used to thinking of the individual agent as negligible just as the individual voter in the most democratic electoral process would be negligible—the individual voters, however, would together get one candidate rather than another elected. Thus Frank Hahn defends himself against those who believe that his analytical methods imply 'that the explanatory emphasis is put on the individual agent when it should be put on social institutions, such as property rights and the social relations which flow from them' (Hahn 1984: 64). This objection to his type of analysis is based on a misunderstanding, he argues, since 'traditional equilibrium theory does best when the individual has no importance—he is of measure zero. My theory also does best when all the given theoretical problems arising from the individual's mattering do not have to be taken into account. The social institutions of property and markets have the dominant role' (ibid.). He sums up: 'to argue that one requires a theory of the action of agents is not at all to maintain that the economy is to be understood by what any one agent wants. For my money, general equilibrium theorists are much closer to Marx than many a Marxist!' (ibid.)

To revert to the example of voting, a theory of democratic government requires that each person be able to vote, not that any one person be decisive, or even contribute substantially to the outcome. But, having granted this, it is still true that, as Roberts correctly points out, this does not entail that economists are used to the individual having no existence whatever. Hahn perhaps goes a little far in his acceptance of the implications of the Aumann/Vind treatment of the individual agent (at least in the passage last quoted, and I think, partly to tease the Marxists!). Elsewhere he does accept 'a continuum or very large number' (Hahn 1984: 50) of agents, but only for households, not for firms. I shall not make much of this, however, since several lines of escape from the problem of the 'disappearing' agent have been developed in recent years, one of them being featured in Hahn's own work.

I begin by noting briefly an escape based upon some rather difficult concepts, from non-standard analysis.[4] Donald J. Brown and Abraham Robinson (1972, 1975) sought an escape from the dilemma of the disappearing agent by the use of non-standard analysis to model a large set of agents. John Roberts has described their idea with notable clarity. In interpreting such non-standard models, one can distinguish between how things look 'from "inside the model" and what they look like from "outside". From outside, these models may have an infinity of (individually negligible, infinitesimal) agents, yet from inside each agent is a well-defined, identifiable entity' (Roberts 1987: 132).

If the agents in a model should become no longer separately identifiable, then the individual may have disappeared as an agent, which would evidently have serious consequences for neo-Walrasian general equilibrium theory, aside from making the doctrine of methodological individualism rather an embarrassment in those models where perfect competition is assumed. But there is as well another sense in which the individual could disappear: the individual agents could be truly reduced to 'locations' for their respective utilities. That such a tendency existed in utilitarianism was noted a number of years ago by Sen and Bernard Williams, who observed that utilitarianism treated agents merely as sites of their utilities: 'Persons do not count as individuals in this any more than individual petrol tanks do in the analysis of the national consumption of petroleum' (Sen and Williams 1982: 4). This tendency in classical utilitarianism certainly always existed; it is further illuminated in the context of the utilitarian's problem with doing

---

[4] On non-standard analysis, the enquiring and dauntless reader might see Robinson 1974.

justice to rights in a recent comment by Sen, where he notes that 'a utilitarian demanding equal weight on every unit of utility cannot, consistently with that, also require equality of freedoms or rights' (Sen 1992: p. x).

There are, however, various different forms of utilitarian positions, as we saw in Chapters 2 and 3. So, as Sen observes in the work just cited, failing to take seriously the distinction between different persons 'may not be a fair charge against utilitarianism in general' (Sen 1992: 14 n. 5). The best candidate for a utilitarian position which escapes the charge of belittling the distinction between persons would probably be the position advocated by James Griffin (1986), who, as we have already seen in Chapter 3, claims to avoid a 'mental state' account of utility altogether. For Griffin, as we noted in our earlier discussion of his work, a person's objective could be that of bringing the world closer to a state of Rawlsian justice, for example. No mental metric need be involved in such an objective. But compare Sen's comments (1992: 53–5). And if Griffin can make his case, it can still be asked whether he is in fact a utilitarian.

Whatever the answer to this may be, it can be claimed that, in so far as the utilitarianism implied in neo-classical theory is of a 'mental state' variety, then this tends to erode the distinctness of persons. And combining this with the tendency inherent in models with a continuum of agents for the individual agent to disappear compounds two separate trends which, especially when united, ought to be resisted strongly by all who care about the separateness, integrity, and rights of persons.

One way in which to avoid these problems is to stay away from 'infinite models' altogether, and instead consider the convergence of finite economies to their limit. This tradition originates in Cournot and Edgeworth and leads to Debreu and Scarf (1963). It was adopted by Arrow and Hahn (1971) and has been further developed in recent work by a number of theorists, who are referred to in Mas-Colell 1982. The Edgeworthian bloodlines of this latter approach should be clear. Writing as early as 1979, when a good deal of this work still lay ahead, Roy Weintraub was already able to claim that the preceding dozen years had seen 'a reformulation of general equilibrium theory in which "markets" and "market behavior" are pushed into the background while the acts of individual exchange are brought into sharper focus' (Weintraub

1979: 128). He stressed the importance of '[t]his game-theoretic approach to microeconomics whose progenitor was Edgeworth not Walras' (ibid.). Hahn also had remarked that 'returning to a line of study first pursued by Edgeworth, it was noticed that a feasible state of an economy in which no coalition of agents could improve themselves would certainly be one for which we would be prepared to say that it could be a resting place of an actual economic process . . . This set of states is called the core of an economy. It is easy to show that every Arrow–Debreu equilibrium is in the core. But the converse is true only under an extremely restrictive postulate' (Hahn 1984: 49).

There would be no reason to expect such states (in the core) of an economy to change—in that sense they would be equilibria. Yet, he points out, these states 'are defined without for instance prices entering into the description at all. Thus, except for the special case when the core and an Arrow–Debreu equilibrium [perfectly competitive equilibrium] coincide, there are really two differing equilibrium concepts of which the core is plainly the more general' (Hahn 1984: 49–50). As we have seen, core and perfectly competitive equilibria coincide where there is a continuum of agents. But apart from this extreme case, and on the (severe enough) assumption that the costs of forming coalitions are zero, 'it can be shown that when the number of agents is large enough (but less than infinite and of course not a continuum), any core state is "near" an Arrow–Debreu [perfectly competitive] equilibrium' (Hahn 1984: 50).

Thus Hahn summarizes what is perhaps the most down-to-earth concept of 'nearly' perfectly competitive equilibrium—'down-to-earth' because it uses neither a continuum of agents nor non-standard analysis—that can still pass muster in present-day neo-classical general equilibrium theory. That the concept is still rarified enough, however, the non-economist reader should need no telling! It requires, as Hahn points out, the costless (and presumably timeless) formation and reformation of coalitions in order to have core states which are 'near' a perfectly competitive equilibrium. And for perfect competition to be approximated, there must be a 'very large number' of agents. Even if one accepted this in the case of agents who are consumers, Hahn is surely right to deny that the idea is acceptable for firms, and to insist that: 'a consideration of these agents leads to great difficulties with the Arrow–Debreu equilibrium which are additional to those which arise from the core ... [T]here are logical difficulties in accounting for the existence of agents called firms at all unless we allow there to be increasing returns of some sort. But where there are increasing returns it may not be possible to show that there are any logically possible economic states which qualify as either Arrow–Debreu equilibria or as members of the core. It may also be wrong to think of a very large number of firms.' (Ibid.)

Taking together the information demanded for an agent to form and reform coalitions (presumably timelessly) and the very large number of agents required even for near perfect competition, the reader may surmise that the implication of the undergraduate texts that perfect competition could ever exist in the real world is more than a trifle optimistic. This consideration—that perfect competition is at best a concept definable for a class of formal models—will be of importance to our appraisal of the concept of Pareto optimality, and thus of the rationality of allocations. Meanwhile we are ready to explore some of the relationships between purely competitive price equilibria, core equilibria, and Pareto optima in the simple context of the Edgeworth box.

Indeed, it will be clear that this model, having only two goods, presents the simplest possible case of a system of relative prices, namely a single price ratio, or rate of exchange. Consider the situation from the point of view of trader A, beginning with the case of bilateral exchange which lies at the opposite extreme from perfect competition. An exchange ratio of B goods for A goods may be indicated geometrically by a straight line such as $t_0 E$ in Figure 6.7(a), whose slope relative to the A goods axis measures the amount of B goods which trader A could obtain for a unit of A goods. Were this rate of exchange to obtain, the vertically shaded region in the figure would be in effect trader A's budget set—that elementary concept from the theory of consumer's behaviour. Likewise the horizontally shaded region would be trader B's budget set.

Now trader A's most highly ranked attainable point, should this price ratio obtain, would clearly be the trade t_1, where I_{A1} is tangent to $t_0 E$, as shown in Figure 6.7(b). However, since the price ratio represented by $t_0 E$ was simply chosen at random, trader B's most highly ranked attainable trade at these prices may be at a point like t_2, where I_{B1} is tangent to $t_0 E$. What this means is simply that for A

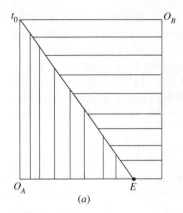 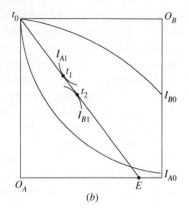

Fig. 6.7.

and B this price ratio is not consistent with an efficient trade—or indeed with any trade: A and B want to trade different quantities of the two goods. Thus the price ratio t_0E cannot be an equilibrium price ratio.

We now need to consider the existence of 'efficient' rates of exchange, and what their properties must be. Notice, to begin with, that an efficient rate of exchange must clearly be between t_0E_1 and t_0E_2 (in Figure 6.8) which go through the end points of the contract curve CC'. Outside this range of relative prices, either A or B would simply not trade: for instance, A would make no offer to trade at a price ratio such as that indicated by the line t_0E_3 in Figure 6.8, since any trade would put the trader at a point in the lower contour set of the no trade position t_0. It goes without saying that B would like very much to trade at this price ratio! B, however, would refuse to trade at the relative prices indicated by t_0E_4. Thus we see that even in the case of bilateral exchange limits can exist to the possible range of those relative prices consistent with trade taking place. Within this range of possible rates of exchange, what are the characteristics of an equilibrium price ratio? Evidently it must be a price ratio at which A and B wish to trade the same amounts. But this can only be where a rate of exchange line is common tangent to an A indifference curve and a B indifference curve. So it must be a point on the contract curve, between C and C', such as the point t_n in Figure 6.8. As already noted, in the case

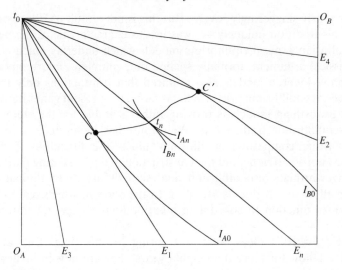

FIG. 6.8.

of bilateral exchange t_n may be anywhere between C and C'. This reflects the fact that, with so few traders, the price ratio depends on their bargaining strengths (embodied in the shapes of their indifference curve).

Now since the limiting exchange ratios consistent with trade are defined by the ends of the contract curve, CC', it is wholly in the spirit of Edgeworth to remark that, as the contract curve shrinks with the balanced addition of clones of A and of B, so does the range of relative prices consistent with trade occurring. Finally, with 'enough' traders of each sort, the core has shrunk to its limit: the perfectly competitive allocations. Now the only equilibrium relative prices left are perfectly competitive prices. Any perfectly competitive equilibrium is necessarily a core equilibrium and thus a Pareto optimal equilibrium. This simple version (without the complications introduced by production) of what is now called the 'first fundamental theorem' of welfare economics is at the heart of Edgeworth's work.

No trades, of course, are consummated at 'false prices' (non-perfectly competitive prices) and the whole 'process' is not to be seen as taking place gradually in historical time. The demands of the model for information, 'timeless adjustment', and so on are obviously staggeringly severe. But this is not a fault of Edgeworth or his tradition uniquely—it was just as characteristic of the neo-Walrasian general equilibrium models which underlay much neo-classical argument: formally spelled out, complete, intertemporal Arrow–Debreu models also required that transactions only take place at equilibrium prices. What is more, the present generation of Edgeworthian models is proving rather suitable for the study of disequilibrium trading. As Weintraub has remarked: 'a neo-Walrasian competitive equilibrium "hides" the difficulties of time and coordination behind the construction of a pre-existing market. Edgeworthian disequilibrium analysis exhibits those difficulties for all to see. It directs attention to the ways in which real institutions function to coordinate inharmonious choice' (Weintraub 1979: 144–5).

Edgeworth's ideas were too daring for his time. But, after lying fallow for more than eighty years, they are now in luxuriant flower. To consider the rationality and optimality claims of neo-classical allocation theory in an Edgeworthian context is thus not to consider the worst case for these ideas, but rather one of the best.

All this having been conceded to Edgeworth, however, it will have been seen that the requirements for the core and for perfect competition, and thus for the applicability of the concept of Pareto optimal perfectly competitive allocations in an Edgeworth economy, are extremely demanding conceptually, quite aside from the much more doubtful claim that they could be realized in any actual society. It will also have been noted that these difficulties beset even a heroically simple model, where all productive activities are abstracted from, and all agents are assumed to be individual persons, thereby satisfying the demands of methodological individualism fully.

In such a model, although no 'black box' agents would exist, coalitions would form, although only when desired by their individual members. Indeed, coalitions might be expected (on a reading of the literature) to form and reform in such Edgeworth economies with a kaleidoscopic frequency unknown in real world organizations. On the one hand, I believe it would be hard to imagine a type of model where the allocations determined by the model were a closer reflection of the choices of the individual persons in the model (given initial endowments) than in an Edgeworth economy in a perfectly competitive core equilibrium. On the other hand such a state of affairs, free from all externalities, from all asymmetric—or even imperfect information, from all organizations which were not instantly formed or abandoned on the wishes of all their members, requires a state of existence totally unlike the life lived by human beings in history.

All this contains an important message for the non-economist concerned about the rationality claims which have their origin in neo-classical theory. The constructed concept of rationality, of which we have seen various versions in previous chapters, drew considerable support from the fact that it was known to be at the heart of elaborate proofs to the effect that a wide class of model economies possessed equilibrium allocations, and that these allocations possessed certain optimality or efficiency properties. The equilibrium allocations, in other words, were the rational dispositions of goods resulting from the rational choices of every individual agent in such models.

Consider a perfectly competitive equilibrium allocation in an Edgeworth economy with 'many' traders. Each person who trades chooses a most highly ranked position which is consistent with the choices of every other trader. A perfectly competitive core allocation reflects the choices of every participant trader. Even today, after all the mathematically sophisticated work that has followed, Edgeworth's idea is still surely one of the most pellucidly clear expressions of the central neo-classical vision: a rational allocation of resources resulting from the rational choices of individual persons.

This vision goes with a particular concept of equilibrium. An equilibrium in the neo-classical tradition is above all else a chosen position. It was necessary to have some understanding of equilibria which are the result of the choices of all the agents in the model to see how deeply the concept of rational choice is embedded in neo-classical theory. There are other concepts of equilibrium, however. A body may be said to be in equilibrium because no force is acting on it which would cause it to move—consider a pendulum. Here choice does not play any role. In Chapters 8 and 9 we shall take a look at some present-day models (derived from the eighteenth- and nineteenth-century classical tradition) in which a large class of agents may be in an equilibrium position which the theory does not attribute to choices on the part of these agents. There may be other agents in the model who do have the power to bring about a change in the model's equilibrium, but who see no reason to do so. Certain features of the world we live in are reflected in these models, but rationality claims concerning what happens in them have not been a leading preoccupation of their authors.

Remarkably, however, it has recently been shown by John Roemer that rational agents (in the sense of neo-classical theory) in such models may be expected to form coalitions and engage in class conflict. Here we see some ideas of coalitions and cores that go back to Edgeworth, reinterpreted in game-theoretic terms, and set to work upon classical themes. Leaving the classical economists and their present-day successors aside until Chapter 8, we may nevertheless pertinently ask here whether Edgeworth's analysis could reflect sharp differences in economic power—say between A traders and B traders.

As it happens, the 'second fundamental theorem' of welfare economics was intended to address the task of repairing the damage which might be expected to ensue to the prestige of the first theorem, should gross inequalities develop. Suppose that the initial endowments of one class of traders, say the A traders, is very poor. A goods, we may imagine, are of little vital importance to anyone, while B goods are essential to life for any trader. Then a perfectly competitive equilibrium allocation might assign the lion's share of the benefits of trade to the B traders. It would still be Pareto optimal. Things, as a matter of fact, could be much worse than might appear from the Figures used in this chapter. As normally drawn, these presupposed that both A and B traders can subsist without trading. The distance between C and C' is limited by the no-trade indifference curves, I_{A0} and I_{B0}. Now, a peasant can perhaps subsist without trading, eating what she has produced. But a present-day working class has only its labour power, which it cannot eat, and so must trade this for food. Edgeworth economies normally have a tacit assumption that all traders can subsist without trade. When this assumption is dropped, the familiar diagram changes fundamentally, as we shall see in the next chapter.

Returning for the moment to the usual Edgeworth economies, Peter Newman, for example, has pertinently commented that

Everything that has been said . . . about the useful properties of equilibrium prices is *relative* to the initial commodity distribution. If that is unfair, no amount of economic and social 'efficiency' in the exchange mechanism will do more than make the best of a bad job—and even that cautious assertion about the merits of the 'hidden Hand' may not really be valid. In any actual situation it might well be that, by any reasonable ethical standards, a coalition of those less well endowed with this world's goods *should* block an allocation on the contract curve. And a competitive 'core' allocation, with everyone playing the market mechanism game according to the rules, would frustrate this desirable change. (Newman 1965: 122, emphasis in original)

The 'second fundamental theorem' addresses this specific deficiency of the Pareto criterion. Essentially, this theorem claims that any desired Pareto optimal allocation can be achieved (and undesired ones avoided) as a perfectly competitive equilibrium for some relative prices and some set of endowments. The required endowments are to be brought about by intervention, specifically by a suitable set of lump-set taxes and transfers imposed upon the traders. This would alter the endowments of the traders, and thus the relative prices and final allocations. Even if this could be done, however, and we shall see in the next chapter some of the problems connected with any attempt to apply this idea in a world lacking just about all the vital features of a perfectly competitive equilibrium, it leaves all the other defects of the concept of Pareto optimality untouched.

The distributional shortcomings of the concept of Pareto optimality are further exacerbated by the fact, noted already in this book, that the canonical presentations of the concept involve a tacit assumption of self-interest. In Chapter 5 we did not yet have before us an explicit model of allocation between agents, and as a consequence certain features of the debate between self-interest and malevolence or benevolence could not yet be conveniently presented. Now they can be.

An exploration of these matters in the context of Edgeworth has a certain irony. He himself declared that 'the first principle of Economics is that every agent is actuated only by self-interest' (Edgeworth 1881: 16). So naturally he has been used as an authority in support of the concept of rationality as self-interest. But as one reads Edgeworth, what is in fact remarkable is how severely he limited the context within which he was willing to accept this assumption.

EDGEWORTH ECONOMIES WITH OTHER-REGARDING CHOICES

Edgeworth had himself written that 'the concrete nineteenth century man is for the most part an impure egoist, a mixed utilitarian' (Edgeworth 1881: 104). Nevertheless, it was to be his fate that overwhelmingly his best-known model (to present-day mathematical economists) would be one based on an assumption of self-interest, something which for him was a special case. His general position was that to be expected of a utilitarian. That this position has not received more attention could be due (at least in part) to a couple of considerations, one applying to readers friendly towards utilitarianism and the other to readers unfriendly to this moral philosophy.

First of all take the case of those readers friendly towards a utilitarian analysis of economic rationality. Now it has fairly recently come to be seen that what has been treated as the leading source for Edgeworth's utilitarianism has in fact been the less appealing of his writings on the subject, namely a piece called 'The Hedonical Calculus', which was originally printed as an article in the philosophical journal *Mind* (1879). This piece is known simply because it was reprinted in Edgeworth's famous book (1881). But as a matter of fact Edgeworth's major work on utilitarianism had been his *New and Old Method of Ethics* (1877), which, as Peter Newman has recently noted, has been virtually unread up to recent years.[5] Thus, even those friendly to utilitarianism seem not to have considered Edgeworth's utilitarianism at its best.

Secondly, consider the case of economists who, since the famous claim of Hicks in 1939, have believed (mistakenly, as we have seen in Chapters 2 and 3) that they had inherited an economics free from utilitarian assumptions. They could be forgiven for accepting gratefully Edgeworth's special assumption of self-interest in the context of his exchange theory, and leaving his utilitarianism to gather dust. Now, however, the case is altered. We have seen in Chapters 2 and

[5] Newman (1987: 89) cites as exceptions to the neglect of this work of Edgeworth the treatments in Howey 1960 and in Creedy 1986.

3 that present-day axiomatic expected utility theory retains important utilitarian features (notably welfarism, consequentialism, and on occasion cardinality). Edgeworth is 'more' utilitarian only in having sum-ranking. On the other hand, since his utilitarianism is an explicit moral philosophy, even if a flawed one, it enables Edgeworth to see the importance of questions lost on those present-day theorists who imagine that an assumption of self-interest and an assumption of value neutrality can be combined to give one a 'scientific' economics.

To see what Edgeworth actually meant by claiming that the kind of person he knew ('concrete nineteenth-century man') could be called a 'mixed' utilitarian, we need to begin with his concept of 'exact utilitarianism'. This is defined as 'the greatest quantity of happiness of sentients, exclusive of number and distribution—an end to which number and distribution are but means' (Edgeworth 1877: 35).

This is in the pure stream of the classical utilitarian tradition (since it comes complete with *sum-ranking*, as well as welfarism and consequentialism), but with all its philosophical faults, it is a position about moral responsibility, and not about self-interest, except in so far as self-interest happened to be consistent with it. Note that the others whose happiness is considered comprise all sentients (including animals as in Bentham), and that Edgeworth makes the striking suggestion that it is more appropriate to interpret each individual sentient as 'infinitesimal with regard to the whole' (Edgeworth 1877: 44). Newman notes that this may be the earliest use of the concept of a continuum of economic agents (Newman 1987: 90). An idea which, as we have seen, was formally introduced into the analysis of exchange models by Aumann (1964*a*) and Vind (1964).

There is, as we already know, a danger that the individual agent may simply disappear in such a continuum of economic actors. Is it then appropriate for the interpreter of Edgeworth's theory to resort to the highly sophisticated move of Brown and Robinson (1972), with a view to leaving each agent (as Roberts has expressed it), though 'infinitesimal' from one point of view, yet a precisely defined and identifiable entity from another point of view?

I think that the answer given to this question must depend (among other things) upon the view taken of the status of the individual person within utilitarianism. Were Sen and Williams, for example, correct in the claim which they made in the passage quoted above, that persons do not count as individuals in utilitarianism any more than individual petrol tanks do in the analysis of the national consumption of petrol? If so then this characteristic of the utilitarian position would certainly support Newman's attribution to Edgeworth of the idea of a continuum of economic actors, with all the possible disappearance of the individual person which this might involve.

Be this as it may, once one sees what Edgeworth means by 'exact utilitarianism'—namely, the greatest quantity of happiness of sentients, exclusive of number and distribution—there should be no problem in seeing what he means by the phrase 'mixed utilitarian'. Moral perfection, for Edgeworth, would require always making the choice which met the requirements of exact utilitarianism. Weak human nature, on the other hand, would produce a mixed utilitarianism—a mixture of moral responsibility and egoism, where these conflicted. We are now ready to consider why Edgeworth used not mixed utilitarianism (as one might expect!), but a special model, based on rationality as self-interest, in his works on exchange.

One of the leading weaknesses of classical, 'mental state' utilitarianism as a moral philosophy, as we know, is its simplistic view of moral responsibility: the claims of responsibilities and of duties of all kinds have to be boiled down into the single objective of maximizing utility. If all choice is about maximizing utility, then the only question is whose utility: the truly good person was then supposed to put the happiness of others first, while the typical son or daughter of Adam was expected to put their own happiness first. The utilitarian, in judging thus, unwittingly became naïve about evil: the worst a person was expected to do was to favour themselves in pursuing utility. This is clear from Edgeworth's own words: having admitted 'that there exists in the higher parts of human nature a tendency towards and feeling after utilitarian institutions' (Edgeworth 1881: 52), he then asks 'could we seriously suppose that these moral considerations were relevant to war and trade; could eradicate the controlless core of human selfishness, or exercise an appreciable force in comparison with the impulse of self-interest' (ibid.). But in fact he is, of course, taking a naïvely optimistic view of human nature: even in its lower elements Edgeworth finds nothing worse than self-interest—he completely ignores malevolence.

The naïvety of the self-interest theory on the question of malevolence has been delightfully exposed by Kenneth Boulding, as we noted in the last chapter. He pointed out that: 'If the rate of benevolence was zero, we, of course, would have indifference or pure selfishness; if the rate of benevolence was negative we would have malevolence, in which case people . . . would be willing to damage themselves in order to damage another' (Boulding 1970: 130).

He went on to offer a striking illustration: 'Rates of malevolence incidentally may frequently be quite high. It apparently cost the United States in 1968 about $4 to do $1 worth of damage in Vietnam, which means our rate of malevolence toward North Vietnam was then at least four' (Boulding 1970: 131).

Selfishness, for Boulding, was thus simply a knife-edge between benevolence and malevolence. If Edgeworth was right that war and trade plunge us into the depths of 'the lower elements of human nature' (Edgeworth 1881: 52), then we would expect to be off the neutral balance of the knife edge, and thus plunged past selfishness deep into malevolence. But the fact is that Edgeworthian exchange models no more naturally call for even an assumption of exclusive self-interest (leaving malevolence aside for the moment) than do other models for the theory of general equilibrium.

Ironically, it turns out that, even in the economic context of an exchange model, and thus of trade and contract, Edgeworth himself had strong suspicions that self-interest alone might lead to disastrous consequences. The passage at issue must be cited in full, and readers allowed to interpret it for themselves. Here it is:

To impair, it may be conjectured, the reverence paid to *competition*; in whose results—as if worked out by a play of physical forces, impersonal, impartial—economists have complacently acquiesced. Of justice and humanity there was no pretense; but there seemed to command respect the majestic neutrality of Nature. But if it should appear that the field of competition is deficient in that *continuity of fluid*, that *multiety of atoms* which constitute foundations of the uniformities of Physics; if competition is found wanting, not only the regularity of law, but even the impartiality of chance—the throw of a die loaded with villainy—economics would be indeed a 'dismal science', and the reverence for competition would be no more. (Edgeworth 1881: 50–1, emphasis in original)

Edgeworth now abandons the self-interest theory and reverts to his general utilitarian position: he finds it 'a circumstance of momentous interest' that one of the settlements between contractors is 'the contract tending to the greatest possible utility of the contractors' (ibid. 53). In a footnote he adds that, if we suppose the traders to be 'actuated in effective moments by a sympathy with each other's interests (as even now in *domestic*, and one day perhaps in political, contracts)', then we might suppose the object which a trader tends to maximize is not the trader's own utility, but this modified by 'a *coefficient of effective sympathy* ... What, then, will be the contract curve of these modified contractors? *The old contract curve between narrower limits* ... As the coefficients of sympathy increase, utilitarianism becomes more pure ... *the contract curve narrows down to the utilitarian point*' (ibid. 53n., emphasis in original).

Let it be freely granted that Edgeworth's position suffers from all the faults of classical utilitarianism. But at least his whole-hearted and above-board utilitarian position may be more easily excused, for his period, than the unconscious and unacknowledged preference utilitarianism (at this present date!) in the writings of economic theorists who rely on the concept of Pareto optimality.

Those with a taste for irony will note that Edgeworth, who was the original source of the concept now called Pareto optimality or Pareto efficiency, was quite ready to abandon the restrictions (now supposed to free one from the need for moral judgements) implied in the concept when those restrictions interfered with his ability to consider seriously the moral implications of his whole theory of contracts. And these implications, as it happens, can be freed from the utilitarian form which Edgeworth gave them, and shown not to be essentially dependent upon this. The easiest way to do this is to construct a simple model, where the traders are assumed to rank distributions of the goods in the model. Within some limits a trader can be supposed to rank bundles higher if they yield a larger own consumption. But beyond some point the trader may not wish for larger and larger own bundles at the cost of dire straits for the other trader. This situation is illustrated in Figure 6.9. In part (*a*) we depict indifference curves which have a shape which may be unfamiliar to non-economist readers, whose acquaintance with microtheory has been confined to one of the standard texts. In

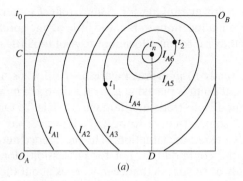

(a)

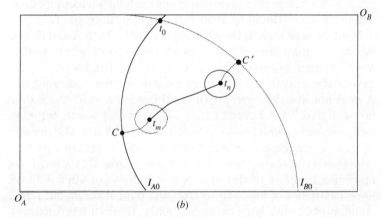

(b)

FIG. 6.9.

Figure 6.9(a) the most highly ranked combination of A goods and B goods for agent A is indicated by the coordinates of the point t_n: A would rank most highly having O_AC of A goods plus O_AD of B goods. More of either good is ranked less highly by A. It is important to note that, in this model, it could be misleading to express this state of affairs by saying that A becomes 'satiated' with more of either good at t_n. A might well personally prefer having more of either or both goods, but judges morally that B needed them more. It is simply the case that A has a target distribution which this agent ranks most highly. (It might not be a single point—the target distribution need not be unique—it could be a small area.) Less highly ranked distributions, such as t_1 or t_2, lie on outer indifference curves, and their lower ranking for A may reflect either the fact that they represent allocations to B of too little of one good or both, or the fact that they represent allocations to A of too little of one or both goods.

We are now ready to interpret Figure 6.9(b). In this figure the initial endowment point is placed at t_0, so A's no-trade indifference curve is I_{A0}, while B's no-trade indifference curve is I_{B0}. One would thus expect the contract curve to be CC'. However, as Kenneth Boulding has expressed the situation: 'The preference here is for a *distribution* of the commodities, not for possession alone. If the parties are highly altruistic, so that each worries about the poverty of the other, the indifference curves may exhibit a maximum point within the box' (Boulding 1966: 628, emphasis in original).

It will be seen that, as shown in Figure 6.9(b), both A and B have systems of indifference curves exhibiting a most highly ranked point for each agent—t_n for A and t_m for B. The contract curve beyond these points has been drawn as a dotted line, indicating that A does not wish, as it were, to drive B beyond t_n to C' and B does not wish to drive A beyond t_m to C. Thus, as Edgeworth put it, we have the '*old contract curve between narrower limits*' (Edgeworth 1881: 53 n., emphasis in original). There is still an area of conflict— *self-interest* still plays a role—but it is more narrowly confined. An appealing property of this idea is that it does not offer only the unreal extremes of pure self-interest and pure altruism, but rather an infinity of points lying between t_n and t_m representing 'mixtures' of the two—surely a reasonable characterization of human imperfection!

Boulding, in the passage cited above, considered the case where each agent 'worries about' the poverty of the other, and this could suggest (although it does not entail) an interpretation of the agent's rankings in terms of 'sympathy'—which could be given a utilitarian interpretation. But the rankings of A and B do not have to be given this interpretation. A, for instance, may be acting from a regard for justice—from a preoccupation with what is right—which would pass muster with a committee made up of history's most dedicated deontologists, such as Kant or Sir David Ross. Edgeworth had grasped an idea which is in fact of sweeping generality and importance, and which must not be lost sight of merely because he stated it in terms of its classical utilitarian special case.

Since the time when Boulding wrote the passage cited above

(1966) there has been an increased attention by economists to concepts like 'benevolence', 'sympathy', and 'altruistic preferences'. Two limitations of this literature (which severely diminish its bearing on our discussion) are, however, important to note. First of all, it has typically been conducted within an ordinal utilitarian context. (I have already commented on this fact in Chapter 5.) Secondly malevolence has, for whatever reason, received rather notably less than its share of attention. (It might be hazarded that this is a reflection of utilitarian naïvety about evil—recall our discussion of Edgeworth above.)

This narrowness of approach may help to explain something which, I think, is otherwise somewhat puzzling. Economists like Peter Hammond are severely critical of the typical ethical presuppositions of neo-classical general equilibrium theory (such as the assumptions of purely self-interested agents, and Pareto optimality). Yet Hammond, for example, has also shown some dissatisfaction with the literature on 'altruistic preferences'. I shall conclude this chapter with an argument that such dissatisfaction is surely warranted, so long as the contrast between self-interested and other choice is made simply in ordinal utilitarian terms, and, as well as that, ignores malevolence.

We may use a simple one-commodity model, in which both malevolence and benevolence can be presented. This model was used by Hammond, but confined to the case of benevolent choices (Hammond 1987b: 85). Boulding had earlier used a one-good model, but he treated malevolent choices as well as benevolent and selfish (Boulding 1967: 69–71). His treatment, however, is marred by the use of a quite unnecessary utilitarian language, which I shall avoid.

Consider, then, a situation where there is a single good and just two agents, Tom and Dick (I do not want these two agents confused with our traders—this is not the Edgeworth box with two commodities and exchange). Points on either axis in Figure 6.10(a) designate quantities of the single good in the hands of Tom or of Dick respectively. Consider first the case of pure self-interest. In this case an income distribution, x_2 (a distribution of the single good between Tom and Dick) will be ranked by one of the agents above another income distribution, x_1, if and only if the agent (say Tom) has more income at x_2 than at x_1. But distributions x_3 and x_4 are equally ranked by Tom with x_2, despite the fact that at x_3 Dick has

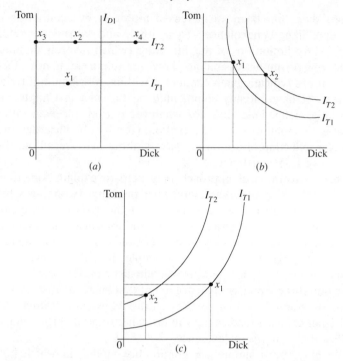

FIG. 6.10.

none of the good (zero income), while at x_4 he has a substantial income. The agent's indifference curves under pure selfishness in this simple model are thus straight lines, horizontal for Tom (such as I_{T1} and I_{T2}) and vertical for Dick (such as I_{D1}). It will be seen that Boulding, in calling pure selfishness a 'knife edge' was hardly over-stating the case.

Now consider, in Figure 6.10(*b*), the case where Dick's income enters positively into Tom's ranking of distributions. Here a distri-bution x_2 may be ranked above x_1, by Tom, despite the fact that under x_2 Tom gets less income, provided that Dick gets sufficiently more. There is clearly considerable choice as to the precise shape of an agent's indifference curves in this case. An agent may become purely selfish at very low levels of income, but on the other hand purely altruistic about any further increases in income above some (supposedly very high) level. Here enters the charitable trust, and the concept, much studied by Boulding, of grants (or one-way transfers).

Now we are ready for the case where Dick's income enters negatively into Tom's ranking of distributions. Consider Figure 6.10(c). Here a distribution x_2 is ranked by Tom above a distribution x_1, despite the fact that Tom's income is somewhat lower at x_2, simply because Dick's income is substantially lower at x_2. Again, the exact shape of Tom's indifference curves will depend on what Boulding has called the 'rate of malevolence'.

Now, looking at this little model, it is surely evident that malevolence, no more than benevolence, need be given an ordinal utilitarian interpretation. Tom may choose to do harm to Dick because it will give Tom pleasure, or because it will increase the 'happiness' of society, etc., but he need not. He may be doing harm to Dick because Dick has violated Tom's rights, and Tom believes Dick should therefore be punished (Tom may accept a 'retributive' theory of punishment). Or his malevolence may come from any number of reasons, good or bad. Tom may be anything from a spiteful busybody to the noblest Roman of them all! He may accept sacrifices in order to damage Dick from patriotic duty, from motives of personal revenge, from loyalty to an injured friend, or from downright cussedness. The theorist who believes that self-interest is a knife-edge does not have to argue for the perfectibility of human nature, nor claim that, fundamentally, human motives tend to be benevolent. Economic theorists who, in arguing for the exclusive adoption of an assumption of self-interest, fancy themselves 'hard-nosed' realists (despite the stupendous unreality of their models) cannot seize this high ground. Just as self-interest could be outflanked in this direction of supposed worldliness by the present-aims theory, as we say in Chapter 5, it can be outflanked by a theory which gives a role to malevolence.

In this chapter we have begun the task of considering questions about the neo-classical constructed concept of rationality which can only be addressed with the aid of models of general equilibrium in the allocation of goods among agents. The concept of Pareto optimality has appeared, and has begun to receive our attention. Now, in Chapter 7, it will play a leading role. Meanwhile, all the prerequisites for a critique of this optimality concept are at hand.

7
PHILOSOPHICAL IMPLICATIONS OF PARETO OPTIMALITY

THE rationality claims of neo-classical theory concerning perfectly competitive equilibrium allocations among freely choosing individual agents are centred upon the concept of Pareto optimality (or Pareto efficiency). We have briefly surveyed the elements of the argument necessary to present this concept in a very austere and simple class of neo-classical models, namely Edgeworth economies. In particular, we glanced at the strikingly demanding requirements for perfect competition among the traders, even in this simple model with no productive activity on stage, and no black-box agents—in other words, with methodological individualism strictly fulfilled. The proposition that any perfectly competitive equilibrium would be in the core (or Pareto optimal) was seen to arise naturally in such models.

When presented in court dress with orders and decorations, this proposition becomes the 'first fundamental theorem' of neo-classical welfare economics. As a theorem concerning human well-being, however, it was early on seen by its most faithful supporters to be in need of supplementing. As we have noted, the second theorem was designed to remedy a glaring deficiency of the first: namely that the first theorem was consistent with virtually any distribution of the model economy's goods among its participants.

The essential point of the second theorem can be put quite simply. Consider an Edgeworth economy in a Pareto optimal, competitive equilibrium with an unacceptable distribution (whatever the specific criteria for this might be). Then any acceptable core allocation could be obtained instead of the objectionable one, by assuming the power to impose upon the model an appropriate set of lump-sum taxes and transfers. There are, in other words, conceivable Pareto optimal equilibria to suit any distributional preferences. It does not follow that such 'desirable'

Pareto equilibria are any more feasible in the real world than any others.

It will be well to remind the non-economist reader here that this second theorem (like the first), which was an integral part of the canonical Arrow–Debreu models, is of course subject to all the vicissitudes which have overtaken such models. It depended upon orderings, perfect competition, and the completeness of an intertemporal system of markets, upon agents possessing the information necessary for this, and of course on the absence of asymmetric information. In the Arrow–Debreu models which (unlike our simple Edgeworth models) included production, the theorem depended upon the absence of all externalities of production. In any model (with or without production) it depended on the absence of externalities of consumption: no consumption by one agent may matter in the least to any other agent (hence the need for the assumption of self-interest).

All this is well known to economic theorists and has been argued, in ever more sophisticated mathematical contexts, over many years. A possibly new element in the debate is the role of asymmetric information, which is of relatively recent origin. It has been shown that asymmetry of information is more damaging to models of perfectly competitive equilibrium than is mere imperfection of information (see the references already given in Chapter 4). Nevertheless, the critics have had great difficulty in penetrating what Sen has called '[t]he enormous standing of Pareto optimality' (Sen 1987: 38). What has given it this teflon quality? Sen argues significantly that the impregnability of Pareto optimality is closely related to 'the hallowed position of utilitarianism in traditional welfare economics' (ibid.).

I believe that Pareto optimality has been able to survive for two reasons, of which one is indeed the utilitarianism which is still at the heart of neo-classical economic theory. This will be explored in the present chapter, and its bearing upon the survival of the prestige of Pareto optimality considered.

The second reason for the survival of the Pareto criterion, I believe, goes very deep, and concerns the analytical structure of neo-classical theory, its concept of the individual choosing agent, and (as already noted) its concept of equilibrium as a chosen position. If every agent in an economy were an individual person, and if every person had an initial endowment which made it possible to survive without trading, then we would know the sense in which any equilibrium of such a model must reflect the choices or actions of each of the individual persons. There might hopefully not be coalitions of a few persons able to determine the equilibrium without any endorsement from all the other agents. It is a deeply believed article of faith, a fundamental component of the neo-classical vision, that this is true. Having worked with Edgeworth enables us to see more clearly why, as was noted in Chapter 1, neo-classics have a strong commitment to the doctrine of methodological individualism. But we also saw in that chapter that the necessity of giving neo-classical theory any links to real life forced the theorist to allow 'agents' which were black boxes to pass muster. Even Debreu (1959), a model justly praised for its chaste abstraction from this vale of tears in which we live, has agents which are corporations and 'consumers' which can be a larger group with a common purpose. So in a neo-Walrasian model, Pedro Gonzalez the night watchman gets his licks in as a 'choosing' agent alongside a multinational with the clout, it may well be, of a reasonably large nation. Chapters 8 and 9 offer, by way of contrast, a sketch of a class of models in which a number of key questions are analysed in terms of economic classes, and no effort is made to insist that a particular class of agents (however large its numbers) must necessarily have any significant input into the equilibrium states of the model. Meanwhile, we must consider the first of the two reasons why I believe the prestige of Pareto optimality has proved so resistant to attack, which has to do with the support it received from the utilitarianism implicit in neo-classical theory.

THE PHILOSOPHICAL ROOTS OF PARETO OPTIMALITY

These roots, it will be suggested, are a strikingly inconsistent tangle of utilitarianism and logical positivism. To see how this came about, however, we have to go back to the original 'old' welfare economics, and the reasons for its fall.

The 'old' welfare economics was a legitimate descendant of utilitarianism—and not of the watered down ordinal utilitarianism of later days either: its great protagonist, Arthur Cecil Pigou, grasped the utilitarian position, sum ranking, welfarism, and consequentialism, with a firm and unwavering grip. I have said hard things about the limitations of utilitarianism as an account of rational choice. But of one fault the economists who developed the 'old' welfare economics cannot be justly accused: they did not suffer from the delusion (nor make the pretence if not deluded) that what came to be called a 'welfare economics' can be constructed without facing up to the necessity for making judgements (at one and the same time judgements of moral philosophy and of political economy) about the distribution of wealth and of income in society. A detailed scholarly re-examination of 'old' or 'Pigouian' welfare economics is indeed overdue, since economists disillusioned with Pareto optimality and decision theorists disillusioned with 'ordinal' expected utility theory have revived certain of its ideas, concerning 'cardinality', while others (see, for instance, Sen 1982: 264–79) have developed them further—in the direction notably of 'partial' cardinalities. For our purposes, however, a brief glance at Pigou's use of 'interpersonal comparisons' must suffice. Referring to 'the old law of diminishing utility' (Pigou [1920] 1952: 89), Pigou states simply that, allowing for every necessary qualification: 'Nevertheless, it is evident that any transference of income from a relatively rich man to a relatively poor man of similar temperament, since it enables more intense wants to be satisfied at the expense of less intense wants, must increase the aggregate sum of satisfaction.' (Ibid.)

Noting that Pigou's views on ethics differed from those of Bentham (in a manner which need not concern us at this moment), Ian Little commented that Pigou 'took over the whole Benthamite doctrine that the welfare of society was the sum total of the welfares of individuals' (Little [1950] 1957: 8). It will perhaps be clear why the works of Pigou and other protagonists of the 'old welfare economics' led to a drastic cooling off in the old, long-enduring love affair of neo-classical economists with Benthamite utilitarianism. Those components of the utilitarian tradition which led to conclusions disturbing to neo-classical economics were now rejected. We have already discussed the rejection of sum ranking, and the retreat to a strictly ordinal utilitarianism in Chapter 2, and we saw that the passion for avoiding all cardinal concepts led to the attempt to present even axiomatic expected utility theory in an 'ordinal' dress. We must now take up the question of interpersonal comparisons, and it is appropriate to do so at this point since we now have the elements of a model of the allocation of an economy's goods among those persons who participate in it.

We need to begin by considering the implications of Benthamite utilitarianism for questions concerning the distribution of an economy's goods among its population. It is important to recognize that Bentham's work had some humanitarian and even radical implications from the beginning. Simply to propose that one should consider the penal laws, the arrangements with regard to property, and the social structure in general, from the point of view of whether or not these maximized the happiness of society as a whole (on any conception of happiness) was a highly radical proposal in Bentham's England. To put into the heads of all those not born to position and consequence the idea that they should have an expectation of happiness in this vale of tears was a highly dangerous idea.

When justice has been done to Bentham's progressive streak, however, the fact must be faced that the classical utilitarian goal of maximizing the sum total of the utilities of individuals is, as Sen pointed out some years ago 'supremely unconcerned with the interpersonal distribution of that sum' (Sen 1973: 16). To get the distributional implication of Bentham's theory which the neo-classics of the 1930s feared, a special further assumption is needed. As Sen put it, if 'everyone has the same utility function, then equating marginal utilities amounts to equating total utilities as well' (ibid.). Versions of this position underlay the use of classical utilitarianism by Pigou and other proponents of the 'old' welfare economics, whose use of interpersonal comparisons will shortly concern us.

Before leaving Benthamite utilitarianism, however, it should be noted that when an assumption of identical (or at least broadly similar) utility functions is not made, classical utilitarianism can lead to some highly unappealing results. Let us return briefly to the two sisters we met in Chapter 3. They are young women now, and tragedy has visited the family. Gwen, overmounted it must be admitted, fell at a stone wall in Ireland and is seriously handicapped for life. Muriel, on the other hand, still enjoys robust health. Suppose that Gwen, since her accident, only manages to get half as much utility from any particular income as does her sister. In such a case classical utilitarianism would give Muriel a higher income than Gwen—making the latter worse off than she would be on an equal division, where her utility level would only be half Muriel's (see Sen 1973: 16–18). Classical utilitarianism gives equal treatment in only one sense: everyone's capacity to generate utility gains gets 'the same weight in the maximizing exercise' (Sen 1992: 14).

Could the neo-classics of the 1930s have stopped short of rejecting Benthamite utility, simply denying that the utility functions of different persons were even roughly comparable? Well, Jevons (who was a fervent Benthamite utilitarian) did just that, and as we shall see, Lord Robbins initially followed Jevons in this. But the arrival of logical positivism shortly offered a more drastic remedy: the chance to reject the Benthamite position, lock, stock, and barrel.

This, of course, destroyed the 'old' welfare economics leaving an unnoticed residue of ordinal utilitarianism, as we saw in Chapter 2, what one might call a tame utilitarianism. As a result of all this, Pareto optimality, which survived the fall of the old welfare economics since it required neither cardinal utilities nor interpersonal comparisons, was in fact immensely strengthened and its prestige greatly enhanced by the ruin of every other welfare-theoretic concept.

Noting that interpersonal comparisons of utility came under fire in the 1930s in an attack led by Robbins, Sen has observed that '[f]or reasons that are not altogether clear, interpersonal utility comparisons were then diagnosed as being themselves "normative" or "ethical"' (Sen 1987: 30). Indeed, he cited a passage from Robbins which shows the latter describing such comparisons as essentially normative (Sen 1987: 30 n. 1). Nevertheless, Sen's view is that the main thrust of Robbins' argument was that interpersonal comparisons were descriptively meaningless, not that they were normative: 'Robbins's well-known attack on interpersonal comparisons as treated by utilitarians was essentially based on denying that there was any descriptive meaning of such comparisons, and not, as often supposed, based on asserting that such comparisons should not be made' (Sen 1982: 265). I took this view in 1970, where I noted the possible influence of Jevons on Robbins: 'Jevons explicitly stated that, as far as he could see, no meaning could be attached to comparisons between the utility experienced by one man and that experienced by another. These were states of mind and, in Jevons' opinion, forever inscrutable. This became the basis of Robbins' famous attack on what he called "interpersonal comparisons of utility" ' (Walsh 1970: 95).

I still believe this view of Robbins to be correct, but I think it may be possible to clarify the distinction between the original position of Robbins and the rather different position of the economists who adopted his slogan of 'denying' interpersonal comparisons. This may in turn do something to clarify the reasons why such comparisons were then diagnosed as normative or ethical. To begin with, the philosophical climate in Britain changed fundamentally in the 1930s as Martin Hollis and Edward Nell have noted: 'Between 1932 and 1935 Logical Positivism gained its ascendancy' (Hollis and Nell 1975: 201).

In its vigorous first youth, logical positivism held a series of positions which were to prove fatally attractive to economists. Crudely, the propositions of logic and mathematics were held to be 'meaningful', but only in the sense that they were tautological, and only one other class of utterance was admitted to be 'meaningful'—namely the empirical statement. What is more, to satisfy the stringent demands of the so-called 'verification principle', each individual empirical proposition had to be separately testable, at least 'in principle'. Moral utterances, since they did not simply state testable facts, were thrown out as meaningless, along with aesthetic judgements, 'metaphysical' utterances, poetry—in fact any utterance which did not fit their absolute dichotomy as fact or tautology. (see Walsh 1987b: 861–3).

Now Robbins's original objections to interpersonal comparisons were emphatically not based on this position. Most citations of his *Essay* are to the second edition (1935), and in this, as Hollis and Nell observe, he had somewhat weakened the position of his first edition (1932) which had been cast in a mould close to philosophical rationalism. Robbins's concessions to the empiricist tide in 1935 were not at all fundamental. But they have tended to obscure the fact that his original argument was in terms of a philosophical tradition fundamentally inconsistent with logical positivism—the new philosophical fashion in terms of which his attack on interpersonal comparisons would be recast by his enthusiastic later followers. Robbins's original argument turns on an extreme position about our (lack of) knowledge of other minds. This position is arguably associated with elements of Cartesian mind/body dualism which have a home within parts of the rationalist tradition. In any case it is not my purpose to argue this case here; my purpose is confined to showing that Robbins's extreme denial of knowledge of other minds would not sit well with the logical empiricist tradition—even in its earliest, most virulent logical positivist form. To see this it should be sufficient to note the position taken by the late Sir Alfred Ayer (whose version of the positivist position perhaps was most influential in Britain) in his brilliant and charming, but also very logical positivist early work. He contended that: 'It does not follow from the fact that each man's experiences are private to himself that no one ever had good reason to believe that another man's experiences are qualitatively the same as his own' (Ayer [1936] 1946: 131–2).

Ayer had good reason as a logical positivist to insist on this, as soon appears. If one instead 'regards the experiences of others as essentially unobservable entities, whose nature has somehow to be inferred from the subject's perceptible behaviour, then . . . even the proposition that there are other conscious beings becomes for him a metaphysical hypothesis' (Ayer [1936] 1946: 132). So a consistent logical positivist who regarded metaphysics as meaningless could not follow Robbins's tack in 1932. Thus Ayer continued: 'For if the contents of other people's sensations really were inaccessible to my observation, then I could never say anything about them. But, in fact, I do make significant statements about them' (ibid.).

This, it will be clear, was all that was needed to give 'descriptive' meaning, in the logical positivist sense, to interpersonal comparisons. Meanwhile, in the philosophy of mind, the tide of opinion was running against the claim that other minds were occult unknowable entities—the view which Robbins's original position on interpersonal comparisons required.

Much of this work in the philosophy of mind was stimulated by the personal influence of Gilbert Ryle on a group of young people then up at Oxford, as well as by the world-wide impact of his book, *The Concept of Mind* (Ryle 1949). Many philosophers, perhaps especially in America, appear to have interpreted Ryle as a behaviourist. But, as ordinarily understood, behaviourism is a claim about what can be observed: it in effect accepts the logic of Cartesian dualism and refuses to acknowledge one of the components of Cartesian ontology, namely the mind. Ryle, on the other hand, both in his writings and in conversation, repeatedly pointed out that he was making a claim not about what things there are, but about language (see Walsh 1954*b*: 250–1). Fortunately, however, we do not need to settle this dispute here and now!

I do not in the least wish to claim that economists as a whole were keeping up with these developments in the philosophy of mind. Indeed, the earliest notable case which I can recall was that of Little, who in the preface to the first edition of his book (Little 1950) explicitly acknowledged the influence of Ryle. I took Little to task at the time (Walsh 1954*b*) for his behaviourist interpretation of Ryle, but as Sen has noted (Sen 1982: 266), Little's behaviourism was only a weak version of this doctrine. What now seems to me important is that Little was perfectly clear that the original attack on interpersonal comparisons was based on 'some vague metaphysical doubt about the existence of minds other than one's own. I say about the *existence* of other minds, because nothing short of denying their existence can entitle one to say that other minds cannot be compared' (Little [1950] 1957: 54, emphasis in original). He also stated clearly that in using this kind of argument against the possibility of interpersonal comparisons, economists were fighting to defend a philosophical position abandoned by philosophers themselves: 'Economists are in this matter a little old-fashioned. I doubt whether there is a philosopher today who would be prepared to say that one cannot compare other people's mental states; that one is not saying anything about the real world when one says "A is happier than B"' (Little [1950] 1957: 55).

Little noted the tendency, already well established by the time he wrote, for economists to make the quite different claim that interpersonal comparisons were value-judgements. He cites Robbins: 'But I still think, when I make interpersonal comparisons, that my judgments are more like judgments of value than judgments of verifiable fact' (Robbins 1938: 641). He insists against Robbins that one should speak of interpersonal comparisons as resting on observation or introspection 'for the good reason that they do rest on such foundations' (Little [1950] 1957: 56).

This exchange shows Robbins falling back on the argument against interpersonal comparisons which logical positivism could live with—that they were without scientific foundation, descriptively meaningless, because of being value-judgements. Note Robbins's use of the logical positivist adjective 'verifiable'. Little, to his credit, was willing to accept neither Robbins's original epistemological claim concerning the unknowableness of other minds, nor the claim that interpersonal comparisons were 'ethical', which had now come into style, and which Robbins, who originally rested his case mainly on the epistemological claim, was here saying that he 'still thinks' is the issue. It would be many years before any large number of economists saw these issues as clearly as Little did in the 1950s.

The claim that interpersonal comparisons were value-judgements would, if it could pass muster (it did not pass muster with Little, but he was a solitary voice), enable economists to borrow the extreme negative position of logical positivism on the status of ethical utterances—that they were literally meaningless. Any stick will do to beat a dog; economists who wanted to keep interpersonal comparisons out of welfare economics had what was then a new and apparently powerful weapon.

The situation had some exquisite ironies: a strict logical positivist philosopher might well have accepted Little's claim that interpersonal comparisons were empirically verifiable factual statements—this followed from their whole position on other minds, as can be seen from the citations from Ayer already given. The economists, however, did not attend to this point. They simply assumed that interpersonal comparisons *were* value-judgements, and then borrowed the logical positivist view of the meaninglessness of value-judgements. The situation which resulted from this in economic theory has been summed up with no less than justice recently by Sen:

I guess it is a reflection of the way ethics tends to be viewed by economists that statements suspected of being 'meaningless' or 'nonsensical' are promptly taken to be 'ethical'. The peculiarly narrow view of 'meaning' championed by logical positivists—enough to cause disorder in philosophy itself—caused total chaos in welfare economics when it was supplemented by some additional home-grown confusions liberally supplied by economists themselves. Positivist philosophers may have been off beam in taking all ethical propositions to be meaningless, but even they had not suggested that all meaningless propositions were ethical! (Sen 1987: 31)

One final irony completes the picture: by the end of the 1950s, logical positivism had retreated to its last line of defence, logical empiricism. But in this necessary withdrawal before its attackers it had had to abandon precisely those clear-cut and uncompromising original positions which had been the whole basis of its denial of the 'meaning' of ethical statements.

As Hilary Putnam has put this:

> The Logical Positivists argued for a sharp fact-value dichotomy in a very simple way: scientific statements (apart from logic and pure mathematics), they said, are 'empirically verifiable' and value judgments are 'unverifiable'. This argument continues to have wide appeal to economists (not to say laymen), even though it has for some years been looked upon as naive by philosophers. One reason the argument is naive is that it assumes that there is such a thing as 'the method of verification' of each isolated *scientifically meaningful* sentence. But this is very far from being the case.... the idea that each scientific sentence has its own range of confirming observations and its own range of disconfirming observations, independent of what other sentences it is conjoined to, is wrong. If a sentence that does not, in and of itself, by its very meaning, have a 'method of verification' is meaningless, then most of theoretical science turns out to be meaningless! (Putnam 1990: 163, emphasis in original)

The economist's logical positivist defence against having to consider interpersonal comparisons had thus lost credibility by the end of the 1950s. The ability to ignore troubling questions concerning the distribution of wealth and income was precious to many economists, however, and since logical positivism had paid such rich dividends in protecting economists from having to face the great historical issues of classical political economy such as poverty and the luxurious waste of riches, they could hardly be expected to become customers for some newer results of philosophical analysis.

There was, nevertheless, supposed to be a subject called 'welfare economics', and since the deep questions concerning distribution which had filled it under the 'old welfare' theorists like Pigou were now taboo, something was needed to fill the vacuum. Pareto optimality had now no rivals—its hour had come.

THE RISE OF PARETO OPTIMALITY

As Sen has noted, with the development of what he calls 'anti-ethicalism', leading to the abandonment of interpersonal comparisons of utility in welfare economics, the only remaining criterion was of course Pareto optimality. If interpersonal comparisons were to be dropped, while utility was still believed to be the only value, then Pareto optimality would be, so to speak, the heir apparent of utilitarianism, 'since it carries the utilitarian logic as far forward as possible without actually making any interpersonal comparisons of utility' (Sen 1987: 38).

The same logical positivist heyday which saw the rejection of interpersonal comparisons of utility saw also the rejection of statements involving the old 'cardinal' utility, and their replacement by ordinal utility theory. This was important because the concept of quantities of utility played an important role in the old utilitarian form of interpersonal comparison. But no quantities of utility were needed for the concept of Pareto optimality. Economists, as we saw in Chapter 2, followed Hicks in believing that they had an economics which was now free from utilitarian assumptions. They went further; they believed that claims concerning the superiority of 'Pareto optimal' over 'non-Pareto optimal' equilibria were not ethical claims!

An explanation sometimes offered for this strange belief turns on the question of unanimity. Recall the Edgeworth box. If the traders are supposed to be at a point off the contract curve, then a suitable point can be found which is on the contract curve and which is so placed as to be preferred by all traders. The truly special thing for the new welfare economists about such a Pareto optimal point was the unanimity with which it could be judged better than the point off the curve. This boils down to the claim that unanimous value-judgements are not really value judgements.

There was, however, a deeper reason why economists were misled into thinking that judgements involving only Pareto optimality were ethically neutral: the value-judgements which they knew and feared were judgements condemning the extreme inequality of wealth and income in existing societies, made by means of interpersonal comparisons of cardinal utilities. Once both cardinal utility and interpersonal comparisons based on this had been banished, they believed utilitarianism (admittedly a moral philosophy) had itself been banished: so ethical judgements were gone from economics! But, of course, ordinal utilitarianism, with its questionable welfarist and consequentialist implications was still deeply entrenched and the whole Pareto optimality argument depended on it.

As Sen has remarked, Pareto optimality can be regarded as

encapsulating one particular aspect of welfarism, namely: 'a unanimous ranking of the individual utilities must be adequate for overall social ranking of the respective states' (Sen 1987: 39). He refers to the relevant literature, and argues further that the use of the Pareto argument in economic policy involves one in consequentialism as well as welfarism. As for consequentialism, the utilitarian tradition of attaching no intrinsic importance to rights is thus carried over into the new welfare economics and its Pareto criterion. Thus the welfarism and consequentialism underlying the Pareto criterion reinforce each other, with no need at any point for sum ranking. The result of all this was to embed the Pareto criterion in a deeply entrenched ordinal act utilitarian economics, whose (ordinal) utilitarianism would, because of its very public rejection of sum ranking and interpersonal comparisons, not be seen as involving utilitarian moral philosophy at all.

Perhaps economists would not have been so ready to dismiss interpersonal comparisons if comparisons of rights (for example) had been considered, instead of simply comparisons of utility. To do them justice, economists would certainly be among the first to condemn the deprivation of every human right, even that of life itself, under the Nazi holocaust, or the appalling deprivation of their rights which was experienced by black South Africans under Apartheid. It would appear that we cannot avoid making interpersonal comparisons of the treatment under law enjoyed by different people, of the differing levels of justice and respect for their rights which they experience. And these comparisons both make factual claims and express moral judgements: they are black with fact but they are assuredly also red with values.

Now the welfarist, consequentialist, welfare economics of which Pareto optimality is the foundation, rules out all these vital comparisons. It enthrones one particularly narrow moral claim—the Pareto criterion—which is not even seen as a moral claim, at the expense of all non-welfarist or non-consequentialist moral claims concerning different states of society—claims based on rights, responsibilities, goals, achievements, duties, indeed any criterion but the Pareto criterion. Recall that the Pareto criterion requires an assumption that all the agents in a model are purely self-interested. Otherwise an agent could suffer negative (or positive) externalities from the poverty or wealth of other agents. But an explicit recognition of the moral importance of rights may force upon economic theory the necessity for recognizing systematic departures from self-interested choice. Any such change, however, as Sen has noted 'can shake the behavioural foundations of standard economic theory' (Sen 1987: 57).

Economic theorists engaged in the intricacies of welfare economics are frequently guilty of an elementary ethical confusion which enables them to obtain ethical results without, as it were, paying the going price for them in terms of openly ethical prior assumptions. What has been called 'preference utilitarianism', in the hands of economic theorists, has been notably hazy about the distinction between some object of choice being 'desired' and its being 'desirable', and between some object being 'preferred' and its being 'preferable'. To say that assault rifles are desired is to make a claim which is certainly true. But to say that their free purchase and sale is desirable is to make a totally different, and ethical claim. We do not normally confuse these claims in our ordinary discourse. But when axiomatic utility theory is used to construct what is known as 'welfare' economics, the neo-classical theorist is forced to perform such a conceptual high wire act that it is hardly surprising if fatal slips occur.

Thus when economists sought (as we saw in Chapters 2 and 3) to free their accounts of rational choice from utilitarian vestiges by speaking only of orders of preference, the unfortunate result of this endeavour was that in fact 'well-being', 'welfare', and 'optimality' became identified simply with what an agent preferred. But the ethical implications of the 'welfare' theorems are not legitimately available (i.e. have not been paid for in terms of the coin of explicit ethical assumptions). For economists to have paid the honest going price for their claims to be talking about 'welfare' or 'well-being' they would have to make their under-the-counter ordinal utilitarianism explicit—as it is, for example, made clear and explicit in Broome.

It is sometimes thought that an axiomatization in terms of 'preferences' is a pellucidly clear and transparent thing—a structure, as it were, of cut glass, like a Waterford decanter, in which nothing can be hidden. Hilary Putnam, however, has argued that this is not so: 'Preference-Function Utilitarianism is really a way of smuggling a second value into utilitarianism . . . In effect, the Preference-Function Utilitarian is insisting that we must make people happy, but we must do this without impairing their freedom to decide for themselves what their Happiness *is*. This is not one value ("Happiness") but two; in fact, it is three' (Putnam 1987: 59–60). The third value, which Putnam claims is assumed by all forms of utilitarianism since Bentham, is of course the principle that every person's happiness is of equal prima-facie importance. He adds that utilitarianism is 'an attempt to make a series of ideas which have deep and complex roots in our culture, values of equality, liberal values of choice, and values of fraternity and happiness, seem simple and non-arbitrary' (ibid.).

These ingredients are all present in the neo-classical doctrine of Pareto optimality. The systematic confusion of what a consumer prefers with what it is preferable for that consumer to have (i.e. in welfarist terms, what will tend towards that consumer's well-being) is often dignified as the doctrine of 'consumer sovereignty'. As Peter Hammond has well argued in recent work, the two efficiency theorems of welfare economics 'acquire all their ethical significance from this particular value judgment' (Hammond 1989: 193). Without the ethical implications of the doctrine of consumer sovereignty, all you have is 'a factual statement about what each consumer would choose' (ibid.).

Consider a possible explicit ethical argument for consumer sovereignty. It could not rest on a welfarist consequentialism. A person's welfare is arguably most promoted if they are legally protected against commodities hazardous to their health or life, dangerous inadequately tested medications, assault weapons, etc. An explicit defence of consumer sovereignty would have to rest on the possible invasion of important rights that could result from legal regulation. But (given its welfarism) an argument based on rights is just what Pareto optimality cannot coexist with, as we shall see spelled out in a later section of this chapter specifically devoted to the incompatibility of Pareto optimality and rights to liberty.

Externalities, as we know, undermine the canonical Arrow–Debreu equilibria, and naturally, as Hammond notes, thus undermine the conclusions of both of the fundamental theorems involving Pareto optimality. Hammond acidly comments that: 'To be able to ignore externalities in a way that their masters in business and even in government find most convenient, *laissez faire* conservative economists need to be able to blind themselves with a suitable theory.' (Ibid.)

Such a theory was of course forthcoming, dependent on the idea that the parties affected by an externality would come together and agree how to create property rights governing the externality—so Pareto optimality would be restored. This leads to what Hammond calls the efficiency tautology. This is the supposition that any possible Pareto improvement in institutional arrangements will always have been found, so that any allocation which has actually taken place must be Pareto efficient. This ensures Pareto optimality by linguistic stipulation, since if there were a possible Pareto improvement 'it would already have been found!' (Hammond 1989: 205.) This tautology obviously leans with crushing weight upon the assumption of intertemporally perfect information, an assumption already fatally weakened by attack on several fronts, notably by the recent theorists of asymmetric information. A giant corporation is rather evidently likely to possess better information concerning externalities it is causing than a private citizen, and can (and often has) suppressed this information—a notable case being the tobacco industry. Hammond notes that a similar objection applies to the core, wherever the unrestricted formation of coalitions is assumed, as is usually the case. Actually, 'since core allocations must be Pareto efficient, when they exist, the core has also been a useful refuge for those whose ethical sensibilities have not progressed beyond the sufficiency of Pareto efficiency' (ibid.). *O tempora! O mores!*—recall, dear reader, how far Francis Edgeworth had progressed beyond Pareto efficiency in 1881!

The first and second theorems of welfare economics are often confused in a significant way, which is convenient for defenders of laissez-faire. As Hammond puts this point: 'Such defenders love to appeal to the first efficiency theorem in order to assert that we should remove all distortionary taxes and other obstacles to perfectly competitive allocations' (Hammond 1989: 207). But the first theorem only asserts that a perfectly competitive equilibrium satisfies the Pareto criterion for some (possibly horrendous) distribution of income. It is, on the contrary, the second fundamental theorem which embodies the claim that virtually any Pareto optimal allocation is a possible perfectly competitive equilibrium allocation. This second theorem, however, holds only subject to the crucial requirement that any required redistribution of purchasing power be actually made through lump-sum taxes or subsidies, so that the new distribution of wealth after the redistribution makes

possible that particular Pareto optimal allocation. In the absence of
such redistribution, the gains of some have to be balanced against
the losses of others (thus introducing those interpersonal comparisons which neo-classical theory professes to avoid like the plague).
But without this one is back with the first theorem, which is devoid
of ethical significance. As Hammond notes: 'There is no guarantee
whatever that *laissez faire* will produce a just distribution of income, or even one that avoids gross injustice, in which some people
barely subsist in abject poverty, while others are extremely affluent.
Indeed, both market and Pareto-efficient allocations can be even
worse than that, because it is quite possible for both to be consistent with widespread starvation.' (Ibid.)

A key assumption, which needs to be carefully examined at this
point, is the assumption that agents can survive without trading.
Sen has argued that most of standard general equilibrium theory
assumes that every economic agent can in fact survive without
trade. Trading, of course, would then simply enhance the trader's
feasible consumption set. Hammond, commenting on this work of
Sen's, concludes: 'So the possibility of the very poor starving in a
world of plentiful aggregate food supplies is virtually excluded by
assumption. Yet Sen (1977b, 1981a, 1981b) has provided much
evidence to show that famine is in fact more often due to gross
inequality of income than it is to the total food supply falling so low
that it becomes impossible to feed all the population adequately'
(Hammond 1989: 211).

Neo-Walrasian general equilibrium without survival has been
seen to pose some technical problems. Having confronted these in
his recent work with J. L. Coles (Coles and Hammond 1986),
Hammond is able to point out that the possibility of the non-
survival of some consumers is not a fundamental obstacle to the
usual theorems on existence, efficiency and so on: 'In particular,
competitive equilibria can occur with a large proportion of the
population below the margin of survival. Such equilibria are even
Pareto efficient, because feeding the starving would require sacrifices from some of those whose survival is not at risk. Really, that
mass starvation can occur in competitive equilibrium, and still be
consistent with Pareto efficiency, merely serves to dramatize the
criticism [of the assumption that Pareto efficiency is sufficient for
ethical acceptability]' (Hammond 1989: 211).

Recall the initial endowment point t_0 in Figure 6.1. It defines a pair of no-trade indifference curves, I_{A0} and I_{B0}, one for each type of trader (t_0 was placed at the upper left-hand corner of the Edgeworth box, but placing the no trade point at, say, t_1 in Figure 6.3(a) will not weaken the argument). The set of possible trades is then confined to the intersection of the upper contour sets of the no-trade indifference curves. The implication of this is that a trader will rank not trading above any point in the box outside the trading set. So it is clearly possible for any trader to survive without trade. Such traders must possess what Sen calls 'trade-independent security'. To put it crudely, they must be able to eat what they possess without trade and thus survive even if all trade breaks down.

Sen remarks that in the literature of general equilibrium it is typically assumed that every agent possesses trade- independent security. He notes that this is a very extreme assumption, not satisfied by most people in present-day economies. The old-fashioned peasant, provided the crops did not fail, may have trade-independent security. But workers in industry or small business, or for government, living in an urban environment and having only their labour power to offer in exchange for food, etc., equally obviously cannot survive without such trade (see Sen 1981a: 173).

In a situation where physical survival is threatened, the standard use of indifference curves may also give a mistaken impression (at least to the unwary). The usual comfortable agent depicted in neo-classical theory may ponder whether to buy a little more entertainment and a little less food, but the starving person does not. The starving are likely to possess what has been (somewhat unhelpfully) called a lexicographic (or lexical) ordering: more food is ranked above more of any other good, up to the point where survival is obtained (just as, in a dictionary, any word beginning with 'a' comes before any work beginning with 'b'). A lexical ordering is illustrated in Figure 7.1. Up to the point marked 'subsistence' on the food axis, more food is ranked above less, irrespective of the amount of other goods available. Thus x_1 is ranked above x_2, despite the amount of other goods available at x_2, because there is less food. On the other hand, of two commodity bundles containing the same amount of food, the bundle with the larger component of other goods is ranked higher. Thus x_2 is ranked above x_0.

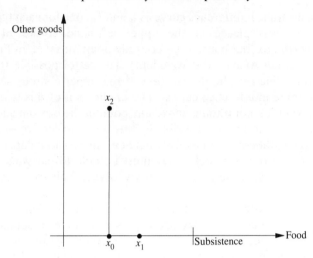

F𝙸G. 7.1.

It is interesting to note that, when lexical orderings are mentioned at all in neo-classical theory, they are usually treated as a curiosity, verging on the pathological. Thus, the usual example offered is that of an alcoholic, of a drug addict. It might, of course, be claimed that all forms of addiction, taken together, make up a not negligible proportion of American consumption and therefore constitute more than a curiosity. For present purposes, however, the relevant comment is that, since Coles and Hammond (and others) have shown that in neo-Walrasian general equilibrium models perfectly competitive equilibria can take place with a large proportion of the population below the subsistence level, neo-classical theory can hardly afford to treat the obsession with food which is a normal concomitant of starvation as 'pathological' or 'irrational'.

Part of the desire to exclude lexical orderings may have technical origins: since there are no equally ranked commodity bundles with such orderings, there are no indifference curves. Indeed, as was shown by Debreu (1959: 55–9) there is no increasing real valued function ('utility' function) which will represent such an ordering. As was remarked by Marcel K. Richter: 'It has been unpleasant for mathematical economists to contemplate foregoing utility functions in theoretical economics. Indeed, it was the simplicity and familiarity of the mathematical techniques of classical analysis for numerical functions which led to the long reign of utility in economic theory' (Richter 1971: 39). After making this interesting claim, Richter cites an extensive literature concerned with alternative 'representations' for such orderings, and presents a sophisticated approach of his own (Richter 1971: 40–5).

We may now construct, in Figure 7.2(*a*), a highly simplified version of an exchange model, where lexical orderings, subsistence levels, and starvation nevertheless all play a role. We give an A trader only the 'other good', and a B trader only food. (There is as usual a balanced set of A and B traders, of arbitrarily large size.) Each A trader initially owns $t_0 O_A$ of 'other goods' and each

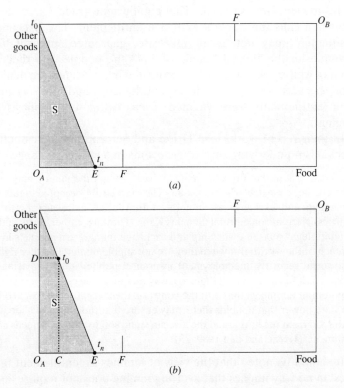

FIG. 7.2.

B trader is initially endowed with t_0O_B of food. The subsistence requirement is assumed to be identical for each trader, whether of type A or type B, and is marked off as O_AF for an A trader and O_BF for a B trader. It will be seen that a B trader can simply retain O_BF of food, while an A trader must acquire all of this by trade.

What Sen calls the starvation set, S, is an attainable set of commodity bundles which does not include a point of minimum subsistence. Up to subsistence, a trader of either type has a lexical ordering over food. (A type B trader, of course, already in fact has more than enough food.) In Figure 7.2(a) we see a situation where the system of relative prices, indicated by t_0E, is such that in perfectly competitive equilibrium the attainable set of an A trader is the starvation set S. At this rate of exchange, the whole of an A trader's endowment will only buy O_At_n food, which is insufficient for survival. The equilibrium trade, t_n, defines what Sen calls the trader's exchange entitlement. This exchange entitlement may not, as in this case, guarantee survival: 'for example, in the Bengal famine of 1943 the people who died in front of well-stocked food shops protected by the state were denied food because of *lack* of legal entitlement, and not because their entitlements were violated' (Sen 1981a: 49, emphasis in original).

In their recent work, Jean Drèze and Sen capture the essential mechanism underlying such tragic events in a striking passage:

The legal system that precedes and survives through the famine may not, in itself, be a particularly cruel one. The standardly accepted rights of ownership and exchange are not the authoritarian extravaganzas of a heartless Nero or some brutal Genghis Kahn. They are, rather, parts of the standard legal rules of ownership and exchange that govern people's lives in much of the world. But when they are not supplemented by other rights (e.g. social security, unemployment insurance, public health provisions), these standard rights may operate in a way that offers no chance of survival to potential famine victims. On the contrary, these legal rights, backed by the state power that upholds them, may ensure that the 'have-nots' do not grab food from the haves, and the law can stand solidly between needs and fulfilment. (Drèze and Sen 1989: 23)

It should be noted that the view of famines as 'entitlement failures' in no way implies that averting famine does not require, as a necessary though not sufficient condition, that adequate food supplies be available (see Drèze and Sen 1989: 25 n. 10). Nor does their analysis require that the famine victims grow no food. As Drèze and Sen note, most of the victims may in fact come from the class of agricultural labourers. The point, rather, is that the contract 'typically includes no right to the output grown by the person's own labour' (ibid. 21). In our simple model, the A traders are directly exchanging their A goods for food, but this does not guarantee their survival (as Figure 7.2(a) shows). Nor is it necessary that the victims possess no food in their initial endowment. The placing of the point of zero trade at the top left-hand corner of the box was dictated solely by the desire for simplicity. One could perfectly well have given each type A trader some food in the initial endowment. Consider Figure 7.2(b), where an A trader's initial endowment is composed of Dt_0 food plus t_0C other goods. At the ruling prices, however, the A traders are still in their starvation set S, since all of their non-food will not exchange for O_AF food. In conclusion, observe that the equilibrium trade t_n (in both (a) and (b) of Figure 7.2) is clearly Pareto optimal, despite the fact that all of the A traders will starve.

It is here that the second fundamental theorem must arrive and save the day. If one Pareto optimal equilibrium results in an intolerable distribution, we are told, there will be a possible alternative Paretian equilibrium with the distribution we seek (whatever that may be). Well, assumptions can be imposed upon an Edgeworth economy powerful enough to restrict it to some set of morally 'tolerable' distributions. To some extent, a very weak version of such an assumption is tacitly present in the standard presentation of an exchange model, since no lexical orderings appear. The position and shape of the indifference curves thus imply that agents of each 'type' can subsist without trade. On the other hand, they are willing to trade on suitably favourable terms, so each type of trader clearly has something on offer which the others want. Entitlement failures, which in the third world can lead simply to death by starvation, can thus be smoothly ruled out. In models with a continuum of traders, the individual trader could hardly get any thinner anyway. Does it make sense to enquire into the nutritional requirements of such agents?

Problems of a serious nature, however, arise when any attempt is made to draw lessons for the real world from the implications of the second theorem. Recall that the implementation of the second theorem requires the imposition of lump-sum taxes and transfers, in order to change distribution and make it possible to arrive at the desired new Paretian equilibrium. But precisely those laissez-faire economists who champion the Pareto optimality theorems have argued strenuously that lump-sum taxes and transfers are bound to distort incentives. Hammond points out that they cannot have it both ways.[1]

The effect of Hammond's argument is to lay bare the fact that, precisely for those who most strongly support the Pareto criterion, the second theorem can be no more than a pious incantation. Without it, however, the remaining first fundamental theorem of welfare economics would stand starkly revealed as having nothing to do with human welfare. The second theorem, thus understood, plays the role which the Duke of Wellington is reputed to have said was that of cavalry in battle: to lend tone to what would otherwise be a vulgar brawl.

Those who would savour the ironies of history need to recall at this point that the whole enterprise of the Pareto criterion became central to neo-classical theory because it was thought to enable one to obtain theorems about 'welfare' without making any value-judgements.

Since those who are most devoted to the Pareto criterion see themselves as the champions of liberty—of the freedom to choose—the theorem now to be glanced at briefly is perhaps the most distressing of all to the devotees of Pareto optimality.

[1] See Hammond (1989: 216–18) and the literature cited there. I have chosen Hammond as an exemplar of the severe criticism of Pareto optimality which has been appearing within neo-classical circles in recent years. He is, by the way, a self-declared neo-classic and welfare economist (Hammond 1989: 186 n.). It should be stressed that he is by no means unique in his critical stance from within the neo-classical tradition. Happily, there is a growing band of younger mathematical economists who were never deeply infected with the anti-ethical position of those who grew up in the shadow of logical positivism, and these younger people are publishing on distributional questions involving a normative analysis. See, for example, the lengthy list of references in Sen (1987: 32 n. 3). The intellectual investment in Pareto optimality on the part of younger theorists is also much lessened as a result of some technical developments which have already been noted in Chapter 5, but should be recalled here. The original canonical Arrow–Debreu models had Pareto optimality as a central feature since they assumed completeness, transitivity, and independence, the absence of externalities (and hence implicitly self-interest), the absence of asymmetric information, of quantity constrained temporary equilibria, and so on. Many of the more recent models have equilibria which cannot be claimed to be Pareto optimal.

THE INCOMPATIBILITY OF PARETO OPTIMALITY AND LIBERTY

I now turn to the argument mentioned earlier, namely that the Pareto criterion is incompatible with the liberty of agents. In a famous paper (Sen 1970), which has led to an extensive literature, Sen argued that a conflict may exist between the Pareto principle (which gives priority to unanimity) and individual liberty (which requires that an individual be decisive over certain personal choices).

First of all we need a condition of minimal liberty—Sen refers to it as condition L (Sen [1970] 1982: 286–7). Some choices should be private to an individual (whether Tom sleeps on his back or his belly) and should be decided by that person only. Minimal liberty requires that there be at least one pair of such choices. It is clearly a very weak condition. The beauty of the impossibility theorem, however, lies precisely in how little liberty there needs to be for this to be in conflict with the Pareto criterion. Sen supposed there is a book, *Lady Chatterley's Lover*, concerning which one is to consider three possibilities: (1) the book is read by prudish A; (2) the book is read by free-thinking B; (3) the book is read by neither A nor B. We may designate these three social states: *a*, *b*, and 0. We now consider the rankings of these three states by A and B. A ranks 0 most highly, then *a* (to keep the book from impressionable B) and finally *b* (see Table 7.1). B, on the other hand, ranks *a* most highly (thinking D. H. Lawrence will give A a useful shaking up) then *b* (it will be enjoyable) and finally 0.

The 'minimal liberty' at issue in this example is the freedom of each individual to choose whether or not to read D. H. Lawrence's novel. On this one issue, then, what an individual prefers is to be

TABLE 7.1 *The rankings of A and B with respect to the reading of* Lady Chatterley's Lover: a *(A reads the novel),* b *(B reads it), and 0 (neither read it)*

A	B
0	a
a	b
b	0

socially permitted (i.e. socially preferred). Hence A is to be allowed a personal preference socially implemented, namely, not to have to read *Lady Chatterley*, so this gives us 0 socially preferred to *a*. Likewise, B is to be allowed his personal preference, which is to read the book, rather than have no one read it, so this gives us *b* socially preferred to 0. But now observe that B reading the novel, option *b*, is Pareto inferior to *a* (A having to read it). So if society follows Pareto optimal ranking we get *a* socially preferred to *b*. Hence, every alternative is worse than some other, there is no best alternative, and thus no optimal choice.

It should be noted that a simple example does not exhibit quite how minimal are the conditions needed in the formal proof. For instance, in a society with many agents, the concept of minimal liberty requires only that at least two individuals should have their personal preferences reflected in social preference over one pair of alternatives each. Any less, as Sen notes, would permit a complete dictatorship! (Sen [1970] 1982: 287.) Secondly, the Pareto principle used is a very weak version, as in Kenneth Arrow (1951*b*). This does not require that, if one agent ranks x above y and all other agents rank x as highly as y, then the society ranks x above y. The weak version requires that the society rank x above y only if every agent ranks x above y. The Pareto criterion has been regarded as an expression of individual liberty. But now it seems that in situations involving more than two alternatives 'it can have consequences that are, in fact, deeply illiberal' (Sen [1970] 1982: 290).

Given what a minimal degree of liberty was involved, it is a staggering illustration of the devotion of economic theorists to the Pareto principle that Sen has to report that many of the contributors to the discussion subsequent to his original paper 'have revealed a preference for resolving the conflict by weakening condition L rather than by weakening the Pareto principle' (Sen [1970] 1982: 294). An example of this is the typical reaction to 'meddlesome' preferences. It has been noted by several authors that the conflict between Pareto optimality and liberty arises when some preferences are 'meddlesome'. Now, as Sen rightly points out, 'libertarian values come into their own in defending personal liberty against meddling' (Sen [1970] 1982: 297). So that the existence of meddling makes these values more, rather than less important. So surely the meddling part of an agent's preferences should be ignored, and the non-meddling part protected against the meddling of others? But this would lead to an attack on that part of the agent's preferences which is embodied in the Pareto principle, and not on the part embodied in the personal rights. This, however, is typically the opposite of what Sen's critics proposed.

It should be observed at this point that through all the debate on Pareto optimality and liberty one hears again a theme which has recurred throughout the present work. The Pareto principle embodies the idea that the only information relevant to judging social states is information as to what individual preferences happen to be—which is, of course, an ordinal act utilitarian view. The present dispute is thus yet another case of the conflict between ordinal utilitarianism (or preference utilitarianism) and moral philosophies which can give due recognition to rights, goals, agency, responsibilities, and duties. The claim, characteristic of utilitarianism, that the maximal attainment of one single objective morally dominates all other moral responsibilities or rights is, as we have seen in Chapter 3, an extreme and contentious moral position. How economists supposedly devoted to 'value-free' science could support such a claim is a mystery. Yet the use made of Pareto optimality rests tacitly upon just that claim—indeed upon a notably extreme example of it, for the objective with sole warrant to attention is composed of the unexamined choices which the members of the society happen to make at a give moment. A revealed whim carries more weight than a fundamental right.

Various attempts have continued to be made to escape from the conflict between Pareto optimality and minimal rights to liberty. One such attempt consists in changing the formal context of the debate. Sen's original impossibility result had been presented as a theorem in social choice theory. Some more recent contributions have been formulated in terms of game theory. One then gets a non-co-operative game, in which each individual is free to choose his or her private component of any final outcome. But it has been argued by Jonathan Riley that 'nonexistence of equilibrium of a libertarian game is analogous to cyclical libertarian social preferences . . . In both cases, theory is unable to explain or justify a particular outcome in a situation where people by assumption enjoy freedom to choose as they most prefer' (Riley 1989: 147). It had been claimed that the social choice theory formulation was itself responsible for the Paretian paradoxes, and that these would disappear when this formulation was abandoned in favour of a number of possible game theoretic formulations. But Riley's theorems 1 and 2 show that 'a cyclical libertarian social choice foundation underlies any libertarian game' (Riley 1989: 161), where the game has the relevant properties. In neither social choice formulation nor game theory formulation does it make any sense for an agent to waive rights to liberty in private matters; on the contrary, they 'should alter their preferences rather than give up their rights to liberty' (Riley 1989: 155). Thus no escape from the paradoxes can be found simply by the transition from the formal language of social choice theory to the formal language of game theory. In the context of game theory, as Riley shows, 'Sen's Paretian libertarian problem is perhaps seen most easily as a finitely repeated [Prisoner's Dilemma] game' (Riley 1990: 38).

A different suggested line of escape has been the argument that the paradoxes could be avoided if the parties to the conflict would voluntarily waive some of their rights, actually choosing to act as if their private objectives were different from what they actually are. A well-known rights-waiving system was that proposed some time ago by Allan Gibbard (1974). This suggestion of voluntary rights waiving has been widely disputed, among others by Kaushik Basu (1984) and Kotaro Suzumura (1989). Basu, in particular, argued that, if one rules out any involuntary waiving of rights as illiberal, so that individuals 'are allowed to waive their rights voluntarily, then there is no guarantee that they will do so in a way that resolves the paradox' (Basu 1984: 413). As Riley concludes, '[t]he problem is that rationality does not dictate either cooperation or noncooperation in this situation. It simply remains ambiguous whether rational agents will and/or should choose to act cooperatively or noncooperatively ... In effect, agents may reasonably keep all their options open by refusing to waive any individual or group rights' (Riley 1990: 47).

Attempts have been made to escape this conclusion by introducing various kinds of defects in the knowledge possessed by the agents (and no one these days wants to deny that agents indeed *may* be imperfectly informed!). However, a model of 'rational' choice or action 'that counts on ignorance for being able to achieve good results, which will fail to be realized if people become better informed, has an element of perversity in it' (Sen 1987: 86).

Can one offer an ethical argument in favour of agents giving up some of their rights, granted that 'rationality' (as variously construed in economic theory) does not guarantee that this will happen? Riley sees a possible case for this in Sen's critique of 'self-goal' choice (already familiar to us from Chapter 5). If one drops the 'self-goal' property as an essential constituent of 'rational' choice, then (as Riley notes) 'sophisticated rational agents may deliberately depart from the immediate pursuit of their own goals in isolation and instead voluntarily commit themselves to follow particular social rules or strategies as instruments for achieving cooperative outcomes' (Riley 1990: 54). It should be noted that these sophisticated rational agents are waiving their personal rights because of having deliberately chosen to act as if they had prefer-ences which in fact they do not have. In effect, these agents have adopted meta-rankings. Rather evidently, however, this response will not resolve the Paretian dilemma at one stroke. Sen has reiter-ated his belief that neither rights to liberty nor Paretian judgements should always prevail. (For a recent statement of this position, see Sen 1987: 87.) So the Paretian paradox does not get a general resolution from these considerations. Riley adds the interesting point (derived from his reading of John Stuart Mill) that 'rights to liberty are essentially claims of individuals and groups to make self-goal choices *with respect to purely private goals*' (Riley 1990: 57, emphasis added). But then such rights would be an inappropriate context in which to wish to see self-goal choice overthrown. The possibly strong arguments for wanting to see self-goal choices curbed where these infringe with disastrous force on others would be absent here, and thus the case for the Paretian judgement corre-spondingly weakened. A second ethical response (noted earlier in the chapter) takes the form, essentially, of arguing that the agents should 'mind their own business'. As Riley puts it: 'a liberal agent must learn to prefer to mind her own business with respect to purely private matters, not give up her rights to liberty or rational-ize her meddlesome conduct in terms of putatively efficient social institutions' (Riley 1990: 59).[2]

Any thinker who takes seriously the claims of rights against what are indeed at best 'putatively efficient' social institutions can say no less. Thus we end our discussion of the 'rationality' claims made in regard to that wide class of models for the theory

---

[2] I received a proof copy of Sen (1995) too late to be able to comment on the discussion of liberty and Pareto optimality therein (Sen 1995: 13–15) in this book. I hope to do so on a later occasion. (Note added Jan. 1995.)

of general equilibrium known as 'Edgeworth models' on a note of sad irony: the concept of Pareto optimality was the battle flag of a tradition in economic theory which proclaimed itself the great defender of freedom to choose, of liberty. But it would appear that the Pareto criterion was an unhappy choice for that purpose.

PARETO OPTIMALITY IN MODELS WITH PRODUCTION

As was noted early in Chapter 6, no claim was made that the 'goods' exchanged in Edgeworth models had not had to be produced—their production was simply kept off stage. It is, of course, possible to bring an element of production on stage by assuming the existence in the model economy, not simply of a given supply of goods, but instead of a given supply of resources from whose services, using a given technology, certain goods could be produced. Harvey Gram and I, in a previous work (Walsh and Gram 1980: 179–268), gave an account of a simple version of such a model, which is usually described as neo-Walrasian. In a neo-Walrasian model the role of Pareto optimality, involving as it does an allocation of the given resources as well as of the commodities produced by the use of their services, is more complicated than in the Edgeworth exchange models which we have considered. The problems concerning the Pareto criterion, however, arise just as much in this more complicated context—indeed the critiques of Pareto optimality which we have been considering were constructed with precisely the more complicated context involving production in view. This is notably true of the work of Sen, Hammond, and the other theorists discussed above. I used the simple context of an elementary Edgeworth model only in order to make the discussion more available to philosophers, social scientists, and other scholars not primarily specialists in general equilibrium theory. The locus classicus of the full dress presentation of Pareto optimality was, I believe, Chapter 6 of Debreu (1959), which is called simply 'optimality'. Current critics of Pareto optimality have this analysis (and its more recent developments) in mind in their work.

Only a brief sketch will therefore be offered here of a method by which production decisions are brought explicitly on stage in a neo-classical discussion of Pareto optimality. It is standardly assumed that, in a given short period or 'elementary time interval', commodities are produced by means of the services of a set of given resources, or factors. (In a standard neo-Walrasian model, all inputs are treated similarly, as the services of given resources.) Thus, instead of amounts of commodities being assumed to be given, amounts of resource services enter into the allocation decision. The concept of Pareto optimality thus has another set of decisions to apply to: decisions about how to combine given inputs so as to produce outputs. 'Pareto efficient' production then requires (very roughly) that, with a given technology and a given supply of resource services, the outputs resulting from production satisfy conditions guaranteeing that more of one output could be produced only if less is produced of some other. Part of what is at issue can be seen by another use of the familiar Edgeworth box, shown in Figure 7.3. For present purposes, however, the sides of the box stand for the given supplies, not of goods, but of factor services. We assume for simplicity that there are two factors, (homogeneous) land and (homogeneous) labour, whose services are used to produce two commodities, wheat and rice. The origins, O_R and O_W now stand, not for individual agents, but for individual goods, to whose production the available factor services may be devoted. The indifference curves, such as I_R and I_W, also have a different interpre-

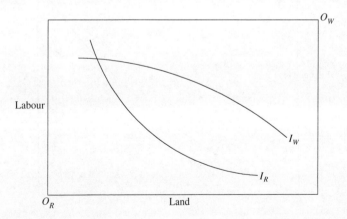

F IG. 7.3.

tation now. Consider I_R: this depicts all the possible combinations of land services and labour services which could be used to produce a given amount of rice—it is in fact the 'iso-product' curve (or 'production indifference' curve) familiar to students of microtheory. The iso-product curve I_W likewise shows the combination of land and labour services which can be used to yield a certain output of wheat. (In the real world, there might only be a finite number of ways of combining inputs to produce a given output; in this case the iso-product curves might have flat facets and corners. A simple analysis of this case can be found in Walsh and Gram 1980: 344–70.)

Now any point in the box is clearly a possible allocation of the total supply of land and labour services to producing rice and to producing wheat. Not all such allocations, however, are Pareto optimal. By analogy from the case of exchange, it will be readily seen that, in Figure 7.4 allocations x_1 and x_2 are *non*-Pareto optimal, whereas allocations x_3 and x_4 satisfy the Pareto criterion. Where a wheat iso-product curve and a rice iso-product curve intersect, more of both wheat and rice could be produced. As in the case of exchange between goods, the locus of tangencies gives us here the set of Pareto optimal input combinations.

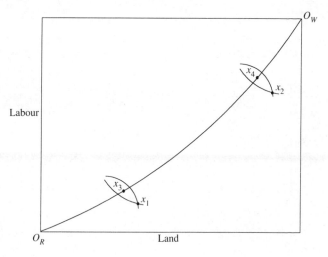

FIG. 7.4.

In standard neo-Walrasian general equilibrium models, a special category of agents is introduced to make production decisions— namely producing agents (often called 'firms'). A Pareto optimal general equilibrium in a model with production thus requires that all of an agent's decisions, those concerning production as well as those having to do with the exchange of the goods produced, satisfy the Pareto criterion. Now, at first glance, the requirements for Pareto optimal production might look (especially to the non-economist) as if they had to do with simply matters of technical efficiency—as if, so to speak, all that is questionable about the Pareto criterion derives from the vastly different positions which may be occupied by different persons under its sway in exchange and consumption. Should this appear to be so, a very little discussion will suffice to dispel this idea. Severe axioms have to be imposed on models of general equilibrium with production in order to ensure that agents in the model will not suffer untoward effects of the production processes themselves. This had been clearly seen by Pigou, famous for his distinction between the private and social costs (and benefits) of production, from whom the whole current literature on 'externalities' ultimately derives. In the development of the formal general equilibrium literature, the necessity for production axioms ruling out interaction between production processes and between such processes and agents' consumption, received an early, but classic statement in Tjalling Koopmans (1957).

To consider just one axiom, that of 'additivity', the implication of this 'is one of noninteraction between productive processes' (Koopmans 1957: 74). Koopmans notes that 'Economic literature abounds with examples of interaction, such as water or air pollution, drawing on subsoil water or oil, effect of deforestation on water runoff, etc . . . such cases constitute exceptions to the propositions about the efficiency of resource allocation through competitive markets' (Koopmans 1957: 75).

The non-economist reader with a nodding acquaintance with our globally warming, toxically polluted, and struggling planet may be forgiven for feeling that these 'exceptions' are in fact the almost universal rule. But, as Koopmans (to do him justice) pointed out long ago, the proof that even perfect competition would allocate resources Pareto optimally in an economy with production depends (among other things) on all these 'exceptions' being ruled out by prior assumption in the construction of the production axioms of the model.

This brief glance at an extremely simple model of Pareto optimal production decisions brings us to the final concern of this book, the topic of Chapters 8 and 9. There not just production, but the conditions of reproduction of certain model economies are considered, and contrasted with what has gone before. Since the equilibria in these reproduction models have not been seen by their authors as particularly reflecting the choices or actions of most of the agents in the models, the concept of methodological individualism has not normally been one of their preoccupations, nor has the concept of Pareto optimality traditionally received any attention. As we shall see towards the end of Chapter 9, however, methodological individualism and the choices of individual agents have found a place in some remarkable recent work on reproduction models.

8

SURPLUS, CLASS, AND CONFLICT IN REPRODUCTION MODELS

In this chapter I wish to consider some properties of very simplified examples of reproduction models. Although these models are of present-day construction (and can be made very formal when presented in full dress) nevertheless their preoccupation with the generation and extraction of a net product or surplus, and with the accumulation of capital, make them strikingly similar to the work of the original eighteenth- and nineteenth-century classical political economists.

These models focus upon the point that an economy, if 'productive', produces a net product (after all necessary inputs have been replaced), and on the question as to which economic class (or classes) in fact obtains this surplus, and on what is done with it. Economic classes are thus differentiated in terms of their control (or lack of control) over this surplus, and over the use made of it. Equilibrium in such models is a strictly long-period position; it need not be a chosen position, except in the case of that class (or classes) in control of the net product. Equilibrium is simply a state from which the model will not move until some force acts upon it to make it do so. Characteristically, there will be a class (or classes) with the power to effect change, should they choose to do so. The choices or actions of such a class may (or may not) exhibit rationality properties in one or another sense. No claim, however, is usually made to the effect that an equilibrium in which such a model finds itself need have any particularly rational or optimal properties that would appeal as such to most of the participants in the model. Some individual persons may be so situated that their choices or actions, taken together, have a significant impact on the model. But this will be simply because of their being members of a class with control over the surplus.

The reader should not imagine for a moment that these features of classical models imply that this tradition has no concern for individual persons. Among the great original classics, Adam Smith, both as philosopher and as economist, gave much importance to individuals—and Smith is the classic of classics. Indeed, he is beloved of methodological individualists! But Smith is also a prime source for the concepts of surplus and economic class which are formalized in today's classical models (see, for instance, Walsh and Gram 1980: 48–81).

The classical argument concerning individuals and class did not (and does not today) have to rest upon some philosophical position about individuals. It is simply that certain deeply important features of an economy's development are seen by classically oriented authors as depending upon what a particular class (or classes), which has control of the surplus, does as a class. Perhaps the clearest illustration of what is being claimed about economic class is David Ricardo's famous argument concerning the effect of the Corn Laws upon capital accumulation in Britain in the early nineteenth century. Gram and I summed up our view of Ricardo's position as follows:

Ricardo always assumed that the landlords, as a class, spent the surplus which they extracted as rent on high living, while the class of industrial capitalists, as a whole, saved the surplus they extracted as profits and devoted it to capital accumulation. In common with other classical economists, Ricardo saw the key importance in his day of economic development. And the pace of development depended, on his assumptions, upon how the surplus was distributed between the landlords and capitalists. Workers, in any event, got a subsistence wage, but it need not be bare physical subsistence, and might be expected to be higher in a growing economy. (Walsh and Gram 1980: 86)

Ricardo had reason to be aware that some individuals might be both capitalists and landlords—he was a capitalist, and became a landlord! He knew that some individual landlords did not behave with the profligacy characteristic of their class. But the point of his argument was not destroyed by isolated exceptions. The Corn Laws (restricting the import of grain) had been passed by a Parliament of which both houses were dominated by landlords, and with population growth farmers were bringing even barren hillsides into cultivation. Naturally the price of corn rose, yielding soaring rents to the owners of the better lands and raising the money cost of a subsistence wage. Profits fell, rents rose, and the surplus was being redistributed from the capitalist class, who (by and large) would use it for the accumulation of capital, to the landlord class, who (by and large) would spend it on luxuries. Hence Ricardo argued with all his strength until his death in 1823 for the repeal of the Corn Laws. But the landlord interest fought this successfully until forced by the Irish famine to give in in 1846.

The final repeal of the Corn Laws broke the separate power base of the landlord class in Britain, and classically oriented writers, after the mid-nineteenth century, have not felt the necessity for a separate landlord class in modelling the British and other developed economies. (Even the simplest model intended to be relevant to third world economies such as those of Central and South America, however, would require a separate landlord class.) In the developed world by the latter part of the nineteenth century, the working class had come on stage as a major participant, and was beginning its struggle for power over the distribution of the surplus. Thus in simple models we find a two-class structure, involving capitalists and workers. With the twentieth century, revolution replaced the capitalist class in Russia, Eastern Europe, China, and elsewhere with a significantly new class of state bureaucrats. Conditions in Eastern Europe and the former Soviet Union have now become propitious for the construction of models explaining the rise and decline of a class of state bureaucrats. Russian and Eastern European thinkers have a classical task to perform (among many others!), namely to construct models which lay bare the role which was played by the state bureaucratic class in extracting the surplus, and diverting it to the ends of that class, and away from the needs of the economy as a whole. Let us hope that no scruples (newly acquired from neo-classical theory) of a methodological individualist nature stand in the way of such work.

A second characteristic of classical thought may now be becoming noticeable. Where there are economic classes, there are likely to be struggles for power, so classical writings, both ancient and present day, give an important role to power and to conflict of interest. These concepts were hardly unknown to Edgeworth, and we have seen his elegant argument that economic power would diminish as the number of agents increased towards what he called 'the practically infinite'. Standard neo-Walrasian general equilibrium models, however, were originally constructed on the basis of

the assumption of perfect competition, where (in the most sophisticated versions), an individual agent has zero economic power;
furthermore, these models (unlike Edgeworth's) gave no role to
any concept of coalitions of agents acting together in defence of
shared interests. Canonical Arrow–Debreu models thus made no
use of the concept of economic class. On the other hand, since the
'individual' agent could be a large corporation (provided it acted
like a perfect competitor!) or a consumer, interpreted as a 'larger
group with a common purpose', it was not totally clear on what
criteria methodological individualism, as it was being practised,
could rule out one of these agents being an economic class.

Recently, of course, models of temporary equilibrium have been
appearing, constructed by classically oriented as well as by neo-
classical authors. Here, agents are allowed to be big enough to be
monopolistic and to fix prices. But these models are not yet sufficiently developed for one to predict whether they will bring classical and neo-classical theory closer together.

What may be somewhat unexpected, perhaps, is that present-day
classical models have on occasion assumed perfect competition,
something fundamentally different from competition in the original classics. The structure of these classical models, however, is
still such as to give an analytical role to at least two economic
classes, and economic power to at least one. (Recently classical
models have begun to be developed, as already noted, where individual producers have economic power and some properties remi-
niscent of monopolistic competitors.)

I turn to the role of conflict. Clearly, conflict was at an all-time
minimum in a canonical neo-Walrasian model, a property of such
models which has led some sceptical minds to accuse them of rather
Panglossian harmonies—as noted recently by Helen Boss (Boss
1990). On the other hand, conflict plays a varying role in classical
writings. The most famous case of a great original classical author
whose work strives to demonstrate the possibility of a remarkable
degree of harmony was surely Adam Smith. Two points need to be
noted, however, about Smith's argument for the existence of harmony. First of all, it addressed quite strictly the conditions of
Smith's own period. A capitalist class was struggling to emerge in
Britain, composed for the most part of numerous small individual
capitalists, each possessing little or no monopoly power and devoting most of their profits to the accumulation of capital. To absorb

the masses which would be driven from the land by the last excesses of the enclosure movement and the hand-loom weavers and spinners who would be ruined by the advent of machinery, the overwhelming need would be for capital accumulation. Smith was right to see a harmony here. His little, struggling, highly competitive capitalists with their insatiable appetite for growth were indeed performing what Marx was later to regard as the historic role of the bourgeoisie.

Secondly, there is plenty of evidence in his work that even in his own day, Smith did not see the harmony as universal. When in an early draft of the *Wealth of Nations* he turns from supporting the right of his little capitalists to be freed from archaic mercantilist restrictions and begins to consider that 'slothful and oppressive profusion of the great' already noted in Chapter 5, a bitter disdain shows unmistakably. His opinion of monopolies, and in particular of the great trading monopolies, such as the East India Company, is too well known to require quotation. Smith knew only trading companies, but one can form a reasonable guess as to what his opinion of giant multinational corporations engaging in production as well as trade might be. As I remarked on a previous occasion, 'The rich are charged with what for Smith, as for any classical political economist, is the unforgivable sin: *squandering the surplus*. He never becomes reconciled to this; he tolerates it insofar as he does, only as a necessary evil whose existence is implied by the system of natural liberty, which he saw as required for maximum accumulation' (Walsh 1987*b*: 865, emphasis in original).

If Smith represents the high point of a belief in the possibility of harmony in the original classics, Karl Marx surely represents the opposite. In making this comparison, I am regarding Marx's work in economics, as Gram and I did (Walsh and Gram 1980: 104–15), as the last great nineteenth-century contribution to the classical tradition. Again, however, one needs to take into account his period of history. As a young man he lived through what Joan Robinson used to call the 'ferocious forties'. The bright dawn of the industrial revolution was long past. The worst savageries of the uncontrolled factory system were everywhere on display, and the arrival of serious reforms in its structure were still in the future. Even more important, perhaps—especially later in the century— the capitalist class had lost the progressive role it had in Smith's day (and even in Ricardo's), and Britain wallowed in a sea of luxury and bad taste which all the current craze for things Victorian should not make us forget. An important feature of Marx's work which helps to give the conflict of classes its stark simplicity, is that he keeps the landlord class off-stage during most of his mature work on economics. Their distinct economic power base had been broken by the repeal of the corn laws as we have noted: the real action was therefore between capitalists and workers.

The highly dramatic quality of Marx's better-known work has tended to mislead some of those less well acquainted with the history of classical economics into assuming that an analysis where the conflict of classes plays a vital role will necessarily be the work of a thinker on the political left. But consider the remarkable case of Ricardo, where the conflict between capitalists and landlords was a crucial part of his analysis, yet Ricardo was notably free of political bias, whether of the right or left. As Marx has noted: 'Ricardo's conception is, on the whole, in the interests of the *industrial bourgeoisie*, only *because*, and *insofar as*, their interests coincide with that of production or the productive development of human labor. Where the bourgeoisie comes into conflict with this, he is just as *ruthless* towards it as he is at other times towards the proletariat and the aristocracy' (Marx [1959] 1968: 118, emphasis in original). What was important for Ricardo was the analytical role of capitalist and landlord classes in generating, distributing, and accumulating the surplus.

If we are to appraise the significance of the form which classical ideas have assumed in the models which have been developed during the twentieth-century revival of this tradition, some fairly technical analysis is unavoidable. What is more, it is of a kind which a reader whose acquaintance with economic theory does not include graduate work may not have met before. At least a sketch of the simplest present-day classical models must therefore be offered here. Fortunately, the special characteristics of these models show up very well in their simplest formulations—their characteristic flavour, as it were, is quite distinctive. On the other hand, the non-economist reader should perhaps be warned that these simple models, because of their very simplicity, may make the issues they depict appear more sharply defined than in fact they are. Later interpretations and qualifications will therefore be necessary. Be that as it may, however, one certainly needs to begin with the simple cases.

THE SIMPLEST CLASSICAL REPRODUCTION STRUCTURES

Somewhat paradoxically, it has been found easiest to approach the understanding of the reproduction of capital by beginning with an economy so simple that capital plays no role. In this model, production takes place, but no capital goods—that is to say produced means of production—are used. Imagine an economy so simple that all production takes place within one time period, or 'week', and neither for consumption nor further production can any goods be stored beyond the 'week' in which they appear. Describing such a model of production without capital, Christopher Bliss has noted that: 'There will be factors of production, labour and land, which persist from one week to the next, but the services which these provide, which is what matters here, will be provided in one particular week, and cannot be stored until another' (Bliss 1975: 15–16).

Bliss also rules out the existence of paper assets or a monetary medium, since these could be used to link up one 'week' with another. It then follows that 'Each week in the history of our economy is a separate and distinct interlude whose outcome can be determined independently of what has gone before and of what will follow' (Bliss 1975: 16).

The detailed requirements for such a model are very stringent, but for present purposes it will suffice to note one or two examples of these requirements here. First of all, the land must not become exhausted from use, and must not need fertilizer to maintain or increase its fertility, otherwise capital has entered the picture. Again, if seed were stored from one week to the next, a capital good would be in use. Perhaps the task of labour, working upon the land, consists in clearing away weeds so that wild wheat can grow. No amount of ingenuity can give this model an appealing degree of reality—nor is realism its function. Its function is to set the stage for the entry of capital goods upon the scene.

A very natural (and highly traditional) way of allowing capital goods to make their appearance is to relax the requirement that seed cannot be stored. We then have a model with a produced capital good. In fact, this is the simplest case of a capital using economy, the one-sector corn model. Of course a model in which the only thing produced is corn and the only produced input is corn can lay no claims to realism—it is much too sparse a model for that—but, again, that is not what is required of it. What the corn model *can* do, is to exhibit, in a clear and striking manner, some of the fundamental concepts of classical analysis, both ancient and contemporary.

Consider, then, a highly simplified economy where the only thing produced is corn. Suppose that land of uniform quality is freely available, and that labour of uniform quality is available in return for corn, so that the only costly input into production is corn. Corn is used to feed the cultivators, and also as seed. There are no iron plows—for the moment. Corn is supposed to be cultivated by hand, or with pieces of stick picked up at random. Shortly I shall introduce an 'iron' sector, but for the moment we must rule out all inputs other than corn. Now suppose that, to simplify matters, there is no choice of technique, and returns to scale are constant. A certain fraction of a unit of corn is then needed to produce a unit of corn, irrespective of the number of units produced. We write this per unit input requirement a_{cc}. Writing Y_C for the gross output of corn, it follows that the product $a_{cc}Y_C$ is the total input requirement needed for a total output of Y_C units of corn. We can now state the viability condition for the corn economy:

$$Y_C - a_{cc}Y_C \geq 0 \tag{1}$$

Or, to state the condition in per unit terms:

$$1 - a_{cc} \geq 0 \tag{1'}$$

The inequality (1) states that, for any level of output Y_C, the input of corn must not exceed the output produced. Inequality (1′) states the viability condition with reference to a unit level of output. A strict inequality in (1) or (1′) means that a surplus or net product exists, whereas a strict equality entails a zero surplus—the economy is then said to be barely viable. In the corn model, surplus is very concrete. It is simply a quantity of corn: $Y_C - a_{cc}Y_C$. The accumulation of capital, in classical models from the simplest to the most complex, depends on the existence of a surplus or net product not needed merely to keep the economy running at the same level. Simple as this one-sector model is, a number of the most fundamental concepts of all models of this type can be illustrated by its use.

To begin with, we can see why present-day classical models are known as commodity reproduction models, or reproduction structures. The only commodity in the simple one-sector classical model, namely corn, is produced by means of corn. More generally, in a classical model, at least one output is also an input into the reproduction of the economy—and this is made an explicit feature of such a model. In standard neo-Walrasian models, on the contrary, all inputs are treated indifferently as the services of a set of given resources. (The resources are owned by households, who derive income from renting their services.) In Bliss's model of production without capital, treating all inputs as the services of given resources is indeed perfectly correct. But in a model where there is even one produced capital good, such as seed, this must be distinguished from resource services if the latter also enter into production (resource services are eliminated by assumption in the simple corn model). Failure to make this distinction prevents a clear light from being cast upon the nature of capital and on the conditions of its reproduction. It should be noted that Bliss is careful to maintain this distinction between produced capital goods and resource services in his capital using models (Bliss 1975: 61–91).

The concept of viability, which is illustrated in its simplest case in the corn model, is without any clear meaning in a model where the only inputs are one kind of object (resource services) and the only outputs are a different kind of object (goods for final consumption). One cannot subtract objects of one kind from objects of another, as one can subtract necessary corn input from corn output in order to establish the viability (or non-viability) of a model economy. The same is true of the concept of net product or surplus, since this is defined in terms of the existence of a more than just viable reproduction structure. This concept of surplus which lies at the core of present-day classical models was also at the core of the original classics, from the work of Sir William Petty (1623–87) onwards (see Walsh and Gram 1980: 19–115).

Just as we can use the simple one-sector corn model to illustrate the very general concepts of viability and surplus, we can also use it to illustrate the concept of subsistence. The input coefficient a_{cc} is made up of the technically determined quantity of corn needed as seed for per unit output, plus the subsistence requirement of the cultivators, also for per unit output. In the corn model, subsistence is simply a quantity of corn, which is pretty dull fare! But in more complicated classical models (models with more sectors), subsistence is a vector of commodities which can contain everything needful for any customary standard of life. The subsistence wage is treated as a datum in the simplest such models, since this yields a clear concept of surplus. Classical models have been constructed in the present century in which the wage is treated as an unknown. In the simple one- or two-sector models we shall consider in this chapter, however, the subsistence wage will always be subsumed in the input coefficients.

Now that the necessary elements in per unit input (seed and subsistence) are specified, we may turn our attention to the net product. As Gram and I noted, the existence of a surplus in this strictly physical sense was 'clearly a necessary prerequisite for the extraction of surplus in the sense of capitalist "profit". The latter demands, in addition, the development of appropriate technical and social relationships for the extraction of the surplus by a social class which owns the means of production and purchases labor-power in return for subsistence' (Walsh and Gram 1980: 13–14).

In our little one-sector model, the only costly input is corn (for subsistence as well as seed) so the 'capitalist' class owns the stock of corn, and uses some of it to hire labor, and some to provide seed. After the needs of reproduction have been met, the net product can be divided by the corn capitalists in any desired proportion between luxury consumption and the accumulation of capital. (Since land is assumed to be freely available, and labour is available in return for subsistence.) Note that the existence of a class not engaged in cultivation implies the existence of a physical surplus. The original classical economists such as Smith and Ricardo were always concerned with economies which yielded a positive net product or surplus: indeed, the enormous productive power of capitalist production was the overwhelmingly visible fact of the period of history in which they wrote. For the classics, the most important economic issue was the allocation of surplus output. The surplus could be allocated to luxury consumption, and the economy would stagnate in the long run, or it could be allocated to increased production: to the accumulation of capital. Growth was the supreme concern of the classics.

Even in the one-sector model we can show the trade-off between luxury consumption and growth. Surplus can be used to support servants, musicians, harlots, priests, soldiers, and others. Or it can be used to accumulate a larger stock of corn to be used as input so that a larger crop can be planted and a larger work-force maintained during the next growing season. For the original classics the accumulation of capital meant that more of those who were born would live. First let us introduce the surplus as a whole, and then see how it may be disaggregated into luxury consumption on the one hand and growth on the other. If we write R_C for the rate of surplus in corn, taken as a whole, we can set out the single quantity relation of the one-sector model as an equation:

$$a_{cc}Y_C (1 + R_C) = Y_C \qquad (2)$$

The trade-off between luxury consumption and growth may then be treated formally by introducing a rate of accumulation g and a fraction of the gross output consumed (over and above subsistence), written λ_C. Assuming that g and λ_C between them absorb the total surplus, we may write the quantity relation of the one-sector corn model as:

$$a_{cc}Y_C (1 + g) = (1 - \lambda_C)Y_C \qquad (3)$$

It should be noted that R and g are both expressed as fractions of the total (corn) capital invested in output $a_{cc}Y_C$, whereas λ is here expressed as a fraction of total output, Y_C. It should also be observed that the extent to which we choose to disaggregate the surplus will depend on the purpose for which we wish to use a particular model.

THE TWO-SECTOR MODEL

Classical models for the theory of general equilibrium are remarkable for the fact that even the one-sector version exhibits in a nontrivial way a number of key concepts: viability, subsistence, surplus, economic class, and the luxury consumption–growth trade-off. Further development of these ideas, however, requires as a minimum the two-sector model. To achieve this, we must add to our little corn model an industrial or manufacturing sector, which I shall call for brevity the 'iron' sector. (The extraction of ores from nature was traditionally treated by the original classics as part of agriculture, so I have in mind a manufacturing sector.) Certain properties of this technology must now be made clear. The original classics, being in Northern Europe, treated the period of production as a *year*, since this was true of the agriculture they were used to. Clearly, there is no reason why the same period of production should apply to industry, but for simplicity I shall suppose that it

does. Our 'year', however, will just be the designation of one production period in our simple model. Clearly corn may either be
consumed in the 'year' after it is harvested, or planted as seed for
the next 'year's' harvest. Iron machines, on the other hand, might
last a long time. Logically, there are three possible assumptions
about machines. One may suppose that they last forever (this has
been assumed, and found of use in certain models). Or one may
suppose that they wear out over a series of 'years', in which case
one treats used machines as a 'joint product'; in a given year, the
iron sector produces so many new and so many used machines
while the corn sector produces corn and so many used machines.
This was done by John von Neumann ([1937] 1945–6) and Piero
Sraffa (1960), and has been further developed in recent years by a
number of others. Finally, one may suppose that all industrial
goods (including machines) wear out completely and must be replaced at the end of one period of production, one 'year'. Purely for
simplicity, and because it will do for our purposes, I shall take the
latter option. In the simple classical models in this chapter the
output of the 'iron' sector will be supposed to last only one period
of production.

Bearing this in mind, we may turn to the examination of the
technology of our two-sector model. It is naturally more complicated than the corn model, since now iron as well as corn is being
produced and used in iron and in corn production. For simplicity,
and since it is quite adequate for our purposes, I wish to treat our
sectors as single product industries.[1] Again, for the sake of simplicity, I wish to stay within the confines of the two-sector model.
This requires that we suppose that the iron sector produces a single
manufactured article, which can be used as an input in both agriculture and manufacturing, and as an item of domestic consumption.
It will be seen that, although the two-sector model is less stark than
the one-sector, it is still so simplified that it cannot be made very
cozy or realistic. Fortunately, in respect of those properties of the
model with which we shall be concerned, the two-sector model is
robust to expansion to an arbitrary finite number of sectors. Thus,

---

[1] Many productive processes necessarily yield more than a single product—the
standard example being the raising of sheep, which produces both wool and mutton.
Such processes are known in the literature as 'genuine' joint production, to distinguish them from the treatment of used machines as 'joint products' of, say, the
production of corn. 'Genuine' joint production has been extensively studied in
recent years: see, for example, the contributions to a volume edited by Luigi
Pasinetti (1980). For a historical treatment, see Kurz 1986.

if one tires of the simple 'manufactured article', it can be supposed that there is a sector producing combine harvesters for agriculture, a sector producing machines for manufacturing, and a sector producing stoves for consumption, in addition to the corn sector.

Returning to the two-sector model, and referring to our single manufactured output simply as 'iron', we write a_{IC} for the per unit 'iron' input into corn. We likewise assume that there is a per unit input of iron implements into iron production: the amount of iron to produce a unit of iron, written a_{II}. Naturally, there must be an input of corn into the iron sector (to feed the iron workers) written in per unit terms as a_{CI}. And finally we still need the per unit input of corn into the agricultural sector, for seed and to feed the agricultural workers. As for gross outputs, we already have the symbol Y_C for total corn output, we now add Y_I for total industrial output. Viability is now more complicated. The two-sector economy is viable if and only if:

Total necessary corn for corn production + total necessary corn for iron production ≤ total corn output   AND
Total necessary iron for corn production + total necessary iron for iron production ≤ total iron output

More formally:

$$a_{CC}Y_C + a_{CI}Y_I \leq Y_C \qquad (4)$$

$$a_{IC}Y_C + a_{II}Y_I \leq Y_C \qquad (5)$$

Observe that the viability condition for the two-sector model is essentially more complex because both (4) and (5) must be satisfied for the economy to be viable. Assuming that the economy *is* viable, and further that surplus is generated in both sectors, we may transform (4) and (5) into equations by introducing the rate of surplus in corn, R_C and the rate of surplus in iron R_I:

$$(a_{CC}Y_C + a_{CI}Y_I)(1 + R_C) = Y_C \qquad (6)$$

$$(a_{IC}Y_C + a_{II}Y_I)(1 + R_I) = Y_I \qquad (7)$$

And, as in the one-sector model, we can disaggregate the surplus to show the luxury consumption/growth trade-off. In a simple model of this type, equilibrium growth is balanced—i.e. in equilibrium, every component of the commodity means of production is growing at the same rate, g. We may then write the quantity equations of the two-sector model of surplus and accumulation:

$$(a_{CC}Y_C + a_{CI}Y_I)(1 + g) = (1 - \lambda_C)Y_C \qquad (8)$$

$$(a_{IC}Y_C + a_{II}Y_I)(1 + g) = (1 - \lambda_I)Y_I \qquad (9)$$

Note that the rates of surplus (R_C and R_I) need not be equal, even in the case of balanced growth, if λ_C and λ_I are different. This leads us to the important question of how the surplus is allocated.

In a strictly interpreted neo-Walrasian model, it will be recalled, what are allocated are the services of given resources. A commodity (say rice) need not be produced at all in that model if households do not want any of it. This is because in such a neo-Walrasian model, commodities are not explicitly treated as part of a reproduction structure, which would not be viable if certain amounts of each commodity were not repeatedly forthcoming. In a classical model, on the contrary, even if no corn is wanted as a luxury, enough must be produced to keep the system viable. Likewise, at least enough iron must be produced to satisfy the iron needs of the corn sector and the iron needs of the iron sector. Given that the input needs of the system are met, however, the surplus can be taken all in corn, or all in iron, or in any mixture of the two. Suppose the economy is so devoted to riotous living that it takes the whole surplus for luxury consumption, and furthermore uses only corn for this. The quantity relations then become:

$$a_{CC}Y_C + a_{CI}Y_I = (1 - \lambda_C)Y_C \qquad (10)$$

$$a_{IC}Y_I + a_{II}Y_I = Y_I \qquad (11)$$

Bismarck, on the other hand, might have wanted to take the whole surplus as iron (at least for a period) if we allow our manufactured article to be also usable as a weapon (war weapons can be a form of luxury consumption!). This illustrates the case where the corn sector is run only for viability. Finally, consider the case of maximum balanced growth, where no luxury consumption takes place (λ_C and λ_I are both zero). So we write the quantity equations as:

$$(a_{CC}Y_C + a_{CI}Y_I)(1 + g) = Y_C \qquad (12)$$

$$(a_{IC}Y_C + a_{II}Y_I)(1 + g) = Y_I \qquad (13)$$

Here the economy is growing by the same proportion in each sector. The ratio of gross outputs is equal to the ratio of inputs and therefore to the ratio of net outputs. It should be noted that this form of modelling leads to certain commodities being given, as it were, a special status. This was true even for the eighteenth- and nineteenth-century classics, who were concerned to distinguish between what they called 'necessaries' and 'luxuries', but the distinction became part of a formal model in the work of Sraffa (1960: 7–8). In Sraffa, when a commodity is needed either directly or indirectly in the production of every commodity (as is the case with our corn and iron), it is said to be a basic commodity. A non-basic is a commodity which may be a necessary input into its own production, but is not (directly or indirectly) a necessary input into all commodities. Clearly a model is a commodity reproduction structure (as I have been using the term) if and only if it contains at least one basic commodity. The input–output system composed of all the basics in the model is the technology which is vital to the model economy's viability. I have been treating luxury consumption simply as a quantity of corn (or iron) devoted to luxury, but instead one can introduce specific sectors, each using corn and iron, and producing some luxury good. Consider the simple case where a single non-basic sector exists, producing a luxury good X by means of corn and iron, and where the whole surplus is devoted to this good. Let a_{cX} and a_{IX} be the corn and iron required per unit of output of the luxury. Then we get:

$$a_{cc}Y_c + a_{cI}Y_I + a_{cX}Y_X = Y_c \tag{14}$$

$$a_{Ic}Y_c + a_{II}Y_I + a_{IX}Y_X = Y_I \tag{15}$$

If we introduce a rate of growth, this will reduce the output, Y_X, of the non-basic. In maximum balanced growth, the surplus is all being used for growth and the output of the luxury sector is necessarily zero—only basic commodities are produced, leaving just the reproduction structure in corn and iron.

It should have become clear from the discussion of the last few pages that in a simple commodity reproduction model with neither choice of technique nor any technical change, every different output mix must imply the existence of a different input mix. The model depicted in equations (10) and (11), for example, is not turning out corn and iron in the proportions needed for the balanced growth depicted in equations (12) and (13). Every different combination of corn and iron in output implies a different combination of corn and iron in input—implies, in other words, a different structure in the capital stock. This is in sharp contrast to the neo-Walrasian model, where inputs are treated as data of the model, and are assumed to be given.

In a classical model, inputs and outputs are both unknowns, determined by the solution to the model. To borrow an image used by Joan Robinson, each different mix of corn and iron (in inputs and therefore outputs) defines the input/output structure of a separate identical island (possessed of the same technology, including subsistence) which has chosen a different composition of surplus output (and therefore of inputs). To speak of 'movement' or 'change' is very misleading in the present context, since it implies going out of one equilibrium and 'getting into' another equilibrium. The models we are considering in this chapter are strictly models of long-period equilibrium, and tell us nothing about the possibility, much less the manner, of getting into such a condition. Recently, classical models have begun to be constructed which attempt the analysis of a process of gravitation towards long-period equilibrium, and something will be said about the implications of this in Chapter 9. For the moment we leave the quantity system of the corn and iron model, and turn to its price system.

THE DUAL PRICE RELATIONS

In a model for the theory of general equilibrium, certain properties of the quantity system are reflected in a system of relative prices (in the formal literature, the price system is said to be 'dual' to the quantity system). This is certainly true of classical models, as we shall now see. The price relations of the model go some way to adding body to the stark input–output conditions upon which we have been concentrating our attention so far.

The quantity system which we have been analysing states the interdependent reproduction conditions for an at least viable classical model. These are technical input–output requirements, however, and tell us little about the social structure of the economy. Luxury consumption out of surplus was identified, but this might be by state bureaucrats, capitalists consuming part of their profits, or even the workers themselves. The growth fraction *g* might likewise be the decision of bureaucrats, capitalists, or workers' councils, depending on the nature of the society. Once one allows for reproducible inputs, however, and thus the concept of surplus becomes defined, some arrangement must be posited for its allocation. In a market economy, it follows immediately that there must be certain categories of income that correspond to the surplus. This is simply a consequence of duality between quantity and price relations in a general equilibrium model of the classical type.

Among the great eighteenth- and nineteenth-century classics, profit on capital stock and rent of land were the two categories of income from surplus. Smith and Ricardo conducted their analyses in terms of three great income classes: capitalists and landlords who divided the income from the net product between them, and workers who received a customary subsistence. In Ricardo's day there were reasons why landowners were an analytically distinct and important economic class and, as noted earlier, Ricardo showed that their interest was sharply opposed to that of other classes, especially to that of the capitalist class whose profits declined as rents rose. Again, as already noted, in a present-day classical model of a developed economic system, rent as a distinct part of the surplus is not normally of key importance to the structure of the model, and so landlords as an analytically distinct class making distinct choices do not usually need to be distinguished.

It should now be clear that, in a simple classical model, 'class' is a strictly analytical category, defined in terms of the structural components of the reproduction system. Capitalists are exactly those who receive profits (the dual of surplus in the price relations, as we shall see). Workers are exactly those who receive a customary subsistence from the wage embedded in the technology. In more complicated models, where workers receive, in addition to subsistence, part of the surplus, then capitalists (or state bureaucrats) must be defined in terms of their control of the capital stock and their power to make choices which determine the rate of growth. In the eighteenth and nineteenth centuries, as the reader of economic and social history and indeed of novels of the relevant period will know, economic class was reflected rather accurately in social class. A landlord spoke, dressed, and behaved in certain characteristic ways, and a capitalist in certain quite different ways. A worker, again, was visibly that. Nowadays, on the other hand, social class (in the sense of the sociologist or gossip columnist) is no reliable guide to economic class. It is with economic class, in the abstract and simplified sense already specified, that present-day classical models are concerned.

In the simplest models, one can get by with just two classes, capitalists and workers. An equally simple model of a planned economy would require state bureaucrats and workers. It should be obvious, however, that any model with pretensions to approaching real world complexity would require more classes, just as it would require many more sectors. More classes have been introduced by, for example, Edward J. Nell (1989: 323–43). In the present simple analysis of income distribution and prices in a minimally complicated classical model, however, our capitalists are assumed, both to own the stock of capital (from which they collect the surplus) and to act as entrepreneurs. There is no separation of ownership and management. Workers, likewise, are assumed to supply homogeneous labour—an enormous simplification.

The original classics, notably Smith and Ricardo, believed that in a real world economy there would be a tendency for profit rates to approach equality across sectors. Twentieth-century classical reproduction models have transformed this tendency into a condition of long-period equilibrium. (Recent models, which go beyond the depiction of steady state or balanced growth, have modified this condition to some extent as will be noted later.) This characteristic of classical prices—that they embody a uniform intersectorial rate of profits—is crucial to their role as prices consistent with the long-period reproduction of the system and to the model's explanation of the allocation of surplus output and of capital goods designed for replacement of used-up inputs.

Relative prices cannot appear non-trivially in the one-sector corn model, since the price of a unit of corn is 1 in terms of itself. The duality between surplus and profit, however, takes its simplest and clearest form in the one-sector model. Consider a one-sector corn model with a positive rate of surplus R. Its single quantity equation is of course:

$$a_{cc}Y_C (1 + R) = Y_C \qquad (16)$$

Now set the total output of corn Y_C equal to 1. Equation 16' then becomes:

$$a_{cc} (1 + R) = 1 \qquad (16')$$

It is now easy to see that the rate of profit, written r, on an investment of corn is then identical with the physical rate of surplus R: the ratio of net output to the stock of corn. Here the role of duality in a present-day classical model is exhibited in its simplest form. To see this, one writes down the single price equation for the one-sector model, introducing rather artificially an indeterminate, nominal price for corn of P_C:

$$P_C a_{CC} (1 + r) = P_C \tag{17}$$

or
$$a_{CC} (1 + r) = 1 \tag{17'}$$

The cost of replacing the means of production ($P_C a_{CC}$ in nominal terms or a_{CC} in terms of corn), plus the rate of profit on the value of this capital investment ($r P_{CC} a_{CC}$ in nominal terms or $r a_{CC}$ in terms of corn), is just equal to the price of corn, P_C or 1 in terms of the commodity itself. The rate of profit is thus a variable determined by technology (which includes the subsistence requirements of labour), while P_C is simply an indeterminate nominal price which cancels out on both sides of (17). In a corn model the rate of profit is a ratio of physically homogeneous quantities: the ratio of net corn output to the stock of corn used up during the period of production.

An important relationship between the rate of profit and the allocation of the surplus is now easy to see. Since (in the subsistence wage model) the rate of profit is determined by the technology alone, it follows that the rate of profit is independent of whether the surplus is used for accumulation of capital, g, or for luxury consumption, λ_C. Furthermore, where $\lambda_C = 0$, the rate of profit equals the rate of growth which is then the maximum rate of growth, g max. In any simple classical model with a subsistence wage, the rate of profit equals the maximum rate of growth. Thus the rate of profit is independent of the conditions of production of non-basic commodities, and depends only on the technology for the reproduction of basic commodities, which here means simply corn.

If we now turn to a model of two (or more) sectors, we find that, in general, in such models we cannot define the rate of profit as a ratio of homogeneous quantities—a physical ratio of surplus corn to corn used up. There is now a necessary input of both iron and corn in each sector, so that the capital stock is now a heterogeneous bundle of commodities which cannot simply be added up, since corn and iron have different units of measurement. If the rate of profit is to be expressed as a ratio of surplus to stock, we need to know the relative prices of the components (corn and iron) of the stock. Only then can we add the value of the iron used in production to the value of the corn used, obtaining the total value of the stock used up in a given sector. Then surplus in a sector can be measured in terms of the units of capital, thereby determining a percentage rate of profit.[2]

In a two-commodity model there is one rate of exchange, which may be expressed as the iron price of corn, P_C/P_I, or as the corn price of iron, P_I/P_C. It is this ratio which we need to know in order to measure the stock of capital in each sector, either as a quantity of corn or as a quantity of iron. We again introduce nominal prices and then choose one commodity as numeraire, in this model, iron. The price equations of the two-sector modern classical model then are:

$$(P_C a_{CC} + P_I a_{IC})(1 + r) = P_C \tag{18}$$

$$(P_C a_{CI} + P_I a_{II})(1 + r) = P_I \tag{19}$$

The ratio of profit to the value of the capital stock used up, r, is uniform across sectors on the assumption that capitalists cannot be in equilibrium (in a chosen position) if they are in a sector where they are making a lower rate of profit than can be made in another sector. Capitalists are thus assumed to be unsatiated, either with growth or with luxury consumption, or with some combination of both. The classical analysis of profits was largely developed by Adam Smith,[3] and has been a characteristic feature of classical

[2] In our present simple model, where a subsistence wage is embedded in the technology, the rate of profit necessarily equals the maximum rate of growth, and so can be discovered if one knows the technology. In the general case, however, where the wage is allowed to be variable and the surplus is divided in some proportion between wages and profits, the maximum rate of growth only equals the maximum rate of profit which, for a given wage/profit trade-off, may not be the ruling rate of profit. Then one indeed must know relative prices to determine the rate of profit. The paragraph in the main text before this note was written to cover the general case.

[3] The concept of a net product or surplus arising throughout industry (and not just in agriculture), and thus the dual concept of a rate of profit tending towards equality across all sectors, was indeed truly the achievement of Smith (see Walsh and Gram 1980: 40–77), but in fact Richard Cantillon (1697–1734) did reach the concept of a uniform rate of profit across all those (agricultural) sectors—where he saw the extraction of a surplus. As I noted some years ago 'the extraction of surplus, and its reflection in a uniform intersectorial rate of profit, is certainly understood by Cantillon for those sectors where capitalist production relations were firmly established in his period' (Walsh 1987c: 319).

models ever since. In a remarkable passage, Smith defined exactly what he meant by profits:

The profits of stock, it may perhaps be thought, are only a different name for the wages of a particular sort of labour, of inspection and direction. They are, however, altogether different, are regulated by quite different principles, and bear no proportion to the quantity, the hardship, or the ingenuity of this supposed labour of inspection and direction. They are regulated altogether by the value of the stock employed, and are greater or smaller in proportion to the extent of this stock. (Smith [1776] 1976: i. 66)

This is exactly what profits are in equations (18) and (19). On the uniformity of profits between sectors, Smith wrote:

The whole of the advantages and disadvantages of the different employ-ments of labour and stock must, in the same neighborhood, be either perfectly equal or continually tending to equality. If in the same neighbor-hood, there was any employment evidently either more or less advan-tageous than the rest so many people would crowd into it in the one case, and so many would desert it in the other, that its advantages would soon return to the level of other employments. (Smith [1776] 1976: i. 116)

Smith writes in a number of passages in such a way that the present-day reader can hardly resist the conclusion that he is de-scribing the uniform rate of profit as being what we would now-adays call a long-run equilibrium concept. In the short run, all sorts of windfall gains (and losses!) may be made in a real economy. The precise condition for a long-run equilibrium in a simple classical model, however, is just the existence of a uniform rate of profit. Smith wrote, for instance:

The establishment of any new manufacture, or any new branch of com-merce, or of any new practice in agriculture, is always a speculation, from which the projector promises himself extraordinary profits. These profits sometimes are very great, and sometimes, more frequently perhaps, they are quite otherwise; but in general they bear no regular proportion to those of other trades in the neighborhood. If the project succeeds they are commonly at first very high. When the trade or practice becomes thoroughly established and well known, the competition reduces them to the level of other trades. (Smith [1776] 1976: i. 131–2)

One aspect of Smith's analysis, however, is missing from our simple classical model. It is evident from the passages quoted that for Smith the long-period equality of rates of profit was a somewhat idealized description of the end-result of a tendency present in a real world economy. He describes economic forces whose effect, if not upset by changes in the situation, would tend to bring the system into long-run equilibrium. Alfred Marshall (1842–1924), having cited Smith's work with approval, described what he called a theoretically perfect long-period in essentially the same way, as a position to which a real world economy would approximate if the conditions of economic life 'were stationary for a run of time long enough to enable them all to work out their full effect' (Marshall 1961: 347). The reader will have seen, however, that our classical model simply sets out the formal properties which the model must possess in order to be in equilibrium. No dynamic adjustment mechanism has been offered which could specify how the system could get into equilibrium from a position where the rates of profit differed between sectors.

This has in fact been (until recently) a deficiency of formal classical models from the beginning of this century, something which was clearly seen by Joan Robinson, who insisted that such models could not be interpreted as the end-result of a real world process of getting into long-period equilibrium. She was led to abandon the view of the original classics and Marshall that long-period equilibrium was the end of a process, and wrote: 'Long-period equilibrium is not at some date in the future; it is an imaginary state of affairs in which there are no incompatibilities in the existing situation, here and now' (Robinson [1979] 1980: iii. 101). The equations of our simple classical model describe exactly a state of affairs where there are no incompatibilities here and now; the system is in equilibrium. In the last few years, however, attempts have been made to give formal accounts of how a classical model which was not in equilibrium might gravitate towards that state. This work, which was inspired by ideas of Adam Smith, will be discussed briefly in the next chapter. Meanwhile it will be sufficient for the non-economist reader to note that, as described by Smith, competition in the classical sense is by no means the perfect competition of the neo-Walrasian formal models. Smith describes a process taking place in real time, among real world capitalists with highly incomplete information. His capitalists are not big corporations, but neither are they infinitesimal. The modelling of this classical competition has been the subject of considerable research effort in recent years, but as Peter Flaschel and Willi Semmler have noted: 'The formal treatment of the classical competitive process is currently in an early phase of development' (Flaschel and Semmler 1987: 13). In the simple model just presented, this dynamic process is off-stage. As regards the properties of the simple model in equilibrium, classical competition simply means that, when thus in equilibrium, the rate of profit is equalized across all sectors of production.

Returning to our two-sector classical model, observe that it is still true (as in the one-sector model) that the input requirements (including subsistence) determine the rate of profit. So it is still true that the rate of profit is equal to the maximum rate of growth. Hence if λ_C and λ_I are set equal to zero (no luxury consumption takes place) and the economy is in maximum balanced growth, then R_C and R_I are identical and equal g max, which equals r. So: $R = g$ max $= r$.[4] In these respects, one- and two-sector models are the same, as in fact are such simple classical models with arbitrarily many sectors. It is an important feature of simple classical models that one set of relative prices together with one profit rate hold in all equilibrium solutions to a given model, regardless of the composition and allocation of surplus.

The reason for this may be put briefly as follows. In order for the economy to reproduce itself, capitalists in each sector must be able to sell corn (or iron) and buy iron (or corn) at such a price ratio as will allow them to reconstitute their capital stock, and sell their output so as to make the uniform rate of profit. Only a price ratio which makes this possible will be an equilibrium price ratio. Given that this equilibrium price ratio rules, suppose that all the surplus is being taken as corn. Since in such models there are assumed to be constant returns to scale, all the corn produced as surplus can be turned out at the same cost, so it will yield the uniform rate of profit. But if instead the surplus were taken wholly in iron, the larger output of iron could likewise be turned out at the same per unit costs, and yield the same rate of profit, at the given price ratio.

---

[4] Recall n. 2 above. Where the wage is allowed to be variable and the surplus is divided between wages and profits, the maximum rate of growth only equals the maximum rate of profit, which may not be the ruling rate of profit. So we get: $R = g$ max $= r$ max. It is still true in our simple model that, for any given division of the surplus between wages and profits, the one profit rate and one set of relative prices hold in all equilibrium solutions to a given model, regardless of the composition and allocation of surplus. (For a detailed analysis of the significance of introducing variable wages and profits into a simple classical model, see Walsh and Gram 1980: 317–36.)

Thus relative prices and the rate of profit are determined by the technical characteristics of the reproduction structure and not by the allocation of surplus. This property holds for all linear (constant returns) models where there are no (or at most one) non-produced inputs and where each process produces a single output. One might imagine all the ways in which the surplus could be allocated on a number of identical islands, with a given technology. Any two identical islands possessing the same technology (including subsistence) would then have the same relative prices and rate of profit, irrespective of the allocation of surplus.

The point of imagining identical islands is to stress the fact that a particular island could not change its tastes, and go overnight from one composition of surplus output to another, without going out of long-period equilibrium. Were such a change in demand to occur, relative prices consistent with reproduction would no longer rule, since one commodity (say, corn) would be being produced in insufficient quantities for the new pattern of demands, while another (say, iron) would be being produced in redundant quantities. A return to conditions of long-period equilibrium, at the new pattern of demands for the surplus, would then require a process of gravitation towards a pattern of inputs and outputs consistent with the long-period reproduction of the system, and characterized by the same set of relative prices and a uniform rate of profit across sectors. This brings us to the examination of questions concerning the role of choice and demand in reproduction models, an area about which there have been some confusions on the part of both sides of the debate as to the significance of these models. The role of demand proves, upon examination, to lead naturally into some of the deeper issues concerning what can, and what cannot, be learned from such models.

One of the most significant of these issues, for the present work, concerns the question as to when the rational choices of a particular class of agents have any effect upon the equilibria of classical models. What rationality claims concerning economic experience do these models suggest may be warranted?

9

CHOICE AND RATIONALITY IN REPRODUCTION MODELS

AT the cost of truly drastic simplifying assumptions, the rudimentary classical model whose quantity and price relations were sketched in the last chapter concentrates a spotlight upon aspects of economic experience which are left in the shadows in standard neo-classical models.[1] As to the rationality of individual agents in general or of the allocations which result from equilibrium positions of the model, however, our simple classical model was almost bare of information. About the only rationality claim made was that the choices and actions of capitalists would ensure that, in equilibrium, there would be a uniform rate of profit across all sectors. The crucial choices, in classical eyes, have always been those concerning the use of the net product. But these choices are made only by those who control the capital stock (capitalists or state bureaucrats) and there is no claim in such models that the choice made, or the resulting equilibrium, will be judged rational by even the majority of the agents in the model. Indeed the spirit of such models (inherited from their classical ancestors, such as Ricardo) is that there will be at least two distinct classes whose interests will be opposed, and which will be engaged in struggle over the surplus.

In the simplest classical models the workers are supposed to obtain a customary subsistence (in more sophisticated present-day models, they contend for a share of the net product, as we shall see). But, where a subsistence wage basket was assumed, the classical theorist was not denying that in the real world members of a working class would have some ability to choose the exact proportions in which they wished to consume the commodities composing this basket. Rather, the point was that an effort to introduce

---

[1] A noteworthy exception is Bliss (1975) where, as remarked earlier, an explicit reproduction structure is distinguished.

these details would only distract the eyes from the great issues which classical theory seeks to throw into relief.

Of course any formal treatment of balanced growth necessarily trivializes the role of choice and demand. The simple classical model does this with its assumption of a customary subsistence. But it also severely simplifies the choices open to the capitalists. The latter must first make what the classical tradition has always regarded as their most important choice: the proportion of the net product devoted to the accumulation of capital. In simple classical models the growth chosen must be balanced. For the rest, the capitalists are assumed to consume the same subsistence basket of commodities as the workers, and they may indulge in luxury consumption in addition. The balanced growth model must then rule out any dependence of the capitalists' preferences—either concerning the rate of growth or the composition of their luxury consumption—upon the level of their income. Otherwise the model is in danger of going out of equilibrium, since it would not (in general) be producing corn and iron in the proportions needed as inputs into the changed output mix.[2]

It should be sufficiently evident by now that the implications of classical theory for questions concerning rationality cannot usefully be addressed until we have considered recent work in the classical tradition which frees the latter from dependence on models of steady state growth.

When the only twentieth-century classical models formulated either did not consider growth at all, as was the case with Sraffa (1960), or considered only balanced growth, as was the case with Neumann ([1937] 1945–6), somewhat overheated claims tended to be made. The less astute proponents of classical models sometimes gave in to the boast that the trivial role played by demand in the versions of these models then available showed the ultimate unimportance of demand at the deepest level in the correct analytical structure. Meanwhile, the antagonists of classical models remarked that what this showed was that such models were only an unimportant special case! Both claims were misunderstandings, and simply tended to hide from view what was really important. In fact, once the simplest classical models are complicated in any one

---

[2] For an elementary discussion of the issues involved see Walsh and Gram 1980: 311–14; for an advanced account see Morishima 1969: 89–114.

or more of a number of ways, choices and the demands resulting from them become important—as was already known to Vladimir Karpovich Dmitriev (1868–1913) around the end of the nineteenth century (Dmitriev [1898–1902] 1974) when the revival of classical ideas in terms of mathematical models was just beginning. But—and this is the important point—the complications which, when introduced into the simple classical models, render choices and demands significant, in fact leave unimpaired the crucial classical insights concerning the net product and the role of the concept of class.

Recall that those concepts were originally laid bare by the eighteenth- and nineteenth-century classical economists and the later—notably Smith and Ricardo—took demand quite seriously.

DEMAND IN THE CLASSICS: ANCIENT AND MODERN

In the original classics such as Smith and Ricardo, and indeed as late as in Alfred Marshall (1842–1924), prices in the short period, known to Smith as market prices, need not be consistent with the continued reproduction of the economic system and need not yield a uniform rate of profit across sectors. The search for maximum profits was then supposed to induce capitalists to transfer some of their stock out of a sector where profits were relatively low, and into a sector where profits were higher. The supply of the commodity which it had been less profitable to produce would shrink, and the supply of the commodity which it had been more profitable to produce would rise. Excess demand would then arise for the commodity whose supply had shrunk, and its price would rise, while excess supply would arise for the commodity whose supply had risen, and so its price would fall. Actual, or 'market' prices would thus tend to gravitate toward their long-period 'natural' level, natural prices being those consistent with the continued reproduction of the system and yielding a uniform rate of profit on the value of capital stock. This dynamic adjustment process, which has been revived in recent models, was explicitly discussed by Smith ([1776] 1976: i. 72–81).

It was obviously the essence of this argument that prices in the short period would not coincide, except by accident, with 'natural' prices (those consistent with continued reproduction). It followed that a significant role was played by demand and supply relations in the short period. But the eyes of the original classics were not usually on these mainly transient phenomena; they were lifted and fixed upon the great drama enacted by the long-period forces of economic life, as these underlying forces determined the structure of natural prices and thus (with Ricardo, especially) the level of profits and the possibility and extent of the accumulation of capital.

It is the most natural thing in the world to simplify the position of the original classics, and of Marshall, by asserting that, for them, demand has no effect upon prices in the long period. If we interpret their long-period positions as the state of our simple classical model (with a subsistence wage) in equilibrium, the conclusion would indeed follow. But that simple model captures only a few of the concepts of the original classics, and distorts others. It captures, as we saw, the concept of surplus throughout industry, and the dual concept of a positive uniform rate of profit. But in the classics, the uniform rate of profit was a tendency, never fully realized or maintained, while in our little model it is a property of the equilibrium which the model depicts.

Even Marshall, perhaps the economic thinker most sensitive to the dangers of mathematically motivated simplifications of models, slipped now and then into the generalization that the classical long period was a stationary or steadily growing state, in which, therefore, demand was of little moment. This was his theoretically perfect concept of the long period. He wrote: 'In a stationary state then the plain rule would be that cost of production governs value...There would be no reflex influence of demand; no fundamental difference between the immediate and the later effect of economic causes. There would be no distinction between long period and short period normal value, at all events if we supposed that in that monotonous world the harvests themselves were uniform...' (Marshall 1961: 367).

But he was clearly restive in that 'monotonous world', and he also had what might be called a work-a-day concept of the long period which is much closer to the original classics: 'That...much misunderstood doctrine of Adam Smith and other economists that the normal, or "natural" value of a commodity is that which economic forces tend to bring about *in the long run*' (Marshall 1961: 364, emphasis in original).

Even when delineating his theoretically perfect long period, Marshall had qualms about the idea of an economy exhibiting constant returns to scale throughout, and really only advanced it as a description of the components of an economy taking one with another. As for his work-a-day long period, if this is an equilibrium, it is an equilibrium only in a statistical sense. Marshall was not describing a linear production model (or constant returns to scale model), where every component is in a mathematical strait-jacket. He was describing a real world economy, where the deep long-period forces were perpetually struggling to assert themselves. This is even more true of Smith. As is well known, a crucial ingredient in Smith's picture of capital accumulation is the yeast-like effect of the increasing division of labour, now in this industry and now in that. But the degree to which labour can be thus divided, with resulting increasing returns to scale, depends on the extent of the market, in other words, on the growth of demand for a particular commodity. This is closer to the idea of structural dynamics, where demand plays a crucial role in the process of growth, and which we shall be looking at later in this chapter, than it is to a present-day linear model of general equilibrium. Those who say that one should not impose linearity upon the original classics where it is not absolutely necessary are indeed correct, as are those who insist that one should describe the long period in the original classics as a long-period position and not as a long-period general equilibrium.

When interest in classical theory revived in the present century, however, what was constructed were rigorous mathematical formulations of long-period steady state general equilibrium models. The concept of surplus throughout industry, and the dual concept of a uniform rate of profit as the equilibrium condition for a system of natural prices in a model subject to no structural change yielded first to mathematical expression.[3] Dynamic considerations had for the moment to be ruled out at two levels, however. No formal

---

[3] The existence of equilibrium in a classical general equilibrium model was demonstrated in a talk given by John von Neumann in 1932, published in German in 1937, but not translated into English until 1945–6. Existence of a system of positive prices for Part I of Sraffa's *Production of Commodities by Means of Commodities* was treated (subject to the restriction that there be no non-basics) by Peter Newman (1962). Treatment of existence in the Sraffa system was extended by Carlo Felice Manara (1980, originally published in Italian in 1968), and further by Bertram Schefold (1980, originally a thesis of 1971). Only the generalized case of joint production causes remaining problems.

account could be given to replace Smith's informal description of the gravitation of market prices towards natural prices in the short period, and no dynamic structural properties could form part of the long period.

Now suppose that one continues to treat the commodities necessary for customary subsistence as embedded in the technology, but allows for the possibility that the surplus may be divided in some proportion between the capitalists and the workers. The actual proportions might be the outcome of class conflict and dependent on relative bargaining strengths, it might be imposed by government, or it might be the result of some other economic forces. As already remarked, a model with a variable wage was presented by Sraffa (1960), and different versions of it have since been offered by a number of authors. We need to be concerned here simply with the role of choice in this slightly more complicated classical model.

Clearly, if the workers obtain any positive share of the surplus, we need an assumption similar to that made about the capitalists' consumption: where the workers consume part of the surplus, the proportions in which they consume corn and iron as luxuries must be unaffected by the level of their income, just as in the case of the capitalists' luxury consumption.

It will be observed that nothing has been said about the workers' preferences concerning the division of the total surplus between luxury consumption and growth. Workers, in models of this type, are typically assumed not to have control of the capital stock, nor, therefore, to make choices concerning the rate of growth. From the point of view of demand, however, there is one important difference in this model: the division of the surplus between profits and wages can affect relative prices. The reason for this lies in the different proportions in which labour and means of production are employed in different sectors. As Sraffa put it: 'It is clear that if the proportion were the same in all industries no price-changes could ensue, however great was the diversity of the commodity-composition of the means of production in different industries. For in each industry an equal deduction from the wage would yield just as much as was required for paying the profits on its means of production at a uniform rate without need to disturb the existing prices' (Sraffa 1960: 12–13).

Since a change in the relative prices of corn and iron may be expected to affect the proportions in which capitalists (or workers) will wish to consume them as luxuries, the student of traditional microtheory may perhaps be forgiven for visualizing a demand curve for, say, corn as a luxury, showing how the quantity demanded will depend on the price of corn, which in turn will depend on the distribution of the surplus between wages and profits. Numerous references to 'wage reduction', 'price movements', 'price variations', etc. (Sraffa 1960: 12–16) in Sraffa's discussion can only encourage these sinful thoughts about demand curves, so this behaviour must be nipped in the bud!

Let the tempted reader be reminded that only one distribution of the surplus between capitalists and workers—only one point on a wage/profit trade-off—can form part of any single classical model. No change in distribution can take place without the model going out of equilibrium. This, of course, was precisely the reason why we needed to make such severe assumptions on preferences, which were designed to rule out another source of disequilibrating changes, those arising from income effects. But if we cannot allow changes due to income effects upon consumption, neither can we allow changes due to substitution effects resulting from different relative prices.[4]

In our simple classical model, all inputs were currently produced commodities. It is natural to ask how the treatment of demand would be effected if non-produced inputs—given resources—were introduced. Now once the workers are allowed to obtain some part of the surplus (over and above subsistence), labour is in effect being treated as a given resource. The explicit treatment of labour as an input can then no longer be avoided simply by embedding a per unit subsistence requirement of corn in a_{CC} and a_{CI} and of iron in a_{IC} and a_{II}, as we did in the subsistence wage model. So in discussing a model with a variable wage we have in fact been considering a model with at least one non-produced input.

The original classics, of course, assumed that any amount of labour needed was available in return for a subsistence wage, and the present-day model with subsistence embedded in the input coefficients formalizes this idea. It follows that in this model, the given technology (including subsistence) determines the maximum possible rate of growth. (The actual rate then being subject to

---

[4] In this discussion of the wage/profit trade-off I have benefited from private conversation with Heinz Kurz.

choice by the capitalists.) But once labour is treated as a given resource, one should consider the possibility that the limitations of the labour supply may be a constraint on the maximum rate of growth. The luxury consumption of workers, like that of capitalists, then limits the actual rate of growth.

Now suppose that land, perhaps as a result of growth, is no longer freely available. It then becomes a scarce resource, and its owners, the landlords, can command a rent, which must come out of the surplus. Again suppose that mineral deposits have become scarce—their owners can command a rent. Clearly in the simple model it must be assumed that (as with the capitalists, and the workers if they get part of the surplus) the proportions in which the landlords consume corn and iron as luxuries must once again be unaffected by the level of their income. (Otherwise the model will go out of equilibrium.) There are more troublesome problems, however, since many complications now enter the model. As continuing growth and rising demand makes land more and more expensive, technical choice must be introduced into the model. (Technical progress is a separate question.) If agricultural land is of uniform quality, more intensive ways of cultivating it must be introduced, while if land is of differing quality, more and more inferior parcels must be taking into cultivation. Similarly for minerals—it will be necessary to resort to more intensive methods or to the use of inferior deposits. Or, of course, one may suppose both of these expedients to be occurring. The least technically demanding treatment of these matters known to me is that of Lynn Mainwaring (1984: 145–62), but the nature of the subject-matter is inherently complex.

Prima facie, it may well be felt that choice and demand ought to play a larger role in such models: increasing scarcities will manifest themselves now in respect of agricultural land, now in respect of some mineral deposits, and some mechanism must exist through which the supplies of land and mineral deposits are brought into line with the demands for them. It is clearly reasonable to expect the scarcity of agricultural land to affect corn production most, and the scarcity of mineral deposits to affect industrial production most. This in turn suggests the likelihood of changes in the relative prices of corn and iron, leading to changes in the amounts of each good demanded as a luxury commodity. But if all this is allowed, the model will clearly go out of equilibrium.

Considering the effects of non-produced factors, such as agricultural land or mineral deposits, in a model with semi-stationary (i.e. balanced) growth, Christopher Bliss has commented:

The assumption of semi-stationary growth demands either that none such should be included in the model or that, being included, the supply of each and every such factor service should expand at [the rate of growth]...One suggestion is that technical progress might be invoked to augment the efficiency of land services in every use, which would have the same effect as an augmentation of the supply. However, this suggestion is not to be taken seriously. Apart from being patently an artifice in the present context, it fails even to provide a reasonable idealization of land-augmenting technical progress, which almost always has the effect of changing the mix of inputs that it is optimal to employ along with land. (Bliss 1975: 67)

As has been observed by a specialist in the effects of non-produced means of production upon commodity reproduction models, Alberto Quadrico-Curzio, 'rent greatly complicates the relations between wages and profits...non-produced means of production create new situations that are not to be found in models with production of commodities by means of commodities alone' (Quadrico-Curzio 1980: 238).

Complexities also arise where joint production is admitted into a model. Our simple classical model had only single-product industries. We had no sectors producing commodities such as wool and mutton, which can not be produced separately. Following Sraffa, however, models with joint production have been extensively developed.[5] Where such commodities exist, demand considerations are again liable to play a disequilibrating role. Here again the interesting possibilities are suppressed if the model cannot be allowed to go out of equilibrium. The same would be true of any attempt to introduce non-constant returns to scale.[6] Where returns to scale are non-constant, per unit costs of production and there-

---

[5] We have already noted a standard reference on joint production to the papers edited by Pasinetti (1980); the reader interested in a survey and analysis of recent technical developments, and copious references to the literature, will find these in Salvadori and Steedman 1988.

[6] The twentieth-century classical tradition which descends from such writers as Neumann and Wassily W. Leontief (1966, 1977) has been quite straightforward in assuming constant returns to scale. Some interpreters of Sraffa (1960), beginning, perhaps with Newmann (1962), have argued that Sraffa also requires a linear technology. A later example of this view is Burmeister 1977. This has been disputed, for example, by Eatwell (1977) and Alesandro Roncaglia (1978). Sraffa himself argued

fore relative prices are not independent of the quantities demanded
of different goods. But the only non-constant returns that would be
consistent with equilibrium would be balanced non-constant returns. Each sector must be supposed to be experiencing in each
period of production the same proportionate increase (or de-
crease) in returns. Clearly this idea is not to be taken seriously.
Recently, however, attempts have been made to specify the
disequilibrium dynamics of classical models, and it is time to take a
glance at some of these writings, since enough has been said for the
reader to see the need for some such development.

CLASSICAL DISEQUILIBRIUM MICROECONOMICS AND DEMAND

A number of studies have recently been devoted to characterizing
the behaviour of a classical model when it is out of equilibrium—
when, that is to say, relative prices are not such as to make possible
the reconstitution of the capital stock and to yield a uniform rate of
profit across sectors.[7] These studies have sought to establish formal
conditions which, if present, would guarantee that a model of this
kind, if out of equilibrium proportions, would return to them.
These formal investigations were inspired, however, by a claim

that 'No changes in output and (at any rate in Parts I and II) no changes in the
proportions in which different means of production are used by an industry are
considered, so that no question arises as to the variation or constancy of returns'
(1960: v.). It has been argued by Neri Salvadori (1983), however, that even in Part
I of Sraffa, and even assuming unchanging inputs and outputs, it can be questioned
whether no assumption on returns is implicitly made by Sraffa. Whatever may be
concluded about Sraffa's model where changes in output do not occur, we are
concerned at the moment with a classical model capable of being in a state of
balanced growth, and the literature of balanced growth models is one of the major
areas where linear production theory has flourished in economics. Non-constant
returns can be introduced into such models only if they are balanced
intersectorially—a rather preposterous requirement.

  [7] Until the 1980s, relatively few theorists had written formal analyses of the
dynamic process which was informally described by the original classics as leading to
equilibrium. What is more, the best-known paper, which had circulated for some
years before final publication, was rather negative. This was the work of H. Nikaido
(1983). Interest in the topic began to spread after a conference on gravitation held
in Paris in 1984, whose proceedings were edited by C. Bidard (1984). Interest was
further stimulated by a second conference, this time in Siena in April 1990. This is
discussed in Duménil and Lévy 1991.

about the history of the notion of equilibrium, and in order to see this recent work in perspective, it will be wise to take a look at its historical roots. In a well-known paper, Pierangelo Garegnani ([1976] 1983) argued that the original classics, and indeed Marshall, 'understood the long-period position as the "centre" towards which the competitive economy would gravitate in the given long-period conditions. The basis of the argument had been laid down by Adam Smith with his distinction between the "market price" and "natural price" of a commodity' (Garegnani [1976] 1983: 131).

For Smith, as we have noted, market prices—the actually ruling prices—might be above or below natural prices, which are those prices consistent with the recovery of all costs and the receipt of profits at the uniform rate. But Smith had insisted that the natural price 'is, as it were, the central price, to which the prices of all commodities are continually gravitating. Different accidents may sometimes keep them suspended a good deal above it, and sometimes force them down even somewhat below it. But whatever may be the obstacles which hinder them from settling in this center of repose and continuance, they are constantly tending towards it' (Smith [1776] 1976: i. 75).

Garegnani's main point was to contrast the long-period positions of the original classics and Marshall with the short-period equilibria found in neo-Walrasian models. Classical analysis always implied the distinction between momentary market prices and long-period natural prices consistent with the reproduction of the capital stock. But in a canonical neo-Walrasian model there was no such thing as a set of disequilibrium prices, and therefore no such thing as a centre of gravity. Garegnani did not explicitly raise the further issue of the relation between gravitation in the original classics and any possible gravitation process in present-day classical models. As has been noted by Luciano Boggio (1984), however, the question of a process of gravitation for today's classical models was largely neglected until the appearance of Garegnani's work. Then in the 1980s, studies of gravitation in classical models proliferated.

It is important to distinguish between two claims. One is the empirical claim that, as Smith believed, real world economies have a tendency to gravitate towards a uniform rate of profit. When a new trade was started up, its profits might for a time be substantially above (or below) the average, and new trades were being started up all the time. Indeed, as already noted, Smith's account of growth gives an important place to the progressive division of labour, whose effect, in giving rise to increasing returns to scale, would not at any moment be uniform across sectors. Smith was not describing general equilibrium in a reproduction model with constant returns. As Willie Semmler has remarked, 'Smith, as well as Ricardo and Marx, does not assume that in any *actual* state of the economy, the profit rate will necessarily be uniform for all sectors' (Semmler 1984: 17, emphasis in original). Crucial to the view of gravitation taken by Smith and the other original classical writers, was a particular view of competition, which we may call 'free competition' and which consisted essentially in the absence of barriers to economic activity. How different this concept of free competition was from the concept of perfect competition embodied in formal neo-Walrasian models may be seen from the following passage by Eatwell describing Smith, which stresses the dynamic ever-changing role of free competition:

Competition creates the tendency toward a uniform wage for each category of labor, a uniform rent for each quality of land, and a uniform rate of profit on the value of capital invested in each particular line as capitalists adjust the composition of the capital stock in search of maximum profits. If these uniformities were established, then commodities would sell at their natural prices. Since in reality, the full effects of competition are disrupted by chance events or specific (as opposed to general) circumstances, commodities will sell at their market prices, which competition will always push toward natural prices. (Eatwell 1982: 208)

This free competition, which by no means implies that there is a 'very large number' of producers, consists rather in the mobility of capital between different industries in search of the highest rate of profit. This was the concept of competition in the original classics.[8] But, it may pertinently be asked, what sort of competition is presupposed by the formal structure of a standard present-day classical model, where a gravitation process is *not* included in the structure of the model? As has been noted by Semmler, 'in the work of some important followers of Sraffa, assumptions pertaining to perfect competition were also made in presenting a theory of

[8] On the classical concept of competition see, for example, the following papers and the references which they contain: Duménil and Lévy 1987, 1989a, 1991a, Flaschel and Semmler 1987.

production prices' (1984: 9–10). I commented on this that: 'Indeed it is a little hard to see why such a model should be always *in* equilibrium unless an assumption of perfect competition is being presupposed. Those who see no reason for the search to find satisfactory gravitation processes might ponder this question' (Walsh 1992: 27, emphasis in original). I noted then, however, that while gravitation models have sometimes used assumptions of perfect competition for simplicity, this has not always been done. Indeed, there is no reason why it should be done.

We are now ready to discuss the second of the two claims which I have said it is important to distinguish. This is the claim that it can be demonstrated that a formal model of the reproduction of commodities, if out of equilibrium, can be provided with a dynamic adjustment process which will take the model back to a general equilibrium with reproduction prices and a uniform rate of profit. Here, though producers can be perfect competitors, they need not be, and the final position of the system is a full-scale general equilibrium—so that one can speak of 'tendencies' only in referring to the process to equilibrium. It will be seen that this second claim is essentially mathematical, concerning as it does the formal requirements for the convergence of a particular model to a particular state.

Often analytical treatments of gravitation processes are confined to two-sector models. I have used two-sector models in this book purely for expository simplicity, but the models which we have studied are robust in respect to expansion to an arbitrarily large finite number of sectors. This is not the situation with formal models of gravitation, where results obtainable by analytical methods for the two-sector case often cannot be generalized. One thus finds that many authors turn to methods of computer simulation in order to study gravitation in larger and otherwise more complicated models, thus losing the generality and force of analytical results in the conclusions then obtained.

Typically, in these models one begins with a given period (which may be regarded as a temporary equilibrium) where market prices will not yield a uniform rate of profit. Production, and thus the quantities of commodities supplied to the market in the next period, then change, resulting in different market prices. There is thus a sequence of temporary equilibria, with the market prices of successive periods tending towards reproduction prices, and thus the rates of profit tending towards uniformity. In each temporary equilibrium producers must find the inputs which they need for the current period among the physical outputs of the preceding period. It may be, then, that some of the last period's (say) iron output is not used up. Or, more seriously, the quantity constraints upon output resulting from the existing input mix may render impossible the outputs now desired, causing agents to be 'rationed'. In extreme cases the model may become non-viable. It is typically assumed that one is dealing with small, local instabilities, and that the reactions called for will not be '*brutales*'—as it is well expressed by Richard Arena, Claude Froeschle, and Dominique Torre (1984: 10), to whom this account is indebted. Greater success has been obtained by the use of computer simulation (subject to the limitations already noted), and to this we shall return.

In models where 'rationing' is a notable feature, a producer does not know what the uniform rate of profit would be were it to rule, nor the prices consistent with reproduction, nor the quantities that would be associated with that uniform profit rate. A firm does know the price of its product in the last period, and the quantity produced then, together with any unsold stocks that remain from the last period. Capitalists may also know the rates of profit of sectors in which they might be inclined to invest. It is assumed that, while a relatively low rate of profit in (say) the iron sector might persuade these capitalists to invest in the corn sector, they would not abandon production in the iron sector. Capitalists are thus assumed to realize that the drop in supply taking place in the iron sector could cause a rise in the price of iron, and that too great an increase in supply in the corn sector would in turn lower the price there. Gérard Duménil and Dominique Lévy note that the behaviour envisaged by the classics implies that the agents engaged in classical competition, namely the capitalists, were aware that negatively sloped demand functions existed: 'ils savent qu'il existe des fonctions de demande à pente négative' (Duménil and Lévy 1984: 11). Otherwise there would be nothing to stop them shifting the whole of their capital upon the appearance of a difference in profit rates. As Duménil and Lévi remark in a later work: 'The classical competitive process is a decentralized dynamic procedure realized in disequilibrium (in particular, markets do not necessarily clear)' (Duménil and Lévi 1987: 133).

In canonical Arrow–Debreu models, it will be recalled, plans were made by all agents in the first elementary time interval of the model for the entire future of that model. No trading was consummated except at the consistent, perfectly competitive equilibrium prices—there were no 'disequilibrium prices' in such a model. Thus markets cleared in these models in every elementary time interval. In recent years, as we have noted, theorists in the neo-Walrasian tradition have been developing models where, with asymmetric information and other complexities, markets need not clear in a given temporary equilibrium. Meanwhile in the present generation of classical models 'market clearing is not required in each period (but obtains asymptotically). The adjustment of supply and demand is progressive, while disequilibrium prevails in the short run (stockpiling, rationing)' (Duménil and Lévi 1987: 137). A fairly standard difference between recent neo-Walrasian and recent classical theorists lies in the stress laid by the neo-Walrasians simply on sequences of temporary equilibria in contrast with the pursuit by the classical theorists of adjustment processes towards long-period prices consistent with reproduction.

The agents whose decisions affect the models in recent classical work are normally the capitalists, although in more complicated models agents known as 'enterprises' may be distinguished from pure capitalists, and there may also be 'banks'. These agents do not look very like neo-classical 'optimizers'. Duménil and Lévi, it should be noted, have explicitly studied the question of rationality in present-day classical models. They suggest that 'very few conclusions actually follow from the consideration of *rational* adjustment, as opposed to the procedure, in which agents respond to disequilibrium in a *sensible* manner' (Duménil and Lévi 1989*b*: 3, emphasis in original).

It takes nothing from the real importance of recent classical work to suggest, as I believe I may, that such a disequilibrium microeconomics might not yield concepts of rationality quite as seductive to social scientists, philosophers, and others, as the magisterial presentations of the canonical Arrow–Debreu models proved to be.

Meanwhile numerous issues concerning the relative importance of long- and short-period modelling have been discussed in a number of contexts among classical theorists in recent years. Despite her lifelong preoccupation with long-period questions of accumulation of capital, Joan Robinson was insistent upon the short-period aspect of the work of Keynes during her last years, engaging in vigorous debate on these matters with Garegnani and others (I have commented elsewhere on her views on short- versus long-period modelling, Walsh 1989: 303–20). It now looks as if some recent work on gravitation may show the way to resolving a number of questions concerning short- versus long-period modelling: Peter Flaschel and Willie Semmler (1988) have explicitly introduced a Keynesian short-period quantity dynamics into the classical long-period process of gravitation. This is designed to close a gap in the classical gravitation process, which had been a purely long-period dynamics. But it also introduces into Keynesian short-period dynamics a more long-period point of view, characteristic of the original eighteenth- and nineteenth-century classical authors. It is noteworthy that, as Flaschel and Semmler have observed, these two types of dynamics do not appear to be exclusive, but instead complementary.

DEMAND IN TRANSFORMATIONAL GROWTH

When classical themes were revived in the twentieth century, the richly dynamic and changing picture painted in words by the original classical political economists could not be attempted at first. Yet remarkable early work had begun shortly after the middle of the present century on the formal treatment of certain processes which lie outside steady state conditions, for example that of Adolph Lowe (1955), of Hicks (1965), and again of Lowe in a later work (1976). A notable pioneer was Richard Goodwin ([1953] 1983), who has influenced a number of younger thinkers. Another author preoccupied early on with problems of the dynamic structural change of a growing economy was Luigi Pasinetti (1965, 1981, 1993). His purpose throughout was to develop a dynamic analysis 'without that fixity of coefficients which had constrained all inter-industry analysis into a static straight jacket' (Pasinetti 1981: p. xii).

Pasinetti's model can undergo fundamental transformations of its structure, not merely small displacements from a balanced state. The model is in a changing equilibrium, not merely returning to an equilibrium from which it was slightly displaced. Pasinetti claims that his model is therefore free from the major defect of the usual formal classical models—their limitation to steady-state equilibria (or to small displacements from such equilibria). Pasinetti's models undergo fundamental changes in technology and—a noteworthy feature—in demand.

Pasinetti argues that the assumptions of zero technical progress and constant returns (normal in balanced growth models) are at least logically possible, whereas the assumption of balanced technical progress plus the uniform expansion of demand 'are not only unlikely, they are impossible' (Pasinetti 1981: 66). He assumes that technical progress is continuously taking place, but at markedly different rates in different sectors; that in some sectors there may be productivity decreases, and that technical progress may involve the appearance of new goods. Demand is emphatically not assumed to expand for each commodity proportionately: as income rises, demand shifts from one group of commodities to another as consumers become satiated with one group after another. Donald J. Harris, who regards Pasinetti's treatment of changing demand as being 'in some ways, the most striking and radically new departure in this model' (Harris 1982: 34) notes that, even in the absence of unbalanced technical change, this changing demand would in itself be sufficient to bring about non-proportional growth. New problems, however, come with this new model: demand must be continually channelled in new directions, so that as Harris remarks, 'the structural dynamics of the economic systems inevitably tend to generate what has rightly been called *technological* unemployment' (Harris 1982: 90, emphasis in original). Harris finds this tendency to unemployment is 'likely to remain dominant' (Harris 1982: 35). As he notes, 'in Pasinetti's scheme there is never a possibility of any set of equilibrium conditions continuing to hold beyond a single period... Consequently there is an ever present tendency towards unemployment owing to the "structural dynamics" of the economy' (Harris 1982: 32). It is true that a number of problems have been found in Pasinetti's model. But it is certainly a daring and fascinating attempt to meet head on what are surely some of the greatest challenges facing classical theorists today: to produce growth models which can successfully embody fundamental technical change and major transformations of demand.

One feature of Pasinetti's model must be noted here, since it is of particular relevance to the present work. A striking feature, especially of his most resent book (Pasinetti 1993), is his methodological device of the 'natural system'. This concept has a number of characteristics which result from technical properties specific to Pasinetti's model which cannot be detailed here. But, as has recently been noted by Angelo Reati, 'the natural system has also a normative dimension because it is characterized by efficiency and fairness, and, as such, it should be taken as a goal for the actual economic system' (Reati 1994: 121). Reati notes that this concept is classically inspired. I would add that, among the great original classics, its inspiration clearly comes from Smith—it was surely not for nothing that Pasinetti subtitled his earlier book on structural change *A Theoretical Essay on the Dynamics of the Wealth of Nations*.

The reader is already familiar with Smith's concept of natural prices. Pasinetti's idea of a whole system of natural determinants of the variables constituting an economy is a much more complex concept, of which prices are only one component. But its Smithian bloodlines can be detected. Pasinetti believes that one can isolate certain primary and natural features of an economic system, which can be seen to be prior to, and independent of, any particular institutional arrangements which might happen to exist in a given case. Ironically, this extension of Smith's notion of underlying naturally necessary features of any economy could have strong appeal for neo-classics. Until, that is, they came up against Pasinetti's conclusion that in his models the naturally called for (and normatively desirable) state of affairs cannot be counted on to come about through the free workings of the market, unless aided by conscious human policy. To take only one example, full employment, as we have noted above, will not exist or continue in Pasinetti's model unless the labour force is being moved from shrinking into expanding sectors.

Pasinetti has pressed well beyond much twentieth-century classical theory in seeking for rationality properties from a specifically classical economic analysis. He is well beyond the simple equilibrium condition of a uniform rate of profit arising from the choices of capitalists. As Reati has expressed it: 'Economic rationality is not defined in the usual narrow sense of profit maximization but rather as the "intelligent" process of learning: the discovery of new and better methods on the production side, and the apprehension of alternative patterns of consumption and the formation of new preferences on the demand side' (Reati 1994: 121).

THE SIGNIFICANCE OF CLASSICAL MODELS

When the only formal classical models which existed were simply depictions of steady state conditions, with all the trivializing of questions concerning choice and demand which that involved, it was sometimes claimed that if these simplifying assumptions were removed the models would lose all their classical character. It should by now be sufficiently clear that this view was mistaken. We have glanced at models which give up just about any of the assumptions of the simple classical model that one can think of, while remaining unmistakably classical. Indeed their authors make a point of acknowledging their descent, in many cases citing Smith as a specific ancestor. But after all, the original classics, such as Smith, never thought in steady state terms and one can see the inspiration for Pasinetti's depiction of transformational growth in Smith's discussions of the effects of growing demand and technical change upon each other.

Proponents of methodological individualism also see Smith (with justice) as one of their forebears. No one conversant with his work in economics, philosophy, political thought, or jurisprudence will wish to deny that he had a deep and vigorous respect for the importance of the individual human person. But this did not in the least hamper his writing an account of the role of the emergent capitalist class of his period, who were making their historically unique contribution to the massive accumulation of capital by choosing overwhelmingly to devote the surplus which they obtained as capitalist profit to growth and not to luxury consumption. With such a truly classical example before us, can there be any justification for riding rough-shod over the valid claims of individual persons on the excuse that great truths concerning classes and power demand this? Or, again, can there be any justification for turning a blind eye to the stark facts about power and class, on the excuse that the individual is the sole and sovereign entity out of which all valid economic arguments must be constructed?

Some questions of interpretation, however, remain, and have, I believe, a certain interest both of an economic and of a philosophical kind. The questions which I have in mind do not mainly have to do with the technical, mathematical, properties of formal classical models. There are many purely formal issues that are being actively debated. But as the non-economist reader may already have seen during our glance at the effects of demand in classical models, these issues are rapidly becoming matters strictly for specialists. Rather, the remaining issues which I wish to discuss concern (for example) the exact interpretation of the key classical concepts when commodities and the surplus no longer assume a simple physical form such as 'corn' or 'iron'.

Begin once more with the one-sector corn model. Here the surplus can be physically seen—it is a pile of corn. Complexities enter the moment one has even one more sector: the surplus no longer has physical units of measurement. The earliest classics experienced surplus in agriculture (see Walsh and Gram 1980: 9–23), which, in Britain, had been transformed into a capitalist mode of production at least a hundred years before manufacturing industry. At the hands of the Physiocrats in France, Cantillon's clear understanding of surplus in various agricultural sectors hardened into the dogma that surplus could arise only in agricultural production (see Walsh and Gram 1980: 23–44). Smith, despite all his admiration for the Physiocrats' analysis of surplus *where they could see it*, nevertheless rejected firmly their confinement of this phenomenon to agriculture. Even in his early works, Smith was quite clear that surplus arose throughout industry, capitalist agriculture being simply one special case of a capitalist industrial undertaking. In Smith, however, there lingered a tendency to seek physical manifestations of surplus—he is most happy when the surplus is embodied in a clearly material form. Along with his great achievements—and indeed reinforced by the just prestige owed to his genius—he passed this cast of mind on to the classical tradition. Is it fanciful to see this influence even in certain characteristics of Sraffa's masterpiece *The Production of Commodities by Means of Commodities*?

Of course, it will be immediately pointed out, the simplest models appear to be those where one or two physical commodities are reproduced by means of themselves. Yet consider what is surely a pretty simple model. Two identical islands (with identical supplies of ordinary labour) produce corn by means of corn. But on one of them there is a group of agricultural scientists who advise the inhabitants on when to plant, how much to water the crop, etc. On the island with the scientists, the output is larger than on the one without (when total input into seed, and into subsistence for ordinary labour, is identical on both islands). On the first island, there is a corn input into agricultural scientists, but even after subtracting this from total output, the surplus is still larger. Suppose this island to be interested (for the present) in maximum growth. If scientists need to supervise closely, then their numbers will have to grow also (new scientists need training by old). So we have:

$$(a_{CC}Y_C + a_{CS}Y_S)(1 + g) = Y_C$$
$$(a_{SC}Y_S + a_{SS}Y_S)(1 + g) = Y_S$$

where a_{CS} is the necessary input of corn into scientists, a_{SC} is the necessary input of scientist services into a unit of corn, and a_{SS} is the necessary input of old scientists into the production of new scientists. (As in our previous two-sector model, land is supposed not to be a binding constraint on output, and ordinary labour is assumed to be forthcoming in needed amounts in return for customary subsistence.) This clearly has the makings of a perfectly recognizable classical model, despite the fact that one of the needed produced inputs (and outputs) is, if you will, an immaterial *service*. The service of a scientist is clearly a Sraffian basic commodity in this model.

Yet the historical fact is that, from the very beginnings of classical political economy, confusions have arisen (and over time, proliferated) over what exactly constituted net product or surplus and what inputs, strictly, contributed to its size. This question, and related issues, have recently been subjected to a detailed examination of considerable subtlety and refinement by Helen Boss (1990). As she notes: 'It was realized by the mid-eighteenth century that *any restrictive definition of the economy and the economic implies a boundary with a non-economic world* raising the question of mutual interaction. On the boundary's economic side, activities designated as "productive" were supposed to yield "produce", "products", "output" that had positive utility. Output increased the welfare of those members of society whose welfare counts. More was better than less' (Boss 1990: 2, emphasis in original). Remarking that the debate as to whether an activity was productive or not was closely connected to 'the question of whether the economy is producing a "surplus"' (ibid.), she adds that 'the boundary problem must be faced by all commentators, except for those who are prepared to deny the existence of either economics or non-economics. Deciding who is a producer and who, implicitly or explicitly is a mere consumer of the fruits, is the fundamental starting point for all who would model socioeconomic action' (Boss 1990: 5).

In a close study of the texts of classical political economy, Boss is able to show how the classics—great as well as minor—fell into what she calls 'input–output error'. This arises when some input into production is at one point or other recognized as being necessary to the production of output, while at another point in the argument the producers of the input in question are treated as 'unproductive'. The charge of 'unproductiveness' may arise because the workers in question do not produce and sell a 'material' good—as was the case with our scientists. Or it may be levelled because the service (in addition to being immaterial) is provided by the state. Or the charge of unproductiveness may be grounded upon the fact that the worker's output is not priced in a market (even if private, and even if material).

Hunting input–output error with even-handed determination, Boss exposes it among the original classics and among the moderns, and equally among the left and the right today: 'In an irony of intellectual history, both *laissez-faire* new Right conservatives and Marxian radicals apply surplus and transfer models to troubles in the mainstream. The public goods-augmented conservative update is more sophisticated in that it allows for the special problems of public goods and public choices, but its conclusions remain directly classical, with unclouded appreciation of Adam Smith's views on parsimony, industry and the incompetence of state authorities' (Boss 1990: 9).

Very little can be said here about her detailed argument concerning the original classics, since this would take us into a lengthy analysis of classical texts for which the present work is not the proper place. One or two points, however, may not be out of order. There can be little question that the overwhelming interest, on the part of Smith and Ricardo, in analysing the surplus and its use, derived from their belief in the desirability of the greatest possible accumulation of physical capital goods in the shortest possible time.

The situation had grown desperate by Ricardo's time. Agricultural labourers, destitute as a result of the ravages of the enclosure movement and of other transformations in agricultural life, had been flooding into the newly industrial towns. At the same time the hand-loom weavers and hand spinners, ruined by the new machine weaving and spinning, were also trying to find employment in the factories. Only a rapid and massive accumulation of physical capital goods—corn for the labourer's bread and machines for them to work at—could begin to address these problems, and so mitigate to some extent the terrible costs of Britain's transformation into an industrial economy.

Perhaps Ricardo, especially, may be forgiven for not having devoted more of his time to the status of what we might today call non-material basics. We know that Ricardo (like Smith) distinguished between commodities which were necessaries, and those which were luxuries. It is natural to translate these as 'basic' and 'non-basic' commodities respectively. But it must be remembered that once one has a formal model of an input–output system (even the little two-sector model) before one, the requirements for a basic become somewhat more starkly inescapable—that it must be an input, directly or indirectly, into every output. Perhaps this is quite a good example of a situation where the necessity to formalize a concept does lead to clarity! So it should be easier to avoid input–output error today.

The Physiocrats, for example, who recognized surplus only in agriculture, nevertheless have the supposed 'sterile' (non-surplus generating) artisan sector able to manufacture luxuries—something which presupposes a more than barely viable technology, and therefore the possibility of surplus in any sector. As Gram and I remarked 'once one sets out the formal relations of the model, it is inescapably there' (Walsh and Gram 1980: 37).

What has been said here should not be taken, however, as implying that problems do not remain concerning the interpretation of the concepts of 'basic commodity' and 'surplus', even in formal classical models. Many of these questions are connected with the concept of subsistence. As we know, in the simplest classical models, workers' consumption is simply treated as part of the means of production. But now suppose that the subsistence requirements were redefined. This would alter the values of the per unit input requirements. With each definition of subsistence, one could expect in general to get a different rate of profit, so that it might seem natural to give up treating subsistence as parametric, and instead introduce a variable wage. Then, defining technology independently of subsistence, a given technology would be consistent with a whole range of wage-profit distributions. Difficulties, however, arise if one drops the concept of subsistence.

As noted earlier, if the subsistence requirement in the wage is dropped, surplus may be positive while the net product is insufficient to support the labour force, let alone providing for growth. As Gram and I noted: 'Surplus then loses its historical significance since a positive surplus no longer implies the basis for accumulation or for the support of the capitalist class. Of course the classical economists never fell into this trap since they always treated wages as a necessary input into the process of production' (Walsh and Gram 1980: 318).

Sraffa, as we have already noted, had suggested a way out of this difficulty. Since, especially in present-day societies, wages, besides subsistence, may include a share of the surplus, one might, he suggested, 'separate the two component parts of the wage and regard only the "surplus" part as variable; whereas the goods necessary for the subsistence of the workers would continue to appear, with the fuel, etc. among the means of production' (Sraffa 1960: 10). Sraffa, though recognizing the case for this separation, chose to treat the entire wage as variable. Gram and I, on the other hand, followed his suggested separation and distinguished two components in wages, thus continuing to define the input–output requirements as containing both technical and subsistence requirements of per unit output.

A number of consequences, of no little importance, follow from these considerations. We noted in the last chapter that the concept of class becomes more starkly analytic when one goes from the original classics to present-day classical models: for writers like Smith and Ricardo, social class was a clear and reliable indicator of economic class—a person was visibly a worker, a capitalist, or a landlord. Not so today. Thus one cannot define the capitalist class (even in a two-class model) as the class which consumes the surplus, if the workers may consume some of it. The analytically important point rather is that the capitalist class, by virtue of its ownership of the capital stock, controls the conditions of its reproduction—in particular, the rate of growth.

Responsibility for the manner of consumption of surplus (to whatever extent it comes into being once the conditions of the reproduction of capital have been decided upon by the capitalists) does not, however, now lie wholly with the capitalist class, with a landlord class (or with a class of state bureaucrats in a centrally planned economy). Any class which can obtain part of the surplus bears some of the moral burden of using it in responsible ways—i.e. in ways which are not environmentally or socially destructive.

Consider next the components of subsistence. These are a subset of the set of basics. (There are, as we know, also technical basics, such as seed, or a manufactured tool used in further production and not as a consumption good, or specialist advice used in production.) It might be argued that the technical basics being, as it were, a matter of engineering necessity, are more easy to specify (or even on a sounder footing) than the basics forming subsistence. But if a consumption good (for which certain inputs are technically necessary) were to be decided not to be, after all, a basic, then this could affect its inputs. Some of the inputs into a putative 'basic' would be technical basics. But some of these might attain this status only if the commodity in question were ranked as a basic. The specialized skill of a wine-maker may be an input only into wine. If wine is a basic, the wine-maker's labour is an input directly into wine, but indirectly into every other output. The fact is that the formal properties of a basic and of a basic system may be rather clear, but this in no way removes the necessity for responsible social choice as to what commodities or services to regard as basics. Recall that the original classics always regarded the components of subsistence as socially determined. In today's world, some pretty sophisticated goods and services are certainly going to rank as basics. We saw that the services of agricultural scientists were basic in our simple model of the present chapter. But in this case they could be regarded as technical basics. There is no reason to require this of every basic which is a component of subsistence, however. A bottle of a simple sound wine or an evening of music surely need not have to be argued to be basic solely because they will enable the recipient to produce more steel per week! They can simply be regarded as parts of subsistence in a civilized society.

Present-day classical models can provide a map of the logical terrain which needs to be understood for responsible thinking about the great issues concerning the proper use of the net product of society, but they cannot grant us a dispensation from the necessity for evaluating the components of a society's output. And here we come face to face with issues over which present-day classical work shows some of the strengths and the weaknesses which have characterized so much of twentieth-century economic thinking as a result of the influence of logical positivism and logical empiricism.

PHILOSOPHICAL STRENGTHS AND WEAKNESSES OF THE CLASSICAL REVIVAL

That some of the greatest figures of the twentieth-century classical revival should have been influenced by logical positivism is surely hardly surprising given the period in which they wrote. In the case of Piero Sraffa, for instance, it has been remarked by John Eatwell and Carlo Panico that a 'compelling empiricism' (Eatwell and Panico 1987: 445) and 'the rejection of the use of subjective concepts, are themes running throughout Sraffa's economics. Economics should be constructed from variables and relationships which are, at least in principle, observable and measurable' (ibid.). They reached the conclusion that Sraffa's critical approach to neo-classical theory 'was motivated by a distaste for "subjective" models, but was conducted in purely logical terms, at least in his later works' (ibid. 451). They note his 'admiration for the "objective" structure of classical theory' (ibid.). This characteristic of the classical tradition has been widely observed, but, of course, in the original classics it was not the result of a logical positivist epistemology. Certainly Sraffa's book (1960), in giving no role (for example) to utility functions, has an 'objective' look—its title itself suggests this.

As Eatwell and Panico themselves remark (and as has been noted by a number of Cambridge and Italian authors), however, the peculiarly sparse look of Sraffa's book is largely dictated by the specific set of topics to which Sraffa wished to confine himself: Sraffa takes as data the size and composition of output, the reproduction conditions, and the wage rate. In doing this he was following the surplus theories of the classics. But if this is so, then Sraffa had an analytic reason for this much noted sparse structure quite independent of logical positivist principles.

On the other hand, several authors have drawn attention to Sraffa's careful avoidance of counterfactual arguments, and, as we shall see, such arguments came under fire from logical positivism. As to Sraffa's avoidance of counterfactuals, Sen, for example, has recently commented that: 'Sraffa tried to explore whether the relationship between prices, productions, and distributions of income cannot be substantially explored without considering any changes—factual or counterfactual—and without, thus, invoking any "marginal" concepts at all (since such concepts take the form of asking what would have happened if something had been one unit more or less)' (Sen 1989: 305).

Sen does not put forward this point as a criticism of Sraffa. On the contrary, he stresses that: 'It is quite remarkable that Sraffa did establish a number of important relationships (e.g. those between the wage rate and the profit rate, and between relative prices and quantities) that could be expected on the basis of certain *given* characteristics (such as the same rate of profits and same wage rates in different enterprises)' (ibid., emphasis in original). He argues that Sraffa had made an important methodological contribution through his analysis of the relation between prices, costs, production, and distribution: 'The concept of "determination" used in this approach is a broader one than that of *causal* relations, which would necessitate counterfactual analysis. It can be argued that Sraffa focused attention on the "coherence" of observed reality and the power of that coherence, showing how observing a part of the reality (e.g. quantities of inputs and outputs and the profit rate) can tell us about another part (in this case, the wage rate and all the relative prices)' (ibid., emphasis in original).

It should be noted, however, that Sraffa's avoidance of counterfactual conditionals goes with his rejection of the use of 'subjective' concepts. For the logical positivists, truly scientific statements were often seen as those that could be translated satisfactorily into Russellian symbolic logic. It was then discovered that counterfactual claims did not translate nicely. This caused great heart searchings during the heyday of logical positivism.

One thus cannot deny out of hand that it would have been quite 'in period' for Sraffa to have wanted to construct an economic analysis wholly 'untainted' by counterfactual utterances. Some considerations tell against this interpretation, however. For one thing, as already noted, Sraffa wanted to take as given exactly what, in his view, the original classics had, and then establish simply certain core relationships between the wage rate and the profit rate, and between quantities and prices. He had, in other words, reasons derived from his reading of the classics and from his views on economic theory for his choice of approach.

And then it can be pointed out that what Sraffa did was in one sense not very logical positivist in spirit. In the passage just after that last quoted, Sen goes on to comment (of Sraffa's focusing on the 'coherence' of reality) that '[t]his type of enquiry has been neglected in modern economics (partly because of the dominance of the positivist methodology and the narrow range of scientific interest in contemporary economics)' (Sen 1989: 305–6).

Finally, it should be noted that there is a marked irony in the possibility that Sraffa had been to any extent influenced by the logical positivists, since as Eatwell and Panico (among others) have noted, 'It was Sraffa who forced Wittgenstein to accept that the theory of language advanced in the *Tractatus Philosophicus* was logically inadequate, paving the way for the recognition of the social content of signs and language presented in *Philosophical Investigations*' (Eatwell and Panico 1987: 445). The later work of Wittgenstein, of course, was the fountainhead of much of that subtle analysis of ordinary language which was one of the acids which ate away at the crude logical positivist analysis of the meaningful uses of language.

Whatever may be true of Sraffa, in the case of another great figure of the twentieth-century revival of classical themes, namely Joan Robinson, there is clear evidence of the damaging effect of logical positivist assumptions upon the effectiveness of some of her arguments. That she had been influenced by positivism I know from conversations as well as from her writings. This did not prevent her from having deep insights which were certainly not morally neutral concerning economic life and theory. However, Daniel M. Hausman has recently claimed that it seriously impaired the consistency of her position. Hausman argues that for her, *the* moral problem was 'the conflict between individual and collective interests' (Hausman 1989: 821). (It was certainly one of the most important moral problems which she recognized, at the very least.) He cites one of her last works. She wrote: 'The philosophy of orthodox economics is that the pursuit of self-interest will lead to the benefit of society. By this means, the moral problem is abolished. The moral problem is concerned with the conflict between individual interest and the interest of society. And since this doctrine tells us that there is no conflict, we can all pursue our self-interest with a good conscience' (Robinson [1979] 1980: 43). Hausman comments that: 'Despite the power and brilliance of

Robinson's writing, neither the moral concern nor the argument for its insolubility are presented clearly, for they are encased within a positivist view of science, metaphysics and morality that must be superseded before one can confront the serious issues' (Hausman 1989: 822).

Noting very properly that it would be unfair to 'take Robinson to task for espousing the philosophical orthodoxy of her day' (ibid.), he shows in detail how her positivist inspired inability to do justice to the place of reason in moral argument, and her enforced dismissal as 'metaphysical' of important concepts with a moral dimension, successively hamstring her argument. It should be stressed here that the confusions which he cites were all typical errors inherent in the position of the logical positivists, and in no way personal mistakes of hers. Her tendency to slip into the despairing view that morality is only a matter of 'feelings' is typical of this period, and it was certainly damaging. As Hausman remarks, to have a serious discussion of the conflict between individual economic behaviour and the dictates of morality, demands that moral argument be taken seriously 'not as the arbitrary heavings of someone's heart, but as imperatives and claims with cognitively significant content subject to rational appraisal and capable of rational influence' (Hausman 1989: 824).

Bereft of a confidence in argument which could properly be both factual (technical or theoretical) and moral, Robinson sometimes spoke and wrote as if the whole of the issues debated so hotly in the controversy between Cambridge, England, and Cambridge, Massachusetts, over the nature and significance of capital, could be reduced to purely technical points of economic theory. At other times, the opposite was true, and she would dismiss certain previously hotly debated technical issues impatiently as 'unimportant'.

Now of course, there *are* technical distinctions between a present-day classical model (in the tradition of Sraffa) and a standard neo-Walrasian model. Some of the simpler of these show up even in the little model of the reproduction of corn and iron which has been sketched here, such as the different treatment of inputs, and the rather prominent role of surplus and economic class in the classical models and their absence from centre stage (to say the least) in the neo-Walrasian models. But if one presents the differences purely in technical terms, one offers Hamlet without the Prince of Denmark. Just as neo-Walrasian models are an incredibly subtle set of variations upon the deep (and morally non-trivial) idea of methodological individualism, believed in but not adhered to by neo-Walrasian theory, so in their turn classical models are a set of variations upon the ancient theme of the ultimate significance of economic class, economic power, and the moral implications of the control and disposition of the surplus. Both side's models are black with fact, white with convention, and red with values;[9] until both sides recognize this, constructive debate and exchange of ideas will be impossible, and the well-known and widely noted bitterness of the controversy between them over the nature and role of capital has provided clear evidence of this state of affairs.

In the specific context of the twentieth-century revival of classical thinking, at least a couple of features of original classical theory (both reasonable enough in their time) served to keep explicit discussion of the moral implications of the developing models off-stage. The original classics had a tendency (not universally adhered to) to treat output and net product as quantities of physical goods—of corn, in the very simplest case. This is discussed at length by Boss (1990), as already noted. The twentieth-century classics, working to formalize and render mathematically precise the earlier insights, rather naturally set up input–output models whose coefficients represented quantities of goods like corn and iron. The existence (and size) of a net product then reduces to a question of fact. In the simplest case: is corn output greater than, equal to, or less than corn input?

But subsistence is a concept with many aspects (nutritional, medical, educational, aesthetic, moral, and so on); ultimately it is the question: what is the morally acceptable minimum standard for a civilized society? If it is left buried in the per unit input requirements, then a deeply important question, which the classical structure is peculiarly suited for laying bare, is left unaddressed.

A second feature of the original classics has tended to shield classical writers from the need to investigate the moral implications of their models. This concerns the use of the surplus. As we have

---

[9] The non-philosopher reader may wish to be reminded that the original image was W. V. Quine's famous comment on the lore of our fathers: 'It is a pale grey lore, black with fact and white with convention. But I have found no substantial black threads in it, or any white ones' (Quine 1963: 406). I took the liberty of adding threads red with values to the weave (Walsh 1987b: 862). For Putnam's comments on the tapestry thus enriched, see Putnam (1990: 163–4).

seen, for the great eighteenth- and even the early nineteenth-century classical economists, the answer was simple: there was an overwhelming need for the accumulation of capital. So the distinction between growth and luxury consumption was at one and the same time the key distinction economically and the key distinction morally. It did not need discussion. But once the early industrial revolution darkened into what Robinson called the 'ferocious forties', this was no longer so.

Granted, much 'anti-growth' writing is thinly disguised romantic reaction; granted that in particular, exhortations to limit growth come ill from the rich world when in effect addressed mainly to the poor countries. Nevertheless, advocacy of growth today must come with clear, explicit provisions for the preservation of the planet. It must, in addition to being scientifically informed, embody a responsible moral position. Nor can one take seriously policy based on models where growth is confined to the balanced expansion of a fixed set of outputs. Here Pasinetti, Lowe, and other thinkers probing beyond the steady state are surely on the right path: fundamental changes in choices and demand (reflecting, hopefully, a more responsible attitude toward nature) and the rapid growth of new, more benign technologies combined with the decline of old pollutant ones, are surely needed.

Joan Robinson, certainly one of those most associated with the revival of classical theory, was concerned throughout her life with the content of growth, and was never uncritical of its being devoted to armaments and conspicuous waste, when it could have provided the necessary infrastructure for a decent life for all. As I have remarked elsewhere: 'She and those influenced by her never saw growth as an objective to be pursued independently of the attempt to find solutions to the problems of distribution' (Walsh 1992: 39). Consistent with this has been the highly original work of Adolph Lowe, in particular his modelling of the recycling of production and consumption residuals in order to reduce the ecologically undesirable side-effects of otherwise desirable kinds of capital accumulation, so that the processes of transforming residuals enter the model as additional circular flows (Lowe 1976: 223–31).

It should never be lost sight of that what Smith wanted was not simply any growth for growth's sake. He did not want the accumulation of capital in order to fatten the coffers of great monopolies, or to feed the 'slothful and oppressive profusion of the great' (Smith [1937] 1978: 655). He wanted the accumulation of capital because it provided the sustenance of industrious people, and because he knew well that the necessaries and comforts afforded to the great mass of the population would be most generous in an advancing state of society and most miserly in a stagnant or declining state. This humanly necessary and healthy consumption was that consumption which he always rightly insisted was the object of all production.

The deepest classical insight concerned the vital importance of the surplus, and the core moral value implicit in classical political economy concerned its responsible use. The detailed description of the criteria for such responsible use have simply become more complex.

Both in respect of the interpretation of the concept of subsistence, however, and of the concept of the surplus, the present-day classical claim to carry on the traditions of classical political economy (a moral science, let us remember), is ill served when we content ourselves simply with the technical properties of these concepts as they appear, embedded in the algebra of a formal input–output system.

CLASSES ARISING FROM THE RATIONAL CHOICES OF INDIVIDUALS

In recent years a remarkable group of theorists has formed. On the one hand, they are dedicated to neo-classical economic theory in general and to methodological individualism in particular. In the words of John Roemer, the leading economic theorist of the group, neo-Walrasian theory is 'one of the great contributions to social scientific method of the past century' (Roemer 1988: 151). And it is insisted by Jon Elster that one must start 'by stating and justifying the principle of methodological individualism' (Elster 1985: 1).

On the other hand, however, they are equally convinced that concepts like surplus, class, and exploitation can be derived within models which are composed solely of individual agents who are rational (in the sense of neo-Walrasian theory), have given endowments which differ in value, and have available a given technology. Indeed they claim much more. They are not seeking a sparse and minimalist treatment of surplus and class such as some have seen as characterizing, for example, Sraffa (1960). They aim at no less than a derivation, in those terms which they regard as necessary for rigour, of the key concepts of specifically Marxian theory. This, it will be seen, is a much richer mixture. It will scarcely surprise the reader to hear that the critical response has been massive.

I shall confine my remarks on all this to Roemer and some of those who have commented on his models, since we are concerned here with economic theory and its concept of rationality. But it should be noted in passing that considerable work has been done in, for example, political science and history by scholars influenced by this movement.

It is normally not denied even by severe critics of Roemer's work that, as James Devine and Gary Dymski have put it, he 'has made important contributions: he has shown that some Marxian theses can obtain even in a Walrasian framework' (Devine and Dymski 1991: 236). A good deal of the criticism of Roemer centres on various ways in which his Walrasian analysis is too sparse to capture the richness of texture of certain Marxian concepts. This critique from the point of view of classical Marxian scholarship is well exemplified by, for example, W. H. Locke Anderson and Frank W. Thompson (1988), and by Michael Lebowitz (1988). This line of enquiry, however, I shall leave to specialist scholars.

I wish to address here only the much more limited question of the bearing of Roemer's work for any present-day model of surplus and class. Compared to a Marxian model, our generic classical model is extremely simple, as the reader will be well aware. If one must link it to a particular ancestor, it is much closer to Smith than it is to Marx. To mention only one glaringly obvious point, our generic classical model makes no use whatever of the labour theory of value. For the historical Marx, the analysis of the exploitation of one class by another was profoundly linked to labour value concepts. It is thus only natural that, when Roemer eliminates labour values, Marxian scholars will protest that he has lost touch with Marx.

With regard to our generic classical model, on the other hand, he is eliminating a concept of which we made no use. What he *is* doing, however, is of key importance to the present work. To see this we have to return to our very first theme: methodological individualism.

As stressed in Chapter 1, it has been possible for a philosophical mind to be drawn to methodological individualism purely from a deep regard for the integrity and standing of the human person. Neo-classical theory, however, has had other fish to fry as well. It has certainly been believed, until Roemer burst upon the scene, that an insistence on this individualist doctrine (even if it was not in fact lived up to) would keep at bay certain concepts which neo-classicism did not wish to embrace, notably the concept of class. But Roemer has demonstrated that one can scrupulously adhere to the neo-Walrasian methodology and yet arrive at a situation where opposed classes have arisen endogenously within a model, and are engaged in conflict. As Michael A. Lebowitz has remarked, Roemer's formal analysis constitutes 'a classic case of hoisting neo-classical economics by its own petard' (Lebowitz 1988: 203).

Lebowitz derives little joy from this, however, since he argues (as have a number of other scholars) that methodological individual-ism in effect stands Marx on his head. I am only too ready to grant that this may indeed be so, since I do not believe that even neo-Walrasian models (which as we know normally abstract from most of the great issues of classical political economy) can embody more than lip service to the individualist doctrine, as was argued at length in Chapter 1.

My present interest in Roemer's results, however, does not re-quire in the least that methodological individualism have any valid-ity whatsoever. I leave that issue aside. I am concerned with the implication of Roemer's argument that even a neo-classical model, and even one which is circumscribed severely enough to conform fully to methodological individualism, can be shown to partition into conflicting classes when all agent's endowments are not iden-tical in value.

The reader is already familiar from Chapters 6 and 7 with neo-classical models which, because of their high level of unreality, can be construed as wholly consistent with individualism. The agents in an Edgeworth economy can be interpreted as individual persons. They can, moreover, form and reform coalitions. Roemer does not have to keep all productive activity off-stage, he simply has to keep the allowed technology elementary enough to prevent the solidifi-cation of impenetrable black boxes. To take the most obvious case, a capitalist (who is a single person) can provide capital (say corn) for a number of workers to plant and cultivate in return for a wage. Roemer can set up an Arcadian scene populated exclusively by exemplary neo-classical agents, each interpreted as a single person and each engaged in choosing and acting in perfect conformity with the axioms which characterize the constructed concept of rationality found in such models. He can then show that the dismal shadow of classical concepts like class conflict can fall even over this pastoral scene. Even in Arcadia, it is there. Thus it appears that one cannot avoid the dark struggle of opposed classes even by living among the tranquil Pareto optimalities of neo-Walrasian competitive equilibrium.

Rationality, it will be seen, is centre stage again; but the agents who are to exemplify it must seek a coalition, forming one class for protection from another. Edgeworth was wont to link war and trade, and echoes of Edgeworth can be heard in Roemer, not least because Roemer's approach is essentially game-theoretic. He argues that, if one is concerned with the analysis of paths of transition, 'of convergence to the new equilibrium, I think class struggle and therefore methodological individualism and game theoretic analyses in particular are key' (Roemer 1982*a*: 514). In his preoccupation with convergence to equilibrium, he recalls the interests of recent classical theorists glanced at earlier in this chapter, and also that of recent neo-Walrasian theorists of temporary equilibrium.

Roemer develops a rich taxonomy of models, purporting to analyse the contrasting class phenomena in feudal, capitalist, and socialist economies. Certain features, however, are typical of these models as a whole. The agents obey the standard neo-Walrasian axioms characterizing rationality. They have given endowments, and face a given technology. Their individually 'optimal' choices, given these endowments and technology, lead to the emergence of different classes. It is shown that the classes arise because of the unequal endowments possessed by the different agents. Some comments on this last point are important.

First, canonical neo-Walrasian models did not require that the endowments of every agent be identical in form, nor that they be identical in exchange value. So Roemer is not making an eccentric or special assumption. Secondly, Roemer's individual agents can be perfect competitors, just like those in canonical neo-Walrasian models. Thirdly, there need be no cheating or coercion. An agent whose endowment is insufficient to support life without working will have to seek employment, but Roemer sees to it that there will typically be alternative employments, so the agent will have a choice. (The exception is in his model of feudalism, where the agent, if a peasant, is coerced to work for a lord.) Fourthly, Roemer's agents can all have the same preferences and the same talents (except in the analysis of socialist exploitation, where differences in agents' endowments of inalienable abilities are a big part of the analysis).

Roemer often attributes the emergence of classes in his models simply to the differential endowments, together with 'the scarcity of capital relative to the labor available for it to employ' (Roemer 1988: 23). But as has been pointed out by James Devine and Gary Dymski, the capacity of the model economy to yield a surplus is also vital: 'the feasibility of surplus output beyond subsistence—is simply asserted on the basis that the capitalist economy *has* a "productive" technology' (Devine and Dymski 1991: 258, emphasis in original; see also p. 263).

Now the non-economist reader may be puzzled by the appearance of the concept of surplus in a neo-Walrasian model. It is true that this concept does not typically appear in such models. Indeed, where all inputs are treated as the services of a set of given resources, the concept of surplus is even without definition in the model. We must observe, however, that models have existed for a long time which are neo-Walrasian in respect of their treatment of the preferences of agents, but which introduce produced capital goods, as well as the services of non-produced factors, into the analysis. A distinguished example already noted is Bliss (1975). In such models, the supply of capital goods produced is normally more than enough to replace those used up, making growth possible. There is thus a net product, or surplus. It should also be noted that neo-classics, such as Hahn (1982) have argued that (for example) Sraffa's model is obtainable from theirs, upon restricting the neo-Walrasian model in various ways.

Roemer's agents seek optimal solutions (which will depend on the particular model) within the constraints set by their given endowments and the technology, and subject to the requirement that the value of their endowments not be run down.[10] Prices are said to

---

[10] It is arguable that over a series of periods of production in some of Roemer's models the requirements for the reproduction of the capital stock, of the labour force, and of surplus and positive profits, might not all be met consistently. Possibilities of such dynamic inconsistency in some of Roemer's models are investigated by (for example) Devine and Dymski (1991: 247–64). Roemer himself notes that 'if my static model is allowed to run for many periods, the accumulation of capital will eventually drive the profit rate to zero (assuming the labor force does not grow at the same rate)' (Roemer 1992: 150). But he adds that there are various ways available in which one can embed his micromodels of agent's choices (found in Roemer 1982*b*) 'in consistent dynamic models of a capitalist economy' (ibid.).

equilibrate the economy 'if, subject to individual optimization, the economy can feasibly reproduce' (Roemer 1982*b*: 34). His term for an equilibrium in a model is a *reproducible solution*. Clearly, the classical reproduction characteristics of these models are as much centre stage as are their neo-Walrasian treatment of the free choices of individual agents.

The agents can all have the same access to the technology, the same preferences, and the same subsistence needs, differing simply in the property they own. Given this difference in endowments, there may well be agents who are unable to reproduce and survive on their own. It may then be possible for a sufficiently rich agent to do no work, instead employing poorly endowed agents. Roemer shows how his simple economies then decompose into a number of classes. An agent 'chooses his class position as a consequence of optimizing against a capital constraint' (Roemer 1982*b*: 77). With capital in the picture, his prices become classical, or Sraffa prices, consistent with reproduction and yielding a uniform intersectoral rate of profit in equilibrium. Again as in Sraffa, Roemer's models can be freed from the subsistence wage assumption, and in fact he frees his concept of exploitation from dependence on subsistence.

He argues that a concept of exploitation in labour terms gets into difficulties when two standard assumptions of reproduction models are dropped: (1) the assumption that every worker contributes the same amount of labour power, and (2) the assumption that labour is homogeneous. Hitherto in his models, with these assumptions he could rank the agents consistently according to three characteristics, wealth, class, and exploitation status. So exploitation status could serve as a proxy for both wealth and class, which 'lends an implicit justification to our calling the phenomenon exploitation, since we got the sensible conclusion that the wealthy were the exploiters and the poor were exploited' (Roemer 1982*b*: 175). But with the introduction of differential labour endowments it becomes logically possible for rich agents to be exploited and for poor agents to be exploiters. Thus he feels bound to abandon a labour theory of exploitation. If, in addition, we introduce heterogeneous labour, he finds it simply unclear how exploitation can be defined as the inability to purchase goods embodying as much labour as an agent supplied. How can different kinds of labour be added? He proposes an alternative theory which includes the labour theory of exploitation as a special case (existing where labour endowments are equal among agents, and labour is homogeneous).

The original classics wrote during a period when it was still fairly reasonable to use an assumption of homogeneous labour. This cannot be said of any classical model today, except where simplicity is an overriding consideration. Homogeneous labour belongs in simple models like the corn model, whose purposes are solely pedagogical. Beyond that, homogeneous labour must join the neo-classical concept of homogeneous capital in much needed retirement.

Now of course, as already noted, present-day classical models do not in general use the concept of labour values, and so the formal concept of exploited labour is not defined in these models. Classes are defined simply in terms of their relation to the net product; thus, historically, a working class has existed in developed economies which did not have control over the disposition of the surplus, while at different times a landlord class, a capitalist class, and a class of state bureaucrats *have* had control over how this surplus was allocated and used. In present-day classical models following Sraffa, the working class may have some share of the surplus, and then must bear some (proportional) share of the responsibility for how it is used.

Roemer's general concept of exploitation, however, makes no use of labour values, being derived simply from differing endowments and the concept of class. It is therefore a notion which can be used 'whenever people use the word "exploit" in reference to economic inequality' (Roemer 1982*b*: 195). Briefly, where N is a society and S is a coalition within N, the coalition S is said to be exploited if and only if:

1. There exists an alternative state of the society in which S would be 'better off'.
2. In the alternative state, the complement to S (i.e. the coalition N–S) which will be designated S' would be 'worse off'.
3. S' is in a relationship of *dominance* over S, i.e. at the least the coalition S' is *preventing* the alternative state coming about.

Recall from our Chapter 6 the concept of the core of an exchange economy. We are familiar with the idea that a coalition may be able to block certain allocations. It can withdraw, and stop trading with the rest of the traders in the model. As Roemer puts it: 'If a coalition S can do better for its members [by] withdrawing, and if the complementary coalition to it, S', does worse after S's withdrawal, then S is exploited under that particular specification of the rules of the game' (Roemer 1982*b*: 195).

In order to understand Roemer's analysis of capitalist production, it is necessary to be aware that his capitalists are not also active in production as managers or entrepreneurs. As an analytical category, for Roemer, capitalists' income is received purely from the ownership of capital which others use. And his concept of capitalist exploitation pertains solely to this income. In his models a high income from entrepreneurial risk taking, administrative talent, etc. *can* contain an element of exploitation. But if it does, this is referred to by the (at first glance) somewhat strange term 'socialist exploitation'. The point of the name is that this category of exploitation persisted and flourished in the socialist regimes of the present century. The concept derives quite simply from the existence of property rights in rare talents. Under socialism as we have seen it develop, high incomes paid for rare talents have, he argues, been the inalienable property of the possessor. Thus the entrepreneur under capitalism and the scientist, ballerina, or artist under socialism or capitalism are examples of this concept.[11]

Socialism and capitalism share in Roemer's work at least one other category of exploitation, which he calls status exploitation. He is referring to the ability of an entrenched bureaucracy to secure high incomes and/or privileges for its top echelons. One can see that the CEO of a large corporation, the apparatchik and the cardinal, are all cases in point.

The models so far considered have constant returns to scale technologies, a common feature of present-day reproduction models. Roemer notes that problems arise when increasing returns, or indivisibilities in production, are introduced. An individual worker may now be unable to use the technology on her own. This poses problems for methodological individualism, and for a concept of exploitation which is stated (as Roemer's is) in scrupulously

---

[11] Roemer's concept of socialist exploitation would thus apply even in an 'idyllic socialist economy where private property is not held in alienable assets, but inalienable assets are held by individuals' (Roemer 1982*b*: 212). This would only disappear if each member of the idyllic society were compensated according to needs. For some comments on the concept of needs, see Sen 1973, 1992, and Walsh 1995.

methodological individualist terms. He seeks to address this problem while preserving the importance of the individual person. The result is an interesting concept of class.

An agent is said to be vulnerable if she belongs to a minimal exploited coalition, and culpable if she belongs to a minimal exploiting coalition. We may then get a partition of the set of agents into the exploited coalition and the exploiting coalition. (There may be a non-empty third coalition, composed of any agents who are neither exploiting nor exploited, referred to as the set of strongly neutral agents.) He sees the collection of all the vulnerable agents as '*the* canonically exploited class in the economy' (Roemer 1982*b*: 224, emphasis in original). His aim is to find a procedure by which agents acting individually would coalesce so as to form the exploited coalition. If they do so coalesce, 'some explanation based on rational behavior could be offered for considering the coalition then formed the canonically exploited coalition' (Roemer 1982*b*: 227). He argues that a process of such coalition formation is the form which class struggle takes in his models.

One does not have to deny that Roemer's models have their share of problems in order to recognize their significance. The implications of the classical concept of a reproduction structure generating a net product, when grafted onto a model society of individual persons with Walrasian rationality characteristics, is surely strikingly illuminated in Roemer's models—as should be visible even from this brief sketch of a few of his concepts.

It is not really a criticism of Roemer to point out that the very nature of his project imports into this treatment of rationality in models with explicit reproduction structures just precisely those shortcomings which are to be found in the formal treatment of rationality in the canonical Arrow–Debreu tradition. A brief notice of this will take us back to our major theme.

WELFARIST CONSEQUENTIALISM IN MODELS OF SURPLUS AND CLASS

In discussing repressive regimes, Roemer asks what should be thought of denials of civil liberties 'which do not have economic consequences' (Roemer 1982*b*: 263 n. 12). He remarks that one could expand the scope of the concept of exploitation 'to include political repression, as that enters into the determination of individuals' *welfare*' (ibid., emphasis added). In the choice of 'welfare' in this passage, Roemer is simply being true to his neo-Walrasian methodology. And it should be noted that he is well aware of the limitations inherent in the treatment of optimal choice in his models: 'They evaluate the improvement in a person's position in a static and simplistic way, by asking if his "utility function" achieves a higher value under the alternative arrangement' (Roemer 1982*b*: 266). He points out that such utility based comparisons will not do when the mode of production changes, and for such historic comparisons abandons utility theory, resorting to a weak criterion based only on income and leisure. He explicitly recognizes the problems of non-comparability arising from efforts to compare the income-leisure bundles of, say, feudal serfs and early capitalist workers. And in discussing the question why people regard the successive elimination of forms of exploitation as good, he chooses to stress the desirability of the self-actualization of persons, citing Rawls's concept of primary goods—necessary for the attainment of life plans and Sen's basic capabilities, which we may lack the means to realize.

There is even a point where he throws off the yoke of that neo-classical idol, Pareto optimality. He notes that the supporter of Pareto optimality might argue that, in eliminating a type of exploitation, it is possible that the basic capabilities of the agents who were previously exploiters would be infringed. But he argues that typically a large exploited class whose poverty seriously impaired their self-actualization has been exploited by a small class much better endowed than they need to be for their development as persons (see Roemer 1982*b*: 272 and n. 8).

When all this has been said, however, one must observe that Roemer's methodology makes it inevitable that most of the time in his formal models he will be confined within the welfarist consequentialism which, as we have seen at length, is embedded in the axiomatic utility theory which forms a central part of the neo-Walrasian formalism. I do not wish to repeat the criticisms of this position already noted in previous chapters. My point here is that axiomatic utilitarian accounts of rationality become even more strikingly and vividly deficient when agents, born and brought up in the placid and sheltered world of canonical Arrow–Debreu models, are confronted with the harsh realities of the struggle between classes for control of the surplus, as they are in Roemer's models.

Choices must now be made, and actions undertaken, by these agents which contrast sharply with the ranking of commodity bundles and the making of marginal adjustments for which such agents were originally constructed. He is (in this respect) simply heir to a tradition which, as Debra Satz has observed, 'attempts to evaluate social and political institutions solely in terms of their consequences for welfare. In particular, proponents of this tradition deny that agents have direct preferences for institutions and procedures that are independent of their consequences for welfare. A conception of justice, that is, a procedure for ordering the claims and interests of different groups, can only be assessed in terms of its consequences for the welfare of the groups in question' (Satz 1990: 315). The quite separate question of the increasing power in the hands of some one class (whether capitalist, feudal landlord, or state bureaucrat) can thus not be posed. These agents cannot decide that their rights mean more to them than bread and circuses.

The stark facts of the dependence of one class upon another for decisions determining the uses of the surplus are not visible in the usual neo-Walrasian model, and some of the more serious deficiencies of the constructed concept of rationality constitutive of such models are thus hidden from plain view. Roemer's axiomatic utilitarian concept of rationality prevents his showing the full implications of the very classical concepts of class and surplus which he has borrowed from the tradition of which Smith, Ricardo, and Marx were leading proponents.

Once self-interest, believed to be so benign by many neo-classical theorists, takes the form, not of the separate self-interested pursuits of innumerable tiny agents, but rather of the concerted self-interest of classes in confrontation with one another, matters become much more serious. Nor is this the worst scenario: a dispossessed class, its labour eliminated and its desperate need for alternatives spurned by a class flushed with the arrogance of overnight success, cannot be expected to feel any sense of community with those who have turned away from it. Then bitterness may well darken self-interest into ill-calculated present aims, and further into malevolence. All those honest, co-operative, and tolerant usages of a civilized society upon which the market economy (which neo-classics see as running on pure self-interest) in fact ultimately depends are then in peril.

To move to a larger canvas, if the poor countries of this earth become desperate enough, and secure nuclear or biological weaponry, stark tragedy is not impossible.

Those who devoted themselves to the revival and restatement of the themes of classical political economy in this century did not set out by concentrating their attention upon the rational choices or actions of an individual economic agent. But it has become more and more evident over the last twenty years or so that classical concepts such as surplus and class, presented in increasingly sophisticated present-day models, hold up a mirror to neo-classical theory in which can be seen dark features of economic reality which have been without representation in the standard neo-Walrasian picture of rational economic agents.

The shortcomings of axiomatic utilitarianism become more clear, and above all the inadequacy of any purely consistency based, 'value-free' concept of rationality. The need becomes obvious for theory to develop strategies which make it possible to curb the pressure of the powerful upon the vulnerable without destroying the whole structure of human society, and which combine measured conflict where necessary with co-operation where possible. And now if ever the moral philosopher needs to keep insisting on the presence of unexamined values woven into the structure of the supposedly scientifically neutral pronouncements of economists and other social scientists and to keep confronting the rationality claims made in terms of constructed concepts from economic theory and decision theory with the morally non-trivial implications of the ways in which we have learned to speak of the rationality of choices or actions in our ordinary discourse.

References

ABRAMOVITZ, M. (ed.) (1955), *Capital Formation & Economic Growth*, Princeton, Princeton University Press.

AKERLOF, G. (1970), 'The Market for Lemons', *Quarterly Journal of Economics*, 84: 488–500.

ALLAIS, M. (1953a), 'Fondements d'une théorie positive des choix comportant un risque et critique des postulats et axiomes de l'École américaine', Paris, *Économétrie*, Colloques Internationaux du Centre National de la Recherche Scientifique, 40, Memoir III, pp. 257–332. Trans. in Allais and Hagen 1979: 27–145.

——(1953b), 'Généralisation des théories de l'équilibre économique général et du rendement sociale au cas de risque', *Économétrie*, Centre National de la Recherche Scientifique, 40: 81–109.

——(1968), 'Pareto, Vilfredo: Contributions to Economics', in *Encyclopaedia of the Social Sciences*, New York, Macmillan, xi. 399–411.

——(1979a), 'The So-Called Allais Paradox and Rational Decisions under Uncertainty', in Allais and Hagen 1979: 437–681.

——(1979b), 'Foreword', in Allais and Hagen 1979: 3–11.

——(1979c), 'The Foundations of a Positive Theory of Choice Involving Risk and a Criticism of the Postulates and Axioms of the American School', in Allais and Hagen 1979: 27–145.

——(1988), 'The General Theory of Random Choices in Relation to the Invariant Cardinal Utility Function and the Specific Probability Function: The (U, θ) Model: A General Overview', in Munier 1988: 231–89.

——and HAGEN, O. (eds.) (1979), *Expected Utility Hypotheses and the Allais Paradox*, Dordrecht, Reidel.

ANAND, P. (1987), 'Are the Preference Axioms Really Rational?', *Theory and Decision*, 23: 189–214.

——(1993), *Foundations of Rational Choice under Risk*, Oxford, Clarendon Press.

ANDERSON, W. H. L., and THOMPSON, F. W. (1988), 'Neo-classical Marxism', *Science and Society*, 52: 215–28.

ARENA, R., FROESCHLE, C., and TORRE, D. (1984), 'Gravitation et reproductibilité: un point de vue classique', in Bidard 1984: 1–36.

ARROW, K. J. (1951a), 'An Extension of the Basic Theorems of Classical Welfare Economics', in J. Neyman (ed.), *Proceedings of the Second Berkeley Symposium on Mathematical Statistics and Probability*, Berkeley and Los Angeles, University of California Press, 507–32.

——[1951b] (1963), *Social Choice and Individual Values*, New York, Wiley.

ARROW, K. J. (1953), 'Rôle des valeurs boursières pour la répartition la meilleure des risques', *Économétrie*, Centre National de la Recherche Scientifique, 40: 41–7.

—— (1967), 'Public and Private Values', in Hook 1967: 3–21.

—— and DEBREU, G. (1954), 'Existence of an Equilibrium for a Competitive Economy', *Econometrica*, 22: 265–90.

—— and HAHN, F. H. (1971), *General Competitive Analysis*, San Francisco, Holden Day.

—— and RAYNAUD, H. (1986), *Social Choice and Multicriterion Decision Making*, Cambridge, Mass., MIT Press.

AUMANN, R. J.(1962), 'Utility Theory without the Completeness Axiom', *Econometrica*, 30: 445–62.

—— (1964*a*), 'Markets with a Continuum of Traders', *Econometrica*, 32: 39–50.

—— (1964*b*), 'A Correction', *Econometrica*, 32: 210–12.

—— (1987), 'Game Theory', in Eatwell, Milgate, and Newman 1987: ii. 460–82.

AUSTIN, J. L. (1961), *Philosophical Papers*, ed. J. O. Urmson, Oxford, Clarendon Press.

AXELROD, R. (1984), *The Evolution of Cooperation*, New York, Basic Books.

AYER, A. J. [1936] (1946), *Language Truth and Logic*, New York, Dover Publications.

AZARIADIS, C., and STIGLITZ, J. E. (1983), 'Implicit Contracts and Fixed Price Equilibria', *Quarterly Journal of Economics*, 98, Suppl., pp. 1–22.

BACHARACH, M., and HURLEY, S. L. (eds.) (1991), *Foundations of Decision Theory: Issues and Advances*, Oxford, Blackwell.

BAIGENT, N., and GAERTNER, W. (1993), 'Never Choose the Uniquely Largest: A Characterization', Mimeographed, University of Osnabruck.

BAR-HILLEL, M., and MARGALIT, A. (1988), 'How Vicious are Cycles of Intransitive Choice?', *Theory and Decision*, 24: 119–45.

BASU, K. (1984), 'The Right to Give up Rights', *Economica*, 51: 413–22.

BATEMAN, B. W. (1987), 'Keynes's Changing Conception of Probability', *Economics and Philosophy*, 3: 97–119.

—— and DAVIS, J. B. (1991), *Keynes and Philosophy: Essays on the Origin of Keynes's Thought*, Aldershot, Elgar.

BENTHAM, J. [1789] (1970), *An Introduction to the Principles of Morals and Legislation*, London, T. Payne and Son. Republished, ed. J. H. Burns and H. L. A. Hart. London, Athlone Press.

—— (1822), *An Introduction to the Principles of Morals and Legislation*, London, T. Payne and Son.

BERNOULLI, D. [1738] (1954), 'Specimen Theoriae Novae de Mensura Sortis', in *Commentarii Academiae Scientiarum Imperialis Petropolitanae*, v. Trans. L. Sommer, *Econometrica*, 22: 23–36.

BEWLEY, T. (ed.) (1987), *Advances in Economic Theory, Fifth World Congress*, Cambridge, Cambridge University Press.

BIDARD, C. (ed.) (1984), *La Gravitation*, Cahiers de la RCP, Systèmes de Prix de Production, 2, 3, Paris, University of Paris, Nanterre.

BIDERMAN, S., and SCHARFSTEIN, B.-A. (1989), *Rationality in Question*, New York, E. J. Brill.

BLACK, D. (1958), *The Theory of Committees and Elections*, Cambridge, Cambridge University Press.

BLISS, C. J. (1975), *Capital Theory and the Distribution of Income*, New York, American Elsevier.

BOGGIO, L. (1984), 'Convergence to Production Prices under Alternative Disequilibrium Assumptions', in Bidard 1984.

BOSS, H. (1990), *Theories of Surplus and Transfer; Parasites and Producers in Economic Thought*, Boston, Unwin Hyman.

BOULDING, K. E. (1966), *Economic Analysis*, i: *Microeconomics*, 4th edn., New York, Harper and Row.

——(1967), 'The Basis of Value Judgements in Economics', in Hook 1967: 55–72.

——(1970), *Economics as a Science*, New York, McGraw-Hill.

BRADLEY, J., and HOWARD, M. (eds.) (1982), *Classical & Marxian Political Economy: Essays in Memory of Ronald Meek*, London, Macmillan.

BRANDT, R. B. (1959), *Ethical Theory*, Englewood Cliffs, NJ, Prentice Hall.

BRAY, M. (1987), 'Perfect Foresight', in Eatwell, Milgate, and Newman 1987: iii. 834–5.

BROOME, J. (1991a), *Weighing Goods: Equality, Uncertainty and Time*, Oxford, Blackwell.

——(1991b), 'Utility', *Economics and Philosophy*, 7: 1–12.

——(1991c), 'A Reply to Sen', *Economics and Philosophy*, 7: 285–7.

——(1992), 'Deontology and Economics', *Economics and Philosophy*, 8: 269–82.

BROWN, D. J., and ROBINSON, A. (1972), 'A Limit Theorem on the Cores of Large Standard Exchange Economies', *Proceedings of the National Academy of Sciences of the USA*, 69: 1258–60.

——(1975), 'Non-standard Exchange Economies', *Econometrica*, 43: 41–55.

BROWN, M., SATO, K., and ZAREMBKA, P. (eds.) (1976), *Essays in Modern Capital Theory*, Amsterdam, North Holland.

BROWN, V. (1991), 'Signifying Voices: Reading the "Adam Smith" Problem', *Economics and Philosophy*, 7: 187–220.

BUCHANAN, J. M. (1987), 'Constitutional Economics', in Eatwell, Milgate, and Newman 1987: i. 585–8.

BURMEISTER, E. (1977), 'The Irrelevance of Sraffa's Analysis without Constant Returns to Scale', *Journal of Economic Literature*, 15: 68–70.

278 References

BUSINO, G. (ed.) (1964–84), *Œuvres complètes de Vilfredo Pareto*, Geneva, Droz.

BUTKIEWICZ, J., KOFORD, K., and MILLER, J. (eds.) (1986), *Keynes' Economic Legacy*, New York, Praeger.

CARABELLI, A. (1988), *On Keynes's Method*, London, Macmillan.

CHIKAN, A. (ed.) (1991), *Progress in Decision, Utility and Risk*, Dordrecht, Kluwer.

CHIPMAN, J. S., HURWICZ, L., RICHTER, M. K., and SONNENSCHEIN, H. F. (eds.) (1971), *Preferences, Utility and Demand*, New York, Harcourt Brace Jovanovich.

COLES, J. L., and HAMMOND, P. G. (1986), 'Walrasian Equilibrium without Survival: Existence, Efficiency and Remedial Policy', Stanford University Institute for Mathematical Studies in the Social Sciences, Economics Technical Report No. 483, Presented at the 5th World Congress of the Econometric Society, Boston.

CONDORCET, M. J. A. N. C. (1785), *Essai sur l'application de l'analyse à la probabilité des décisions rendues à la pluralité des voix*, Paris, Imprimerie Royale.

COPLESTON F. [1950] (1962), *A History of Philosophy*, ii: *Mediaeval Philosophy*, Part I, New York, Image Books.

COTTRELL, A. (1993), 'Keynes's Theory of Probability and its Relevance to his Economics: Three Theses', *Economics and Philosophy*, 9: 25–51.

COURNOT, A. A. [1838] (1929), *Recherches sur les principes mathématiques de la théorie des richesses*, Paris, Hachette. Trans. N. T. Bacon, New York, Macmillan.

CREEDY, J. (1986), *Edgeworth and the Development of Neo-classical Economics*, Oxford, Blackwell.

CUBITT, R. P. (1993), 'On the Possibility of Rational Dilemmas: An Axiomatic Approach', *Economics and Philosophy*, 9: 1–20.

DABONI, L., MONTESANO, A., and LINES, M. (1986), *Recent Developments in the Foundations of Utility and Risk Theory*, Dordrecht, Reidel, 215–29.

DAVIS, J. B. (1990), 'Cooter and Rapoport on the Normative', *Economics and Philosophy*, 6: 139–46.

DEBREU, G. (1951), 'The Coefficient of Resource Utilization', *Econometrica*, 19: 273–92.

——(1954), 'Representation of a Preference Ordering by a Numerical Function', in Thrall, Cooms, and Davis 1954: 159–65.

——(1959), *The Theory of Value: An Axiomatic Analysis of Economic Equilibrium*, New York, Wiley.

——(1967), 'Preference Functions on Measure Spaces of Economic Agents', *Econometrica*, 35: 111–22.

——and SCARF, H. (1963), 'A Limit Theorem on the Core of an Economy', *International Economic Review*, 4: 235–47.

DEVINE, J., and DYMSKI, G. A. (1991), 'Roemer's "General" Theory of Exploitation is a Special Case: The Limits of Walrasian Marxism', *Economics and Philosophy*, 7: 235–73.

DEWEY, J., and TUFTS, J. H. (1932), *Ethics*, New York, H. Holt.

DMITRIEV, V. K. [1892–1902] (1974), *Ekonomicheskie Ocherki*, trans. D. Fry, V. K. Dmitriev, *Economic Essays on Value, Competition and Utility*, ed. D. M. Nutti, Cambridge, Cambridge University Press.

DRÈZE, J., and SEN, A. K. (1989), *Hunger and Public Action*, Oxford, Clarendon Press.

DUMÉNIL, G., and LÉVY, D. (1984), 'Une restauration de l'analyse classique de la dynamique concurrentielle', in Bidard 1984: 1–48.

——(1985), 'The Classicals and the Neo-classicals: A Rejoinder to Frank Hahn', *Cambridge Journal of Economics*, 9: 327–45.

——(1987), 'The Dynamics of Competition: A Restoration of the Classical Analysis', *Cambridge Journal of Economics*, 11: 133–64.

——(1989*a*), 'The Analysis of the Competitive Process in a Fixed Capital Environment: A Classical View', *Manchester School of Economic and Social Studies*, 57: 34–57.

——(1989*b*), 'Micro Adjustment Behavior and Macro Stability', *Seoul Journal of Economics*, 2: 1–37.

——(1991*a*), 'The Classical Legacy and Beyond', *Structural Change and Economic Dynamics*, 2: 37–67.

——(1991*b*), 'Convergence to Long-Period Positions, with the Benefit of Hindsight', Paris, CEPREMAP, LAREA-CEDRA.

EATWELL, J. (1977), 'The Irrelevance of Returns to Scale in Sraffa's Analysis', *Journal of Economic Literature*, 15: 61–8.

——(1982), 'Competition', in Bradley and Howard 1982: 203–28.

——and MILGATE, M. (eds.) (1983), *Keynes's Economics and the Theory of Value and Distribution*, New York, Oxford University Press.

——and NEWMAN, P. (eds.) (1987), *The New Palgrave: A Dictionary of Economics*, London, Macmillan.

——and PANICO, C. (1987), 'Sraffa, Piero', in Eatwell, Milgate, and Newman 1987: iv. 445–52.

EDGEWORTH, F. Y. (1877), *New and Old Methods of Ethics*, Oxford, James Parker.

——(1879), 'The Hedonical Calculus', *Mind*, 4: 349–409.

——(1881), *Mathematical Psychics: An Essay on the Application of Mathematics to the Moral Sciences*, London, Kegan Paul.

ELSTER, J. (1985), *Making Sense of Marx*, Cambridge, Cambridge University Press.

——and HYLLAND, A. (eds.) (1986), *Foundations of Social Choice Theory*, Cambridge, Cambridge University Press.

ESSLER, W. K., PUTNAM, H., and STEGMÜLLER, W. (eds.) (1985), *Epistemology, Methodology and Philosophy of Science: Essays in Honor of Carl G. Hempel on the Occasion of his 80th Birthday*, Dordrecht, Reidel.

FEIWEL, G. R. (ed.) (1989), *Joan Robinson and Modern Economic Theory*, London, Macmillan.

FELLNER, W. (1967), 'Operational Utility: The Theoretical Background and a Measurement', in Fellner *et al.* 1967: 39–74.

——*et al.* (eds.) (1967), *Ten Economic Studies in the Tradition of Irving Fisher*, New York, Wiley.

FISHBURN, P. C. (1979), 'On the Nature of Expected Utility', in Allais and Hagen 1979: 243–57.

FLASCHEL, P., and SEMMLER, W. (1987), 'Classical and Neo-classical Competitive Adjustment Processes', *Manchester School*, 55: 13–37.

——— (1988), 'On Composite Classical and Keynesian Micro-dynamical Processes', Working Paper, Dept. of Economics, University of Bielefeld.

——— (1989), 'On the Integration of Dual and Cross-Dual Adjustment Processes in Leontief Systems', *Richerche economiche*, 42: 403–32.

FOLLESDAL, D., and HILPINEN, R. (1970), 'Deontic Logic: An Introduction', in Hilpinen 1970: 1–35.

FOOT, P. [1983] (1988), 'Utilitarianism and the Virtues', *Proceedings and Addresses of the American Philosophical Association*, 57: 273–83. Repr. *Mind*, 94 (1985), pp. 196–209, cited from Scheffler 1988: 224–42.

FRANKFURT, H. G. (1971), 'Freedom of the Will and the Concept of a Person', *Journal of Philosophy*, 68: 5–20.

FRASSEN, B. VAN (1973), 'Values and the Heart's Command', *Journal of Philosophy*, 70: 5–19.

FRIED, C. (1978), *Right and Wrong*, Cambridge, Mass., Harvard University Press.

GALE D., and MAS-COLLEL, A. (1975), 'An Equilibrium Existence Theorem for a General Model without Ordered Preferences', *Journal of Mathematical Economics*, 2: 9–15.

GARDENFORS, P., and SAHLIN, N.-E. (eds.) (1988), *Decision, Probability and Utility*, Cambridge, Cambridge University Press.

GAREGNANI, P. [1976] (1983), 'On a Change in the Notion of Equilibrium in Recent Work on Value and Distribution', in Brown, Sato, and Zarembka 1976: 25–45. Cited from Eatwell and Milgate 1983: 129–45.

GARFINKEL, A. (1981), *Forms of Explanation*, New Haven, Yale University Press.

GEORGE, D. (1984), 'Metapreferences: Reconsidering Contemporary Notions of Free Choice', *International Journal of Social Economics*, 11: 92–107.

——(1989), 'Social Evolution and the Role of Knowledge', *Review of Social Economy*, 47: 55–73.

——(1993), 'Does the Market Create Preferred Preferences?', *Review of Social Economy*, 51: 323–46.

GEORGESCU-ROEGEN, N. [1936] (1966), 'The Pure Theory of Consumer's Behavior', in Georgescu-Roegen 1966: 133–70.

——(1966), *Analytical Economics*, Cambridge, Mass., Harvard University Press.

GIBBARD, A. (1965), 'Rule Utilitarianism: Merely an Illusory Alternative?', *Australasian Journal of Philosophy*, 93: 211–20.

——(1974), 'A Pareto-Consistent Libertarian Claim', *Journal of Economic Theory*, 7: 388–410.

GILSON, E. [1938] (1966), *Reason and Revelation in the Middle Ages*, New York, Scribner.

GOODWIN, R. M. [1953] (1983), 'Static and Dynamic Linear General Equilibrium Models', in Goodwin 1983: 75–120.

——(1983), *Essays in Linear Economic Structures*, London, Macmillan.

GORMAN, W. M. (1968), 'The Structure of Utility Functions', *Review of Economic Studies*, 35: 367–90.

——(1984), 'Towards a Better Economic Methodology?', in Wiles and Routh 1984: 260–88.

GRAM, H. N. (1976), 'Two-Sector Models in the Theory of Capital and Growth', *American Economic Review*, 66: 891–903.

——(1985), 'Duality and Positive Profits', *Contributions to Political Economy*, 4: 61–77.

——(1989), 'Ideology and Time: Criticisms of General Equilibrium', in Feiwel 1989: 285–302.

——and WALSH, V. C. (1983), 'Joan Robinson's Economics in Retrospect', *Journal of Economic Literature*, 21: 518–58.

GRIFFIN, J. (1986), *Well-Being*, Oxford, Clarendon Press.

GROSSMAN, S., and HART, O. (1983), 'Implicit Contracts under Asymmetric Information', *Quarterly Journal of Economics*, 71: 123–57.

HAGEN, O. (1979), 'Introductory Survey', in Allais and Hagen 1979: 13–24.

——and WENSTØP, F. (eds.) (1984), *Progess in Utility and Risk Theory*, Dordrecht, Reidel.

HAHN, F. H. (1982), 'The Neo-Ricardians', *Cambridge Journal of Economics*, 6: 353–74.

——(1984), *Equilibrium and Macroeconomics*, Cambridge, Mass., MIT Press.

——(1989), 'Robinson–Hahn Love-Hate Relationship: An Interview', in Feiwel 1989: 895–910.

——and HOLLIS, M. (1979), *Philosophy and Economic Theory*, Oxford, Clarendon Press.

HALEVI, J., LAIBMAN, D., and NELL, E. J. (eds.) (1992), *Beyond the Steady State: A Revival of Growth Theory*, London, Macmillan.

HAMMOND, P. J. (1987a), 'Uncertainty', in Eatwell, Milgate, and Newman 1987: iv. 728–33.

——(1987b), 'Altruism', in Eatwell, Milgate, and Newman 1987: i. 85–6.

——(1988a), 'Orderly Decision Theory: A Comment on Professor Seidenfeld', *Economics and Philosophy*, 4, pp. 292–7.

——(1988b), 'Consequentialist Foundations for Expected Utility', *Theory and Decision*, 25: 25–78.

——(1989), 'Some Assumptions of Contemporary Neo-classical Economic Theology', in Feiwel 1989: 186–257.

HAMPTON, J. (1994), 'The Failure of Expected-Utility Theory as a Theory of Rationality', *Economics and Philosophy*, 10: 195–242.

HARE, R. M. (1976), 'Ethical Theory and Utilitarianism', in Lewis 1976: 113–31.

——(1981), *Moral Thinking: Its Levels, Method and Point*, Oxford, Clarendon Press.

HARRIS, D. J. (1982), 'Structural Change and Economic Growth: A Review Article', *Contributions to Political Economy*, 1: 25–45.

HARROD, R. F. (1936), 'Utilitarianism Revisited', *Mind*, 45: 137–56.

HARSANYI, J. C. (1983), 'Rule Utilitarianism, Equality and Justice', Working Paper CP-438, Center for Research in Management Science, University of California at Berkeley.

HART, O. and HÖLMSTROM, B. R. (1987), 'The Theory of Contracts', in Bewley 1987: 71–155.

HAUSMAN, D. M. (1989), 'On Justifying the Ways of Mammon to Man', in Feiwel 1989: 821–32.

HELLMAN, G. P., and THOMPSON, F. W. (1975), 'Physicalism: Ontology, Determination, and Reduction', *Journal of Philosophy*, 72/17: 552–64.

HERZBERGER, H. (1973), 'Ordinal Preference and Rational Choice', *Econometrica*, 41: 187–237.

HICKS, J. R. (1939), *Value and Capital*, Oxford, Clarendon Press.

——(1956), *A Revision of Demand Theory*, Oxford, Clarendon Press.

——(1965), *Capital and Growth*, Oxford, Clarendon Press.

——and ALLEN, R. D. G. (1934), 'A Reconsideration of the Theory of Value', Parts I–II, *Economica*, 1, Pt. I, pp. 52–76, Pt. II, pp. 196–219.

HILPENIN, R. (ed.) (1970), *Deontic Logic: Introductory and Systematic Readings*, Amsterdam, Reidel.

HIRSCHMAN, A. O. (1982), *Shifting Involvements: Private Interest and Public Action*, Princeton, Princeton University Press.

HOLLIS, M., and NELL, E. J. (1975), *Rational Economic Man: A Philosophical Critique of Neo-classical Economics*, Cambridge, Cambridge University Press.

HÖLMSTROM, B. R., and MYERSON, R. B. (1983), 'Efficient and Durable Decision Rules with Incomplete Information', *Econometrica*, 51: 1799–820.

Hook, S. (ed.) (1967), *Human Values and Economic Policy: A Symposium*, New York, New York University Press.

Howey, R. S. (1960), *The Rise of the Marginal Utility School*, Lawrence, University of Kansas Press.

Hume, D. [1739–40] (1978), *A Treatise of Human Nature*, Oxford, Clarendon Press.

Jeffrey, R. C. (1974), 'Preferences among Preferences', *Journal of Philosophy*, 71: 377–91.

Jevons, W. S. (1871), *The Theory of Political Economy*, London, Macmillan.

——(1879), 'John Stuart Mill's Philosophy Tested. iv: Utilitarianism', *Contemporary Review*, 36: 521–38.

Kahneman, D., and Tversky, A. (1979), 'Prospect Theory: An Analysis of Decision under Risk', *Econometrica*, 47: 263–91.

Keynes, J. M. [1921] (1973), *A Treatise on Probability*, repr. in Keynes, *Collected Writings*, viii.

——[1937] (1973), 'The General Theory of Employment', *Quarterly Journal of Economics*, 57: 209–23, repr. in Keynes, *Collected Writings*, 14: 109–23.

——(1971–88), *The Collected Writings of John Maynard Keynes*, ed. D. Moggridge, London, Macmillan for the Royal Economic Society, 1–30.

Khalil, E. L. (1990), 'Beyond Self-Interest and Altruism: A Reconstruction of Adam Smith's Theory of Human Conduct', *Economics and Philosophy*, 6: 255–73.

Kim, T., and Richter, M. K. (1986), 'Non-transitive Non-Total Consumer Theory', *Journal of Economic Theory*, 38: 324–68.

Kincaid, H. (1986), 'Reduction, Explanation, and Individualism', *Philosophy of Science*, 53: 492–513.

Knight, F. H. (1921), *Risk, Uncertainty, and Profit*, Boston, Houghton Mifflin.

Koopmans, T. C. (1957), *Three Essays on the State of Economic Science*, New York, McGraw Hill.

Kuhn, T. S. (1957), *The Copernican Revolution*, Cambridge, Mass., Harvard University Press.

——(1962), *The Structure of Scientific Revolutions*, Chicago, Chicago University Press.

Kurz, H. D. (1986), 'Classical and Early Neo-classical Economists on Joint Production', *Metroeconomica*, 38: 1–37.

Lall, S., and Stewart, F. (eds.) (1986), *Theory and Reality in Development*, London, Macmillan.

Lancaster, K. J. (1966), 'A New Approach to Consumer Theory', *Journal of Political Economy*, 74: 132–57.

Lawson, T. (1985), 'Uncertainty and Economic Analysis', *Economic Journal*, 95: 909–27.

LAWSON, T. (1987), 'The Relative/Absolute Nature of Knowledge and Economic Analysis', *Economic Journal*, 97: 951–70.

——(1988), 'Probability and Uncertainty in Economic Analysis', *Journal of Post-Keynesian Economics*, 11: 38–65.

——and PESARAN, H. (eds.) (1985), *Keynes' Economics: Methodological Issues*, London, Croom Helm.

LEBOWITZ, M. A. (1988), 'Is "Analytical Marxism" Marxism?', *Science and Society*, 52: 191–214.

LECKY, W. E. H. (1913), *History of the Rise and Influence of the Spirit of Rationalism in Europe*, London, Longmans, Green.

LEONTIEF, W. W. (1966), *Essays in Economics: Theories and Theorizing*, New York, Oxford University Press.

——(1977), *Essays in Economics*, vol. ii, White Plains, NY, M. E. Sharpe.

LEROY, S. F., and SINGELL, L. D. (1987), 'Knight on Risk and Uncertainty', *Journal of Political Economy*, 95: 909–27.

LEVI, I. (1986), *Hard Choices*, Cambridge, Cambridge University Press.

——(1989), 'Reply to Maher', *Economics and Philosophy*, 5: 79–90.

LEWIS, H. D. (ed.) (1976), *Contemporary British Philosophy*, London, Allen and Unwin.

LITTLE, I. M. D. [1950] (1957), *A Critique of Welfare Economics*, Oxford, Clarendon Press. Cited from 2nd edn.

LOOMES, G. and SUGDEN, R. (1982), 'Regret Theory: An Alternative Theory of Rational Choice under Uncertainty', *Economic Journal*, 92: 805–24.

LOWE, A. (1955), 'Structural Analysis of Real Capital Formation', in Abramovitz 1955: 581–634.

——(1976), *The Path of Economic Growth*, Cambridge, Cambridge University Press.

LUCE, R. D., and TUCKER, A. W. (eds.) (1959), *Contributions to the Theory of Games IV*, Annals of Mathematics Studies, 40, Princeton, Princeton University Press.

MABBOTT, J. D. (1956), 'Interpretations of Mill's "Utilitarianism"', *Philosophical Quarterly*, 6: 115–20.

McCLENNEN, E. F. (1988), 'Ordering and Independence: A Comment on Professor Seidenfeld', *Economics & Philosophy*, 4: 298–308.

MACHINA, M. J. (1989), 'Dynamic Consistency and Non-expected Utility Models of Choice under Uncertainty', *Journal of Economic Literature*, 27: 1622–68.

——and ROTHSCHILD, M. (1987), 'Risk', in Eatwell, Milgate, and Newman 1987: iv. 201–5.

McKENZIE, L. W. (1954), 'On Equilibrium in Graham's Model of World Trade and Other Competitive Systems', *Econometrica*, 22: 147–61.

——(1959), 'On the Existence of General Equilibrium for a Competitive Market', *Econometrica*, 27: 54–71.

McMurrin, S. (ed.) (1980), *The Tanner Lectures on Human Values*, i, Salt Lake City, University of Utah Press.

McPherson, M. S. (1984), 'On Hirschman, Schelling, and Sen: Revising the Concept of the Self', *Partisan Review*, 51: 236–47.

Maher, P. (1989), 'Levi on the Allais and Ellsberg Paradoxes', *Economics and Philosophy*, 5: 69–78.

Mainwaring, L. (1984), *Value and Distribution in Capitalist Economies*, Cambridge, Cambridge University Press.

Manara, C. F. (1980), 'Sraffa's Model for the Joint Production of Commodities by Means of Commodities', in Pasinetti 1980: 1–15.

Markowitz, H. M. (1994), 'Robin Popes's Findings on Elaborated Outcomes', Paper presented to the Seventh International Conference on the Foundations and Applications of Utility, Risk & Decision Theory, Norwegian School of Business, Oslo.

Marshall, A. (1961), *Principles of Economics*, ed. C. W. Guillebaud, London, Macmillan, for the Royal Economic Society, 1.

Marx, K. [1959] (1963), *Theorien über den Mehrwert*, ii, Berlin, Dietz Verlag. Cited from the translation, *Theories of Surplus Value*, ii, Moscow, Progress Publishers.

Mas-Collel, A. (1974), 'An Equilibrium Existence Theorem without Complete or Transitive Preferences', *Journal of Mathematical Economics*, 1: pp. 237–46.

——(ed.) (1982), *Non-cooperative Approaches to the Theory of Perfect Competition*, New York, Academic Press.

——(1985), *The Theory of General Economic Equilibrium: A Differentiable Approach*, Cambridge, Cambridge University Press.

May, K. O. (1954), 'Intransitivity, Utility, and the Aggregation of Preference Patterns', *Econometrica*, 22: 1–13.

Mayer, T. F. (1989), 'In Defense of Analytic Marxism', *Science and Society*, 53: 416–41.

Maynard Smith, J. (1982), *Evolution and the Theory of Games*, Cambridge, Cambridge University Press.

Menger, K. (ed.) (1937), *Ergebnisse eines mathematischen Kolloquiums*, 8, Vienna.

Mill, J. S. (1949), *A System of Logic*, 8th edn., London, Longmans.

Mirman, L. J. (1987), 'Perfect Information', in Eatwell, Milgate, and Newman 1987: iii. 836–7.

Mirowski, P. (1984*a*), 'Physics and the "Marginal Revolution"', *Cambridge Journal of Economics*, 8: 361–79.

——(1984*b*), 'The Role of Conservation Principles in 20th Century Economic Theory', *Philosophy of the Social Sciences*, 14: 461–73.

——(1987), 'Shall I Compare Thee to a Minkowski–Ricardo–Leontief–Metzler Matrix of the Mosak–Hicks Type?: Or, Rhetoric, Mathematics, and the Nature of Neo-classical Economic Theory', *Economics & Philosophy*, 3: 67–95.

——(1988), *Against Mechanism: Protecting Economics from Science*, Totowa, NJ, Rowman & Littlefield.

——(1989), *More Heat than Light: Economics as Social Physics, Physics as Nature's Economics*, Cambridge, Cambridge University Press.

MIZUTA, H. (1975), 'Moral Philosophy and Civil Society', in Skinner and Wilson 1975: 114–31.

MORGENSTERN, O., and TUCKER, A. W. (1962), *Advances in Game Theory*, Proceedings of the Princeton University Conference, Philadelphia, Ivy Curtis Press.

MORISHIMA, M. (1969), *Theory of Economic Growth*, Oxford, Clarendon Press.

MORTON, A. (1991), *Disasters and Dilemmas*, Oxford, Clarendon Press.

MUNIER, B. R. (ed.) (1988), *Risk, Decision & Rationality*, Dordrecht, Reidel.

——(1994), 'Hammond's Consequentialism: A Qualification', Paper presented to the *Seventh International Conference on the Foundations and Application of Utility, Risk and Decision Theory*, Norwegian School of Business, Oslo.

NAGEL, T. (1986), *The View from Nowhere*, New York, Oxford University Press.

——(1988), 'Autonomy & Deontology', in Scheffler 1988: 142–72.

NELL, E. J. (1989), 'On Long-Run Equilibrium in Class Society', in Feiwel 1989: 323–43.

NEUMANN, J. VON [1937] (1945–6), 'Über ein öekonomisches Gleichungs-System und eine Verallgemeinerung des Browerschen Fixpunktsatzes', in Menger 1937, trans. as 'A Model of General Economic Equilibrium', *Review of Economic Studies*, 13: 1–9.

——and MORGENSTERN, O. [1944] (1947), *Theory of Games and Economic Behavior*, Princeton, Princeton University Press.

NEWMAN, P. (1962), 'Production of Commodities by Means of Commodities: A Review', *Schweizerische Zeitschrift für Volkswirtschaft und Statistik*, 98: 58–75.

——(1965), *The Theory of Exchange*, Englewood Cliffs, NJ, Prentice-Hall.

——(1987), 'Edgeworth, Francis Ysidro', in Eatwell, Milgate, and Newman 1987: ii. 84–98.

NIKAIDO, H. (1983), 'Marx on Competition', *Zeitschrift für Nationalökonomie*, 43: 337–62.

NITZAN, S., and PAROUSH, J. (1985), *Collective Decision Making: An Economic Outlook*, Cambridge, Cambridge University Press.

NOZICK, R. (1993), *The Nature of Rationality*, Princeton, Princeton University Press.

O'DONNELL, R. M. (1989), *Keynes: Philosophy, Economics and Politics*, New York, St Martin's Press.

PARETO, V. [1898] (1966), 'Comment se pose le problème de l'économie pure', in Busino 1964–84: ix. 102–9.

PARFIT, D. (1984), *Reasons and Persons*, Oxford, Clarendon Press. Citations from reprinting (with corrections) 1987.

PASINETTI, L. L. (1965), 'A New Theoretical Approach to the Problems of Economic Growth', Vatican City, *Pontificiae Academiae Scientiarum Scripta Varia*, 28.

——(ed.) (1980), *Essays on the Theory of Joint Production*, London, Macmillan.

——(1981), *Structural Change and Economic Growth: A Theoretical Essay on the Dynamics of the Wealth of Nations*, Cambridge, Cambridge University Press.

——(1993), *Structural Economic Dynamics: A Theory of the Economic Consequences of Human Learning*, Cambridge, Cambridge University Press.

PETTIT, P. (1991), 'Decision Theory and Folk Psychology', in Bacharach and Hurley 1991: 147–75.

PIGOU, A. C. [1920] (1952), *The Economics of Welfare*, London, Macmillan. Cited from 4th edn.

POPE, R. E. (1983), 'The Pre-outcome Period and the Utility of Gambling', in Stigum and Wenstøp 1983: 137–77.

——(1984), 'The Utility of Gambling and of Outcomes: Inconsistent First Approximations', in Hagen and Wenstøp 1984: 251–73.

——(1985), 'Timing Contradictions in von Neumann & Morgenstern's Axioms and in Savage's "Sure-Thing" Proof', *Theory & Decision*, 18: 229–61.

——(1986), 'Consistency and Expected Utility Theory', in Daboni, Montesano, and Lines 1986: 215–29.

——(1988), 'The Bayesian Approach: Irreconcilable with Expected Utility Theory?', in Munier 1988: 221–30.

——(1991), 'Lowered Welfare under the Expected Utility Procedure', in Chikan 1991: 125–33.

——(1994a), 'The Elusive Positive and Negative Utility of Chance: Part 1 from Adam Smith & Blaise Pascal to Post World War II', Harvard, Kress Seminar Series, June.

——(1994b), 'The Irrationality of the Expected Utility Procedure: Its Omission of Loans and Other Serious Business Considerations Dependent on Credit Risk', Paper presented to the *American Economic Association*.

——(1994c), 'The Expected Utility Procedure's Inability to Include Loans Even with So-Called "Elaborated Outcomes"', Paper presented to the

Seventh International Conference on the Foundations and Application of Utility, Risk and Decision Theory, Norwegian School of Business, Oslo.

PUTNAM, H. (1978), *Meaning and the Moral Sciences*, London, Routledge.

——(1981), *Reason, Truth and History*, Cambridge, Cambridge University Press.

——(1985), 'Reflexive Reflections', in Essler, Putnam and Stegmüller 1985: 143–54.

——[1986] (1989), 'Rationality in Decision Theory and in Ethics', *Critica: Revista hispanoamerica de filosofia*, 18: 3–16, cited from Biderman and Scharfstein 1989: 19–28.

——(1987), *The Many Faces of Realism*, La Salle, Ill., Open Court.

——(1988), *Representation and Reality*, Cambridge, Mass., MIT Press.

——(1990), *Realism with a Human Face*, Cambridge, Mass., Harvard University Press.

QUADRIO-CURZIO, A. (1980), 'Rent, Income Distribution and Orders of Efficiency and Rentability', in Pasinetti 1980: 218–40.

QUINE, W. V. (1963), 'Carnap and Logical Truth', in Schilpp 1963: 385–406.

RADFORD, R. A. (1945), 'The Economic Organization of a P.O.W. Camp', *Economica*, NS 12: 189–201.

RAMSEY, F. P. (1931), *The Foundations of Mathematics*, London, Routledge & Kegan Paul.

RAPHAEL, D. D. (1975), 'The Impartial Spectator', in Skinner and Wilson 1975: 83–99.

——(1985), *Adam Smith*, Oxford, Clarendon Press.

RAPOPORT, A. (1985), 'Application of Game-Theoretic Concepts in Biology', Bulletin of Mathematical Biology, 47: 161–92.

——(1987), 'Prisoner's Dilemma', in Eatwell, Milgate, and Newman 1987: iii. 973–6.

RAWLS, J. (1955), 'Two Concepts of Rules', *Philosophical Review*, 64: 3–32.

——(1958), 'Justice as Fairness', *Philosophical Review*, 67: 164–94.

——(1971), *A Theory of Justice*, Cambridge, Mass., Harvard University Press.

REATI, A. (1994), 'New Developments on Structural Change and the Labor Theory of Value', *Review of Radical Political Economics*, 26: 118–31.

RICHTER, M. K. (1971), 'Rational Choice', in Chipman, Hurwicz, Richter, and Sonnenschein 1971: 29–58.

RILEY, J. (1989), 'Rights to Liberty in Purely Private Matters: Part 1', *Economics and Philosophy*, 5: 121–66.

——(1990), 'Rights to Liberty in Purely Private Matters: Part 2', *Economics and Philosophy*, 6: 27–64.

ROBBINS, L. R. (1932), *An Essay on the Nature and Significance of Economic Science*, London, Macmillan, 2nd edn., 1935.

—— (1938), 'Interpersonal Comparisons of Utility: A Comment', *Economic Journal*, 48: 635–41.

ROBERTS, J. (1987), 'Large Economies', in Eatwell, Milgate, and Newman 1987: iii. 132–3.

ROBINSON, A. (1974), *Non-Standard Analysis*, rev. edn., Amsterdam, North Holland.

ROBINSON, J. V. (1962), *Economic Philosophy*, London, C. A. Watts.

—— [1979] (1980), *Collected Economic Papers*, i–v, Oxford, Blackwell (in the USA, 1980, Cambridge, Mass., MIT Press).

ROEMER, J. E. (1981), *Analytical Foundations of Marxian Economic Theory*, Cambridge, Cambridge University Press.

—— (1982a), 'Methodological Individualism and Deductive Marxism', *Theory and Society*, 11: 513–20.

—— (1982b), *A General Theory of Exploitation and Class*, Cambridge, Mass., Harvard University Press.

—— (1986), *Value, Exploitation, and Class*, New York, Harwood Academic Publishers.

—— (1988), *Free to Lose*, Cambridge, Mass., Harvard University Press.

—— (1992), 'What Walrasian Marxism Can and Cannot Do', *Economics and Philosophy*, 8: 149–56.

ROMILLY, S. (1840), *Memoirs of Sir Samuel Romilly*, citation from Raphael 1975.

RONCAGLIA, A. (1978), *Sraffa and the Theory of Prices*, New York, Wiley.

ROSEN, S. (1985), 'Implicit Contracts: A Survey', *Journal of Economic Literature*, 23: 1144–75.

ROSENBERG, S. E. (1986), *The Christian Problem: A Jewish View*, New York, Hippocrene Books.

ROSS, W. D. (1930), *The Right and the Good*, Oxford, Clarendon Press.

ROTHSCHILD, E. (1992), 'Adam Smith and Conservative Economics', *Economic History Review*, 45: 74–96.

RUNDE, J. (1990), 'Keynesian Uncertainty and the Weight of Arguments', *Economics and Philosophy*, 6: 275–92.

RYLE, G. (1949), *The Concept of Mind*, London, Hutchinson.

SALVADORI, N. (1983), 'Was Sraffa Making No Assumption on Returns?', working paper, Department of Economics, Faculty of Political Science, University of Catania, Italy.

—— and STEEDMAN, J. (1988), 'Joint Production Analysis in a Sraffian Framework', *Bulletin of Economic Research*, 40: 165–95.

SAMUELSON, P. A. [1952] (1966), 'Utility, Preference and Probability', abstract of a paper given at the conference 'Les Fondements et applications de la théorie du risque en économétrie', Paris, repr. in Stiglitz 1966: 127–36.

SATZ, D. (1990), 'John Roemer's *Free to Lose: An Introduction to Marxist Economic Philosophy*', *Economics and Philosophy*, 6: 315–22.

SAVAGE, L. [1954] (1972), *The Foundations of Statistics*, New York, Dover.

SCARF, H. (1962), 'An Analysis of Markets with a Large Number of Partici-pants', in Morgenstern and Tucker 1962: 127–55.

SCHEFFLER, S. (1982), *The Rejection of Consequentialism: A Philosophical Investigation of the Considerations Underlying Rival Moral Conceptions*, Oxford, Clarendon Press.

——(ed.) (1988), *Consequentialism and its Critics*, Oxford, Clarendon Press.

SCHEFOLD, B. (1980), 'Fixed Capital as a Joint Product and the Analysis of Accumulation with Different Forms of Technical Progress', in Pasinetti 1980: 138–217.

SCHELLING, T. C. (1984), 'Self-Command in Practice, in Policy, and in a Theory of Rational Choice', *American Economic Review* (Papers and Proceedings), 74: 1–11.

SCHICK, F. (1984), *Having Reasons: An Essay on Rationality and Sociality*, Princeton, Princeton University Press.

SCHILPP, P. A. (ed.) (1963), *The Philosophy of Rudolph Carnap*, La Salle, Ill., Open Court.

SCHUMM, G. F. (1987), 'Transitivity, Preference, and Indifference', *Philosophical Studies*, 52: 435–7.

SCHWARTZ, T. (1986), *The Logic of Collective Choice*, New York, Columbia University Press.

SCOTT, W. R. (1937), *Adam Smith as Student and Professor*, Glasgow, Glasgow University Publications, 46.

SEIDENFELD, T. (1988), 'Decision Theory without "Independence" or with-out "Ordering": What is the Difference?', *Economics and Philosophy*, 4: 267–90.

SEMMLER, W. (1984), *Competition, Monopoly, and Differential Profit Rates*, New York, Columbia University Press.

SEN, A. K. [1969] (1982), 'Quasi-transitivity, Rational Choice and Collective Decisions', *Review of Economic Studies*, 36: 381–93. Cited from Sen 1982: 118–34.

——[1970] (1982), 'The Impossibility of a Paretian Liberal', *Journal of Political Economy*, 78: 152–207. Cited from Sen 1982: 285–90.

——(1971), 'Choice Functions and Revealed Preference', *Review of Economic Studies*, 38: 307–17.

——(1973), *On Economic Inequality*, Oxford, Clarendon Press.

——[1976] (1982), 'Liberty, Unanimity, and Rights', *Economica*, 43: 217–45. Cited from Sen 1982: 291–326.

——[1977a] (1982), 'Rational Fools: A Critique of the Behavioral Foundations of Economic Theory', *Philosophy and Public Affairs*, 6: 317–44. Cited from Sen 1982: 84–106.

——(1977b), 'Starvation and Exchange Entitlements: A General Approach and its Application to the Great Bengal Famine', *Cambridge Journal of Economics*, 1: 33–59.

——[1980] (1982), 'Equality of What?', in McMurrin 1980. Cited from Sen 1982: 353–69.

——(1981a), *Poverty and Famines: An Essay on Entitlement and Deprivation*, Oxford, Clarendon Press.

——(1981b), 'Ingredients of Famine Analysis: Availability and Entitlements', *Quarterly Journal of Economics*, 95: 433–64.

——(1982), *Choice, Welfare and Measurement*, Cambridge, Mass., MIT Press.

——(1985), 'Rationality and Uncertainty', *Theory and Decision*, 18: 109–27.

——(1986), 'Adam Smith's Prudence', in Lall and Stewart 1986: 28–37.

——(1987), *On Ethics and Economics*, Oxford, Blackwell.

——(1989), 'Economic Methodology: Heterogeneity and Relevance', *Social Research*, 56: 299–329.

——(1991), 'Utility: Ideas and Terminology', *Economics and Philosophy*, 7: 277–83.

——(1992), *Inequality Reexamined*, Cambridge, Mass., Harvard University Press.

——(1993a), 'Money and Value: On the Ethics and Economics of Finance', *Economics and Philosophy*, 9: 203–27.

——(1993b), 'Internal Consistency of Choice', *Econometrica*, 61: 495–521.

——(1994), 'The Formulation of Rational Choice', *American Economic Review* (AEA Papers and Proceedings), 84: 385–90.

——(1995), 'Rationality and Social Choice', *American Economic Review*, 85: 7–24.

——and WILLIAMS, B. (eds.) (1982), *Utilitarianism and Beyond*, Cambridge, Cambridge University Press.

SENSAT, J. (1988), 'Methodological Individualism and Marxism', *Economics and Philosophy*, 4: 189–219.

SHAFER, W. J. (1976), 'Equilibrium in Economics without Ordered Preferences or Free Disposal', *Journal of Mathematical Economics*, 3: 135–7.

SHUBIK, M. (1959), 'Edgeworth Market Games', in Luce and Tucker 1959: 267–78.

SIDGWICK, H. [1874] (1907), *The Methods of Ethics*, London, Macmillan.

SIMON, H. A. (1982), *Models of Bounded Rationality*, 2 vols., Cambridge, Mass, MIT Press.

SKINNER, A. S., and WILSON, T. (eds.) (1975), *Essays on Adam Smith*, Oxford, Clarendon Press.

SLUTSKY, E. [1915] (1952), 'Sulla teoria del bilancio del consumatore', *Giornale degli economisti e rivista di statistica*, 51: 1–26. Trans. 'On the

292 *References*

Theory of the Budget of the Consumer', in Stigler and Boulding 1952: 27–56.

SMITH, A. [1937] (1978), An early draft of part of the *Wealth of Nations*, in Scott 1937. Cited from Smith 1978: 562–86.

——[1776] (1976), *An Inquiry Into the Nature and Causes of the Wealth of Nations*, ed. R. H. Campbell, A. S. Skinner, and W. B. Todd, Oxford, Clarendon Press (1st pub. London, Strahan and Cadell).

——[1790] (1976), *The Theory of Moral Sentiments*, ed. D. D. Raphael and A. L. Macfie, Oxford, Clarendon Press.

——(1978), *Lectures on Jurisprudence*, ed. R. L. Meek, D. D. Raphael, and P. G. Stein, Oxford, Clarendon Press.

SPENCE, A. M. (1973a), 'Job Market Signalling', *Quarterly Journal of Economics*, 87: 355–74.

——(1973b), *Market Signalling: Information Transfer in Hiring and Related Processes*, Cambridge, Mass., Harvard University Press.

SRAFFA, P. (1960), *Production of Commodities by Means of Commodities: Prelude to a Critique of Economic Theory*, Cambridge, Cambridge University Press.

STIGLER, G. J. (1987), 'Competition', in Eatwell, Milgate, and Newman 1987: i. 531–6.

——and BOULDING, K. E. (eds.) (1952), *Readings in Price Theory*, Homewood, Ill., Irwin.

STIGLITZ, J. E. (ed.) (1966), *The Collected Scientific Papers of Paul A. Samuelson*, i, Cambridge, Mass., MIT Press.

——(1986), 'Theories of Wage Rigidity', in Butkiewicz, Koford, and Miller 1986: 153–221.

——and WEISS, A. (1981), 'Credit Rationing in Markets with Imperfect Information', *American Economic Review*, 71: 393–410.

STIGUM, B. P., and WENSTØP, F. (eds.) (1983), *Foundations of Utility and Risk Theory with Applications*, Dordrecht, Reidel.

STRAWSON, P. F. (1959), *Individuals*, London, Methuen.

SUGDEN, R. (1985), 'Why be Consistent?', *Economica*, 52: 167–84.

——(1989), '*Well-Being: Its Meaning, Measurement, and Moral Importance*, James Griffin', *Economics and Philosophy*, 5: 103–8.

SUZUMURA, K. (1983), *Rational Choice, Collective Decisions, and Social Welfare*, Cambridge, Cambridge University Press.

——(1989), 'Can Pareto Libertarian Paradox be Resolved by Voluntary Exchange of Libertarian Rights?', The Institute of Economic Research, Hitotsubashi University.

THRALL, R. M., COOMS, C. H., and DAVIS, R. L. (eds.) (1954), *Decision Processes*, New York, Wiley.

TUCKER, A. W., and LUCE, R. D. (eds.) (1959), *Contributions to the Theory of Games*, iv, Annals of Mathematics Studies No. 40, Princeton, Princeton University Press.

TULLOCK, G. (1964), 'The Irrationality of Intransitivity', *Oxford Economic Papers*, 16: 401–6.

URMSON, J. O. (1953), 'The Interpretation of the Moral Philosophy of J. S. Mill', *Philosophical Quarterly*, 3: 33–9.

VARIAN, H. R. (1987), 'Microeconomics', in Eatwell, Milgate, and Newman 1987: iii. 461–3.

VIND, K. (1964), 'Edgeworth-Allocations in an Exchange Economy with Many Traders', *International Economic Review*, 5: 165–77.

WALSH, V. C. (1954*a*), 'The Theory of the Good Will', *Cambridge Journal*, 7: 627–37.

—— (1954*b*), 'On Descriptions of Consumers' Behaviour', *Economica*, NS 21: 244–51.

—— (1958*a*), 'Scarcity and the Concepts of Ethics', *Philosophy of Science*, 25: 249–57.

—— (1958*b*), 'Ascriptions and Appraisals', *Journal of Philosophy*, 55: 1062–72.

—— (1961), *Scarcity and Evil*, Englewood Cliffs, NJ, Prentice Hall.

—— (1964), 'The Status of Welfare Comparisons', *Philosophy of Science*, 31: 149–55.

—— (1967), 'On the Significance of Choice Sets with Incompatibilities', *Philosophy of Science*, 34: 243–50.

—— (1970), *Introduction to Contemporary Microeconomics*, New York, McGraw Hill.

—— (1987*a*), 'Models and Theory', in Eatwell, Milgate, and Newman 1987: iii. 482–3.

—— (1987*b*), 'Philosophy and Economics', in Eatwell, Milgate, and Newman 1987: iii. 861–9.

—— (1987*c*), 'Cantillon, Richard', in Eatwell, Milgate, and Newman 1987: i. 316–20.

—— (1989), 'Joan Robinson and "Getting Into Equilibrium"', in Short and Long Periods', in Feiwell 1989: 303–10.

—— (1992), 'The Classical Dynamics of Surplus and Accumulation', in Halevi, Laibman, and Nell 1992: 11–43.

—— (1994), 'Rationality as Self-Interest versus Rationality as Present Aims', *American Economic Review*, 84: 401–5.

—— (1995), 'Amartya Sen on Inequality, Capabilities and Needs', *Science and Society*, 59, Winter 1995–6.

—— and GRAM, H. N. (1980), *Classical and Neo-classical Theories of General Equilibrium: Historical Origins and Mathematical Structure*, New York, Oxford University Press.

WEINTRAUB, E. R. (1979), *Microfoundations: The Compatibility of Microeconomics and Macroeconomics*, Cambridge, Cambridge University Press.

WERHANE, P. H. (1991), *Adam Smith and his Legacy for Modern Capital-*

294　　　　　　　*References*

ism, New York, Oxford University Press.

WIGHTMAN, W. P. D. (1975), 'Adam Smith and the History of Ideas', in Skinner and Wilson 1975: 44–67.

WILES, P., and ROUTH, G. (eds.) (1984), *Economics in Disarray*, Oxford, Blackwell.

WRIGHT, G. H. VON (1951), 'Deontic Logic', *Mind*, 60: 1–15.

—— (1963), *The Logic of Preference*, Edinburgh, Edinburgh University Press.

Index